Kinship Care

The Placement Choice for Children and Young People

Edited by
Bob Broad

Russell House Publishing

30130 161430623

First published in 2001 by:
Russell House Publishing Ltd.
4 St. George's House
Uplyme Road
Lyme Regis
Dorset DT7 3LS

Tel: 01297-443948
Fax: 01297-442722
e-mail: help@russellhouse.co.uk

© Bob Broad and the various contributors

The moral right of Bob Broad and the various contributors to be identified as the authors of this work has been asserted by them in accordance with The Copyright Designs and Patents Act (1988).

All rights reserved. No part of this publication may be reproduced, stored in a retrieval system or transmitted in any form, or by any means, electronic, mechanical, photocopying, recording or otherwise, without the prior permission of the copyright holder and the publisher.

British Library Cataloguing-in-publication Data:
A catalogue record for this book is available from the British Library.

ISBN: 1-898924-96-1

Typeset by The Hallamshire Press Limited, Sheffield

Printed by Bell and Bain, Glasgow

Russell House Publishing

is a group of social work, probation, education and youth and community work practitioners and academics working in collaboration with a professional publishing team. Our aim is to work closely with the field to produce innovative and valuable materials to help managers, trainers, practitioners and students. We are keen to receive feedback on publications and new ideas for future projects.

**Thurrock
Council Libraries**

Contents

Acknowledgements   v
About the authors   vii
Introduction   ix
Bob Broad

PART ONE : LEGAL, RESEARCH AND THEORETICAL PERSPECTIVES

1 Overview of the Legal Position of Grandparents as Kinship Carers   1
Jennifer Jenkins

2 Grandparents and the Care of Children: The Research Evidence   11
Lynda Clarke and Helen Cairns

3 Family and Friends who are Carers: A Framework for Success   21
Ann Wheal

4 Kinship Care, Child Protection and the Courts   29
Joan Hunt

5 Keeping Children in Kinship Placements Within Court Proceedings   39
Suzette Waterhouse

6 Family Dynamics in Kinship Foster Care   47
Roger Greeff

7 Contributions from an Irish Study: Understanding and Managing Relative Care   59
Valerie O'Brien

8 Children Reunited with their Parents: A Review of Research Findings   73
Elaine Farmer

PART TWO : KINSHIP CARE POLICIES IN PRACTICE: EXPERIENCES AND LESSONS

9 Kinship Care: A Family Rights Group Perspective   85
Robert Tapsfield

10 Making Kinship Partnerships Work: Examining Family Group Conferences   93
Paul Nixon

11 Assessing Grandparent Carers: A Framework   105
David Pitcher

12 Looking After Children Within the Extended Family: Carers' Views   115
Sophie Laws

13 Training Materials for Kinship Foster Care   127
Ronny Flynn

PART THREE : WAYS FORWARD FOR KINSHIP CARE

14 Promoting Kinship Foster Care: Preserving Family Networks for   135
Black Children of African Origins
Lynda Ince

15 Comparing American and United Kingdom Kinship Care: A Practitioner's View   147
Jean Stogdon

16 Kinship Care: Learning from the Past and Looking to the Future   155
Bob Broad

Acknowledgements

There are a number of important acknowledgements to make. First of all it is important to record that this book would not have been possible without the motivation, commitment and help of all the book's contributors, and subsequently, the valued advice from RHP the publishers, especially Geoffrey Mann, Martin Jones and Ann Wheal. I am also grateful to Professor David Ward, De Montfort University for his sustained energy and support for this project. The book's genesis was a conference in Leicester hosted by De Montfort University and I wish to thank all those who attended, gave presentations, and helped organise it (namely the Centre for Social Action, especially Helen Douds). It was the interest by delegates in improving the circumstances of children and young people in kinship care and of their kinship carers, which also motivated me. I would also like to thank Elizabeth Lightowler at De Montfort University for her support with this project. Also I would like to extend a special thanks to Denise Lawes, my wife, on two counts. First if Denise had not brought the situation of children in kinship care placements, through her practice as a senior social worker in the London Borough of Wandsworth, to my attention in the first place, then the kinship care research I have had the privilege to conduct, and this book, would not have been possible. Second a particular thanks to Denise, and also to our lovely children Jonathan Broad and Jenny Broad, for their continued love, support, and patience throughout my long periods of concentrated work on this book, and related research matters.

A special thanks is also in order to the kinship carers and young people whom I have had the privilege to interview as part of our kinship care research. My overall hope is that as a result of this book and ongoing work by others that kinship care practice and policy improves for children and young people living within their extended families whether or not those families warrant or wish for the support of welfare services. Finally, as with all edited collections, so with this one, the responsibility for its overall coherence rests with me, as editor.

About the Authors

Dr Bob Broad is Professor of Children and Families Research in the Faculty of Health and Community Studies, De Montfort University, Leicester. A trained social worker, he was awarded his PhD in 1988 and has undertaken a number of funded research projects about young people leaving care, kinship care and youth justice. His publications include *Young People Leaving Care: Life after the Children Act 1989* (Jessica Kingsley, 1998).

Helen Cairns is based at the London School of Hygiene and Tropical Medicine. She was the Research Officer at the Family Policy Studies Centre working on the ESRC project on grandparenthood in Britain. She previously worked at the Centre for Policy on Ageing, WHO Special Programme of Research, Development and Training and the Population Activities Unit of the UNECEF in Geneva.

Lynda Clarke is Senior Lecturer in Demography at the London School of Hygiene and Tropical Medicine and Head of Demography at the Family Policy Studies Centre. She specialises in family demography, particularly the circumstances of children and health and family policy. She is directing a current ESRC project on grandparenthood in Britain.

Dr Elaine Farmer is a Senior Research Fellow in the School for Policy Studies at Bristol University where she is also Programme Director for the Masters Degree in Child Welfare. Her books include *Trials and Tribulations: Returning Children from Local Authority Care to their Families* (HMSO, 1991), *Child Protection Practice: Private Risks and Public Remedies* (HMSO, 1995) and *Sexually Abused and Abusing Children in Substitute Care* (Wiley, 1998). Her latest study is on the fostering task with behaviourally difficult adolescents.

Ronny Flynn is a Black woman lecturer in the School of Health and Social Welfare at the Open University. Her involvement in family placement work began as training manager for National Foster Care Association in 1989. She is principal

author of two open learning handbooks on kinship care published by NFCA.

Roger Greeff teaches social work at Sheffield Hallam University. He has interests in children's rights, social work in the care system, and in anti-discriminatory social work, especially in the area of racism. He edited *Fostering Kinship: An International Perspective on Kinship Foster Care.*

Joan Hunt practised as a social worker before entering academic life in 1985. She is currently Senior Research Fellow in Oxford University's Centre for Socio-Legal Studies. Her research interests are children's law, the operation of the family justice system and the interface between legal institutions, families and social welfare agencies.

Lynda Ince is a part-time senior lecturer at the University of Hertfordshire and a freelance training consultant and researcher for local authorities. Her teaching interest is children and families and in particular the needs of black and minority ethnic children who are looked after. Lynda is currently a PhD student at the University of Birmingham. Among her publications is a study titled *Making it Alone* (1998) on the experiences of young black people leaving care, a chapter in Barn (Ed.) (1999) *Preparing Young Black People for Leaving Care* and *Overcoming the Obstacles* (Richards and Ince, 2000) a national study on black and minority ethnic children looked after by local authorities.

Jennifer Jenkins was formerly the manager of the family law team at the Law Commission. She currently works as a family law consultant. Jennifer is the honorary legal consultant to the Grandparents' Federation and chairperson of the legal group of British Agencies for Adoption and Fostering.

Dr Sophie Laws is an independent researcher/consultant, Honorary Research Fellow at North London and South Bank Universities. Last post held was Head of Research at the College of Health. Recent

viii   *About the Authors*

publications include *Pride and Prejudice: Working with Lesbian and Gay Young People* (Save the Children, 1999), and *Hear Me! Consulting with Young People on Mental Health Services* (Mental Health Foundation, 1998). Forthcoming from Sage with Save the Children is *Research for Development: A Practical Guide*.

Paul Nixon is the Commissioning Officer (Family Group Conferences) for Hampshire County Council Social Services Department. His main interests are partnership practice, community involvement and family support. He is co-author of *Empowering Practice? A Critical Appraisal of the Family Group Conference Approach* (Policy Press, 1999).

Dr Valerie O'Brien is a lecturer in the Department of Social Work and Social Policy at University College, Dublin. Her special areas of interest are child welfare, child placement and systemic theory, and she is particularly interested in practice research. She is immersed in practice through her membership of the Irish Adoption Board and she works as a systemic consultant in the Clanwilliam Institute Dublin, principally in the areas of family and organisational contexts.

David Pitcher works in Plymouth as a field social worker in a Child Care Team. He runs 'Parents Again' a local support group for grandparents who are caring for their grandchildren. He holds the Advanced Award in Social Work and is a recognised family mediator.

Jean Stogdon obtained her CQSW in 1971. She worked for 30 years as social worker, manager, and Guardian ad Litem and has a lifelong personal and professional interest in the

extended family. She was awarded a Churchill Fellowship in 1999 to study grandparents and kinship care in USA. She launched a new voluntary organisation *Grandparents Plus* (with Lord Michael Young) in 2000 and was a contributor to *Grandmothers of the Revolution* (2000) and *Family Business* (Demos, 2000, with Lord Young).

Robert Tapsfield is Chief Executive of the Family Rights Group. He is a qualified social worker with over twenty years experience of working for local authorities as a social worker and as a manager. He has been very involved in the introduction and development of family group conferences.

Suzette Waterhouse works as both a social work practitioner and researcher. Her practice has included employment with Social Services Departments, a child guidance clinic and the NSPCC. For 16 years she has acted in children's court cases as a Guardian ad litem and is continuing to work for the new CAFCASS service in this capacity. She has published research relating to parental contact with children in care, kinship care, fostering service organisation and placement choices for children in temporary foster care.

Ann Wheal joined the Department of Social Work Studies at the University of Southampton in 1990 following a successful career in teaching in inner city multi-racial schools and colleges. Since then she has been involved in research projects and writing and editing books mainly on foster and residential care. She is on several Government working groups and is a governor at a special needs nursery. She was also a kinship carer.

Introduction

Bob Broad

The book's aims and structure

This book is concerned with practice, policy and research developments concerning kinship care placements for children and young people whose welfare concerns are brought to the attention of social services, and who can no longer live with their birth parents. The vast majority of the contributions describe developments in the UK although there are regular references to developments in the USA, where kinship care is much more developed than in the UK. There is also a specific chapter, by Ince, about kinship care developments for black children and families, based on the American literature. It is argued here that kinship care, also sometimes known as extended family care, or family and friends care, is a topic of considerable importance and increasing interest. This book is for children, young people and family social workers, social work managers, senior policy makers, family researchers and academics working in the children, young people and family social work and social policy arenas. Each chapter identifies, explains and addresses different aspects of the core topic, kinship care, and this structure should assist readers to readily identify and locate what they need. For example, for those with a particular interest in the legislative framework within which kinship care placements can be made there is a separate chapter dedicated to the relevant legislation by Jennifer Jenkins, a family law consultant. Other chapters are similarly concerned with different aspects, as will be detailed below in this introduction. Whilst of course many of the discussions in this book are explicitly or implicitly about child care placements and options, a deliberate attempt has been made here to highlight specific kinship care issues, and not repeat and reproduce information about residential or foster care, already comprehensively covered, for example, regarding the latter, by Professor David Berridge at the University of Luton, or about the former, by Professor Ian Sinclair at the University of York. The book is in three parts. Part one concerns policy, legal and theoretical perspectives, part two focuses on the applied practice of kinship care in the field, and part three focuses on examining possible ways forward for kinship care. First let me outline the book's origins.

The book's origins

The idea for this book came from a conference entitled *Kinship Care: The Role of The State*, hosted by the Department of Social and Community Studies, De Montfort University in Leicester in 1999, and it followed on from a kinship care research project I had previously undertaken. At that conference there were a number of speakers and workshops focusing on key issues about kinship care. Speakers and workshop leaders at that conference included Professor David Berridge (University of Luton), Helen Jones (Department of Health), Robert Tapsfield (Family Rights Group [FRG]) Ronny Flynn (Open University), Ann Wheal (University of Southampton), David Pitcher (Plymouth Social Services), Roger Greeff (Sheffield Hallam University), Jennifer Jenkins (then legal advisor to The Grandparents Federation) and myself. There were also stalls from the Grandparents Federation, the National Foster Care Association and others.

There seemed to be a genuine interest from delegates in taking kinship care issues forward, and since that conference there have been occasional seminars on the topic co-organised by De Montfort University and the FRG. The FRG is undertaking further development work in this area; I am undertaking research, with Christine Rushforth and Ruth Hayes, on a Joseph Rowntree Foundation funded kinship care research project. At the University of Bristol Elaine Farmer and Sue Moyers are also undertaking funded (Department of Health) work in this field. John Hunt (University of Oxford) is undertaking a Department of Health funded review of kinship care. There will likely be other developments in this emerging field. The Department of Health regards kinship care as another viable placement option, which sits neatly within its Quality Protects Initiative (DoH, 2000a, 2000b). It is also the case that kinship care of children and young people is a much wider subject than simply, but importantly, another 'placement choice' for hard pressed social service departments. This 'wider social agenda' concerns the changing structure of families, and the growing acknowledgement of grandparents as full citizens, with entitlements, and not 'only', as described here, as family carers. Also family, cultural and racial diversity is more the norm and not, as might have been the case forty or fifty years ago, the exception. Although this might make the idea of kinship care more acceptable, and less stigmatised, whether this is of any assistance to hard-pressed grandparents bringing up a child in need, remains very doubtful.

Yet formal kinship care, in other words those arrangements whereby courts and/or social services make or authorise financial, legal or support packages, may be an 'issue of its time' for a number of reasons. These reasons include kinship care being regarded as the preferred choice for some children and families, a perceived crisis of confidence in public care, and pragmatically, a shortage of placements for children at risk. There is also a growing recognition that for children who can no longer live with their birth parents, kinship care, particularly by grandparents, (and in practice that often means grand-mothers), *if properly supported*, provides very valuable support in terms of that child's identity, and the family network's functioning and well-being.

This edited collection then is in part De Montfort University's contribution to the emerging debate about kinship care and one response to all those at that 1999 conference who wanted to take things further than one conference and who expressed a genuine interest in keeping up to date with research and practice developments on the subject. Many local authority delegates also wanted to take back ideas to their local authorities about how to develop and build services, within or in addition to, existing structures and budgets.

All those who gave presentations at the conference were invited to make a written contribution and many have stayed the course and made the time to write a chapter and it is thanks to their efforts that this collection appears at all. The time it takes to produce an edited collection also provides a welcome opportunity for editors to update and add to collections and this is the case here. Thus other key players and writers were invited to make a contribution enabling post 1999 issues to emerge and for the

book to be even more topical and relevant for readers. I am very grateful to all the contributors and especially to those whose kinship care work was not known to me at the time of the De Montfort University conference, and whose work has enriched this collection enormously.

The book's contents

As we have seen, this book's overall aim is to present and analyse practice, policy and research information, about kinship care of children and young people in the UK. It seeks to record the major developments in this important emerging field, making reference to key legal, welfare, professional, assessment, financial, training and research issues.

The book is in three parts:

1. Part one focuses on legal, research and theoretical perspectives on kinship care.

2. Part two concentrates on emerging kinship care policies and practices set within various social services settings and contexts.

3. Part three provides different perspectives, including international ones, about kinship care and examines possible ways forward and agendas for action.

What follows is an introduction to each chapter within each of the three parts.

Part One: Legal, Research and Theoretical Perspectives

Jenkins' chapter presents an overview of the legal position of grandparents as kinship carers. Jenkins outlines all those provisions within the Children Act 1989 which govern their legal position. Her chapter examines the key legal issues in relation to parental responsibility, grandparents and social services, legal considerations and requirements regarding looked after children, Residence Orders, guardians, and adoption. The terms of the Private Law (where, for example, the parents have died) as well as the relevant sections of the Human Rights Act 1998, are also included, and a case for more Department of Health guidance is made as a means of promoting and safeguarding standards, and equity of support and services, principally from social services departments.

Clarke and Cairns' chapter summarises the research evidence about grandparents and the care of children and, in so doing, draws out wider themes about changing family trends, and the changing role of grandparents, including 'custodial grandparents'. The chapter reports on findings from the 1998 British Social Attitudes Survey, which, for the first time, looked at grandparenting, using a nationally representative sample of grandparents. It reviews the different levels of satisfaction held by grandparents about caring for their grandchildren, the effects of caring on grandparents' well-being and lifestyle, and provides important data about daytime care and babysitting by grandparents. The authors explain the types of situations which led to grandparents taking on a parenting or custodial role and raise a number of key policy questions about the changing role of grandparents, kinship care, and inter-generational family care. This chapter complements the book's other, more social services focused chapters about kinship care, by focusing on the broader policy context of grandparents and the care of children.

In the following chapter Wheal, drawing on her considerable experiences as a grandmother, researcher and educator, puts forward a strong case for social services to be much more strategic and responsive to children's and families needs when support is required. She recommends that social services departments initially plan for a 'family and friends placement', rather than it being regarded only as a crisis response, with assessments following after a placement has been made or agreed. She also argues that there needs to be a universally agreed kinship care definition and 'family and friends as carers' framework for such placements which require more consistent and higher level support by local authority social services departments. Wheal acknowledges the difficulties in some cases of maintaining family unity and the need for additional professional help and guidance when a child lives with family and friends as carers. Wheal's chapter presents an agenda for action. She suggest three groupings; state interventions, private interventions and neighbourhood fostering, to assist and clarify priorities, and as a way of separating out key issues, rights and responsibilities.

In Hunt's chapter about kinship care, child protection and the courts, the author presents detailed research findings, and outcomes for children where kinship care placements were made in court proceedings, and for another, post-court group, of children in kinship care placements. The chapter vividly illustrates the limited involvement and rights of grandparents

and other extended family members in court decisions where safeguarding the child, and welfare issues are prominent. Her chapter concludes by arguing that kin support for children involved in child protection court proceedings is often viewed more favourably than other options, and may be receiving a higher profile. She also argues that these developments come with a critical rider, namely that the intentions of the Children Act 1989 requiring local authorities to first consider and place a child with a member of the child's extended family 'unless it would not be consistent with the child's welfare' (Section 23 (6)) need more acknowledgement if they are to fully develop.

Waterhouse's chapter discusses issues relating to the use of kinship care within a family proceeding framework through a presentation of key findings from a large scale research study that examined kinship care placements, as an outcome of court care proceedings, as part of a wider study. The research in question examined a maximum cohort of 650 children who were the subject of care and supervision orders, over a four year period, and at the point of final court hearing. Her wide ranging research findings point to a rising use of kinship care placements direct from care proceedings. She provides considerable empirical data in this under-researched area. She identifies those extended family members who were involved in the placement, reviews the advantages of kinship placements in care proceedings and tackles the important issues of assessment thresholds, and supportive framework required for kinship carers.

Moving away from legal and court perspectives on kinship care, Greeff's chapter about systems perspectives provides a theoretical analysis, and models of family dynamics of kinship care. He looks at key issues of motivation, guilt, and new roles for the parent and grandparent (as the 'normal' kinship carer). He argues that an understanding of the family history is vital to an understanding by the extended families and social workers of current behaviour, roles and expectations of family members. He also argues for more open understandings within extended families, and for more open working relationships between extended families and agencies, both of which acknowledge family difficulties and any child neglect issues. Examples of a number of types of family systems such as 'open system' (clear but permeable system boundaries), 'closed system' (parent excluded), and 'shared care' (parent integrated into parent/adult sub-system) are presented and evaluated.

O'Brien's chapter summarises the key findings of her study into the development of relative care in Ireland, the care careers of the children, and the processes involved at the decision-making, assessment, and post-assessment stages. The different routes giving rise to the relative care placements are illustrated although the chapter focuses predominantly on key findings arising at different junctures of decision making assessment, support and access and concludes with a discussion of the implications for practice. One of its key contributions, based on the author's research findings, is its new kinship care conceptual and practice model called *ENORC* (Evolving Networks Of Relative Care) aimed at speeding up and clarifying responses, within a clear conceptual framework.

Farmer's chapter concentrates on a vital, yet often overlooked, policy area, namely that of acknowledging, and reviewing the research-practice evidence about children returning to their families, the developments and outcomes for them, and the factors which differentiate between successful and unsuccessful returns. Such a chapter is included here to highlight the important point that the vast majority of children who have been looked after return to live with their parents, (something, which the author notes, child care research seems to overlook at times!). Whilst there is not then, deliberately so, a specific focus on kinship carers, Farmer's chapter discusses many of the family dynamics and social work practice-policy issues, about children leaving and returning to 'a family'. These findings are not only of direct relevance to all children and young people moving in between private, family care and public, residential or foster care, but to all those who work to unite or re-unite children and families. The chapter also highlights the tendency in the UK care system for there to be 'moves in and out of care', and, therefore, in and out of different family, including extended family, situations. The transition back to the child's family is identified as a particularly crucial time and one which requires more recognition, and planned and highly skilled social work involvement.

The second part of the book concentrates more on kinship care practice, whether drawn from experiences within a local authority or voluntary sector setting, and the subsequent practice and policy lessons that can or should be learnt from such experiences.

Part Two: Kinship Care Policies in Practice: Experiences and Lessons

Tapsfield's chapter draws on the difficulties experienced by kinship carers, as reported to the Family Rights Group (FRG) advice service, to make out a strong case for local authorities to have clear and comprehensive policies to support kinship carers. Of critical importance, he also explores the reasons why many local authorities seem reluctant to promote and support kinship care and then recommends what is needed for them to overcome their reluctance, and act in more supportive, consistent and less defensive ways. This FRG perspective, bedded in reported experiences of kinship carers, embraces legislative, policy, financial and practice elements.

Nixon discusses the role, developments and limits of family group conferences (FGCs) potentially, as a highly relevant way for social services to work with extended families to make kinship care arrangements. He makes the case for extended family placements to become a preferred choice for children and families by citing the origins of and key developments in FGCs in New Zealand. In so doing he anticipates and highlights many of the emerging issues about kinship care placements in the UK, namely the need for new ways of including kin in child welfare/family decisions, of acknowledging professional power and resource issues, continuity of identity issues, and the organisational structures and decision making strategies needed for more family-friendly, and kin focused, social work practice.

When a child cannot be looked after by his or her own parents, somebody else must take on this task. The responsibility for assessing such alternative carers is one of the most important the local authority has. This is especially the case because a child in need of substitute care may well have been affected by abuse, neglect or traumatic experiences, and will need carers who are not just competent, but who are able to understand difficult or perplexing behaviour, and who can help repair some of the damage that has been done. For those professionals working with vulnerable children, there can surely be few skills more needed than those in assessing those who will care for them.

Pitcher's contribution, from a practitioner's perspective, is to describe a framework devised by him and other Plymouth City Council colleagues, for assessing grandparent carers. The framework is based on understanding the experiences of grandparents, through a piece of practitioner research undertaken by him, in Plymouth, of grandparents who were known to be caring for grandchildren who would otherwise be in local authority care. Pitcher presents both the findings of that research study and the recommendations made to social services, and a full description of the assessment framework that was devised. The chapter is an excellent example of a practitioner research project which has had impact.

The principle virtue of Laws contribution, alongside Stogdon's, (in Part Three) is that it contains the all important views of kinship carers, as expressed by them in a research project. Her chapter reports on the experiences of a small number of kinship carers from one local authority about what it is like being a kinship carer, the help received and needed from social services and their views of such help. In many ways this chapter captures the main dilemmas about kinship care, the changing nature and role of nuclear and extended family, and the role of the state when short and longer-term crises occur in the care and upbringing of children. The issues of greater recognition of kinship carers needs, their lack of financial parity with foster carers, the continued under-valuing of caring, and the call for more ongoing social work support for carers and children, are all discussed.

Flynn's chapter summaries the training materials produced for the National Foster Care Association (NFCA) for kinship carers (including those who were foster carers) and social workers. The training materials aims included raising the status of family and friends foster care; improving the care and support of this group of children; assisting carers and social workers to develop skills; and challenging discrimination and promoting equality. The materials concentrated on kinship carers of children who were in public care, and as Flynn comments, driven by NFCA's policy of seeking to give kinship carers equal status and recognition with other foster carers. It is of note that the materials presented drew on the direct experiences of kinship foster carers and social workers, and the views of some children and young people, by including case material and quotations. The 'training portfolio' in social work often picks up on unresolved policy issues and this is also the case here about the existence, focus, and entitlements of local authority policies for kinship carers. Flynn also raises questions about

how kinship care is or could be organised within local authorities, for example within foster care, or family placement, teams? Flynn concludes on a policy level by arguing that until many of these organisational and policy tensions are openly debated, then children's services will continue to fudge the issue of supporting kinship care as a viable option.

Part Three of the book builds on present understandings of kinship care, and by drawing on wider racial, cultural, national or international perspectives, points to the changes required in order for kinship care policy and practice developments to be developed and sustained in the UK.

Part Three: Ways Forward for Kinship Care

Ince's chapter focuses on how kinship care needs to be promoted in order to preserve and sustain black and ethnic minority family networks. It provides a detailed overview of what lessons can be learnt from the United States of America about developments in kinship care generally and specifically in relation to black families. It is argued by Ince that many of those lessons could be applied here providing that a number of major professional and policy changes are invoked. It offers a critique of current child welfare practice, policy and information gathering in the way that these often exclude consideration of the needs of black children and families, and indeed extended families generally. The chapter ends by identifying the main changes necessary to make kinship care a more mainstream placement option for children who have to live away from their birth parents.

There is considerable research, and practice development material available about formal and informal kinship care in the USA. Stogdon writes as a grandparent, as an experienced social worker and social work manager, and as someone who can make direct comparisons between the UK and the USA by virtue of her funded USA kinship care study tour. Stogdon puts the argument that for children who can no longer live with their birth parents, kinship care by grandparents or other extended family members should be the preferred placement choice. Her hypothesis is that child welfare in the UK, through the Children Act 1989, acknowledges the importance, the primacy even, of the extended family, but that cultural and organisational factors have mitigated against those legislative intentions being even partially realised. Stogdon provides an overview of the changes she considers are necessary to make kinship care happen but implies that practical concerns, such as continued shortage of foster carers, rather than legislation or permanence principles, are more likely to make kinship care develop in the UK in a planned, and supported way.

The final chapter, by me as editor, draws together the main themes and key issues raised in this volume in respect of future developments in kinship care. In so doing it contains statistical information about the increasing numbers of children looked after, emphasising the importance of evaluating kinship care, and suggests ways in which this could be done. It ends by arguing for more public debate about kinship care, and funded research and policy development work to be conducted, and calls on the Department of Health to work with the voluntary sector, social services and academic institutions, to take a lead.

Having outlined the book's origins, and its aims and structure, I want to share with you why kinship care for children and young people is potentially so important to me, not only in respect of my professional search for helpful and productive welfare responses, but more widely, in respect of future child welfare and child protection issues.

Kinship care: a personal reflection on what has been and what might be

Throughout my professional life in the social welfare fields, my main interest, like others, is in seeking out, promoting, and identifying practice and research which makes a positive difference to people's lives. This has also involved setting out agendas for action, where necessary, as in the case for kinship care. The sorts of 'big questions' that this involves me in seeking to address or answer, include; 'Why do some children and families have serious problems and others do not?' and 'What can be done when problems arise?' 'What works best in helping children and families in need?' 'Why do some children and young people display problem behaviours,

whereas others (brought up in similar fashion) do not?' 'Where they exist, how can 'cycles of deprivation' be broken? and 'Are such patterns of family interaction inevitable and immutable?' or, 'When such patterns are destructive, how best can they be changed and by whom? 'Why has comparatively little been done to tackle racism?' are all further examples of these 'big questions'. That is quite a list, viewed perhaps as somewhat disconnected: yet the link between them is a genuine search to uncover, to use the jargon, 'problem causation-problem resolution' i.e. 'What works?' For whom? and Why? in resolving individual, family and societal problems.

My particular professional interest in kinship care (it could also be about 'user power' or children's rights) stems from a combination of long-standing practice and research interests about children and young people's welfare and service responses. Having been a secondary school teacher in London, and then a probation officer in the 1970 for many years, and keeping statistical information about my probation caseload, I became increasingly aware of the high proportion of offenders who had behaviour problems, who came from what were then termed 'broken homes' or had had some sort of loss or separation in their early life, were living in deprived circumstances, and seemed to lack consistent parenting. My earlier teaching experiences also confirmed this view about the links between a child's background, feelings of personal insecurity, poverty and behaviour, and in a sense such associations are obvious. I was and still am struck and moved by the extent of ongoing poverty and unhappiness experienced by some children and families, which together with other family and societal dynamics seem to underpin, fuel and define the nature and extent of any subsequent offending, or indeed other harmful behaviour by members of that family.[1] I was and am also struck by the resilience and selflessness of many families living in difficult circumstances. As a social work lecturer and tutor in the 1980s I found many of the students on second year DipSW placements in social services, working on complex and demanding child protection tasks. Time and time again those students on placement in children and families

---

1. It is also fully recognised that differential policing strategies also have a direct impact on the reporting, and recording of official crime rates. Yet the point that the key risk factors for offending include those mentioned i.e. specific individual, family, and societal factors, (as well as criminal opportunities and situational influences) is long established and widely recognised by those eminent in the field (Farrington, 2001).

teams were in the front line, seeking to deal with the most intransigent children at risk and family problems by looking to support families in ongoing- or post-crisis mode. Sustained family support, and indeed group work initiatives, often seemed to begin with the arrival of the student and end when the social work placement ended.[2] Undertaking practitioner research and, subsequently, funded academic research, I seek to understand, explain or evaluate social welfare issues, initially concerning offending, and the impact of probation work (Broad, 1991), and latterly, the impact of child care legislation on young people leaving care (Broad, 1998). In relation to the latter, for example, it has become ever more apparent and widely accepted that despite the best efforts of many projects, (leaving care teams for example), the outcomes for care leavers in terms of levels of educational attainment, physical and emotional health, pregnancy rates, and, when older, employment rates, remain very poor indeed. Indeed, it may well be that the principle 'success' of leaving care teams is in the critical area of 'being there,' being available and offering personal support and guidance, and this may or may not ultimately lead to 'better' education, health or other outputs.

All of these experiences have led me to ask if the family, in addition to the state, can, should, would want to, play an even larger part in helping and supporting family members who present seriously problematic and needy behaviour. For example, to take the obvious one here, could or should extended families play a larger part in caring for a child or young person within their family who will otherwise be removed from home and taken into care? This immediately reminds one of the Family Group Conferences aims, and subsequently, its patchy implementation involving complex partnerships between the state, the child and the family. Also, again in respect of young people leaving care, despite the laudable aims of the Children Act 1989, which placed more duties on local authorities, including those concerning young

people leaving care, many of the deep-seated problems for care leavers continue. Why? Yet it should be the case, alongside other government initiatives, that the Children (Leaving Care) Act 2000, implemented from October 2001, will produce much better and more consistent outcomes than before for care leavers. Other wider social policy initiatives about parenting, employment, education, reducing social exclusion, housing, employment, training, and mentoring will, in this author's view, likely to have at least as much impact on young people leaving care as the leaving care legislation.[3] Also many children and young people are still placed in inappropriate residential or foster care placements because that is all that is available and there are no other longer-term alternatives considered. For black and other ethnic minority children especially, and indeed white children, questions about how their identities, resilience, and futures are nurtured and sustained, or disrupted and weakened, by inappropriate (non-family and friends) stranger care, need to be asked. Care experiences can often compound and contort existing problems, and in some, appalling cases, the 'care system' itself has become a source of further abuse. It is also the case that foster and residential care, generally regarded as a much safer and more supportive place than being in an abusing and harmful home situation, 'works' for many children and is valued and necessary. It is the lack of a 'real' choice of placement for children at risk which is at issue here, and it would seem that the child remaining or placed within the extended family is often overlooked as a preferred option.

Returning to care leavers briefly, and whilst recognising that young people leaving care are not a homogeneous group, (and increasingly do not enter care until they are early teenagers), they often share the emotional burden of being or feeling rejected, separated from their immediate family, and of then becoming labelled as 'troublesome and troubled young people' (to quote a previous Secretary of Health). This then raises the question, given the continuing recorded

---

2. I am very pleased to see that one of the contributors to this collection, David Pitcher, runs a support group for grandparents as a part of his job.

3. It is also worth reminding ourselves that it is increasingly the children from families where there are already serious welfare, mental health and/or child protection, behavioural issues, and in some cases victims of severe bullying and/or institutional racism (in the form of poor quality and/or discriminatory services), who are taken into either residential care or foster care in the first place. In other words the problems of young people in the care system are not all, or at all, problems that have arisen suddenly because of the care system but are primarily a result of their previous individual and family history which led them to be placed in care in the first place. I emphasise this point because, surprisingly perhaps in some of the literature, it is as if the care system causes all the problems, which is not the case.

poor outcomes for the majority of young people leaving care, 'Is removal from the family home the best or appropriate or the only way to deal with a child presenting serious behavioural and emotional problems and/or child protection concerns?' Or are there other family-based options? Perhaps so long as social services act as an emergency service, and as a child policing agency, and not a primary preventive service, removing the child from an abusing home will continue to be the only available option. Yet for some children, either those who might be placed in care, or returned to care, or who are at risk of 'serious harm,' kinship care remains a largely unexplored option. This will depend on whether and when kinship care features higher on the Department of Health placement choice policy menu as another real choice, properly funded, driven and supported by progressive policies. Perhaps one starting point in connection with kinship care is for there to be a full and informed national debate about family support and preventive work with families. As well as the policy level, and when kinship care becomes more developed, it will also require far more training input, both at the qualifying and post qualifying levels (on the latter see Flynn's chapter on training in this volume). Social work students and social workers could be helped increasingly to understand and assess the strengths of all extended families, and acknowledge much more than has hitherto been the case the strengths of black extended families, and also the capacity of families to change.

Thus my interest in kinship care stems from a mix of:

- **Hope** that the extended family be regarded as a more positive child placement option for many children than removal from the family network.
- **Reservations** about the efficacy of all professional welfare interventions.
- **Concern** that the needs of black and minority ethnic children and extended families be more fully recognised.

- **A wish** that kinship care can become a more fully recognised partner and adjunct to state care.
- **A need for political and professional recognition of kinship carers** including a sustained kinship care campaign, built on a measured analysis of its contribution.
- **A recognition that partnerships** between the state and the family require further re-examination.

In this volume then a wide range of informed professional and user perspectives are provided and cumulatively they make out a strong case for kinship care to become a much more recognised and supported placement choice for children in need. I hope that this edited collection has a positive and sustained impact on emerging kinship care discussions and developments, and that the direction, nature and level of vitality of these developments will flow from carers and users views, and other research and practice developments reproduced here, at least as much as local and national interests.

References

Broad, B. (1991). *Punishment Under Pressure: The Probation Service in the Inner City.* London: Jessica Kingsley.

Broad, B. (1998). *Young People Leaving Care: Life After the Children Act 1989.* London: Jessica Kingsley.

Broad, B. (1998). Kinship Care: Children Placed with Extended Families. *Childright*, 155: pp 16–17.

Broad, B. (2001). Kinship Care: Supporting Children in Extended Family and Friends Placements. In *Adoption and Fostering*, forthcoming.

DoH (2000a). *Tracking Progress in Children's Services: An Evaluation of Local Responses to the Quality Protects Programme Year 2 National Overview Report.* London: DoH.

DoH (2000b). *Planning and Providing Good Quality Placements for Children in Care.* London: DoH.

Farrington, D. (2001). *Understanding and Controlling Crime.* British Psychological Society Centenary Conference Lecture, 5th January, London, Royal Society.

1 Overview of the Legal Position of Grandparents as Kinship Carers

Jennifer Jenkins

Introduction

Most of this chapter and the rest of the book are concerned with the situation where a local authority social services department is involved with a family. However, this chapter also considers two different kinds of cases where grandparents bring up their grandchildren independently of social services. These are first, where the parents have died and secondly, where the parents are unable or unwilling to look after their children. It will also highlight key Articles in the European Convention on Human Rights recently incorporated into domestic law by the Human Rights Act 1998. Although the chapter is written from the perspective of grandparents it applies equally to other members of the extended family.[1]

Children are born to parents but are also part of their wider family. Sometimes, because of family quarrels, social relationships in the family are damaged temporarily or even broken permanently but legal relationships continue throughout the child's life unless the child is adopted or freed for adoption. Where parents refuse to let children have contact with other family members, mediation can be helpful if the problems cannot be resolved directly.[2] Court proceedings are best avoided if possible.[3]

Family problems can also lead to members of the wider family bringing up the children. Many grandparents enjoy a close relationship with their grandchildren. The amount of time they can spend together will depend on various factors including practical issues such as how far apart

they live. Grandparents may be asked to look after the grandchildren to enable the parents to go to work, to have a holiday on their own or even to allow individual time for brothers and sisters. However, some grandparents are not secondary carers of their grandchildren assisting the parents but primary carers providing full time care of their grandchildren. The reasons for this and the processes that bring it about affect their legal status as carers. In some cases the position is complicated because a local authority also has responsibilities towards the children. Whatever the circumstances the legal position is governed by the Children Act 1989.[4] This Act makes an important distinction between parents, guardians and persons with a residence order who are entitled to make an application to the court for an order, and grandparents. Grandparents must first obtain permission (leave) from the court before they can make an application.[5]

The Legal Framework

The Children Act 1989, implemented on 14 October 1991, reformed and simplified much of the law about children previously contained in a number of different statutes. An important feature of the Act was that it brought together in one place private law (which deals with individuals) and public law (where a local authority is involved). As a result, a court making a decision about a child's upbringing has much more flexibility in determining what order(s) to make.

---

1. In the Wandsworth research grandparents were the kinship carers in 39 per cent of the cases. Laws, S., and Broad, B. (2000). *Looking After Children within the Extended Family: Carers' Views*, p13. Department of Social and Community Studies De Montford University.

2. Mediation is a process in which an impartial third party meets with those in dispute so that they can talk through their problems and try to reach agreement.

3. Application can be made for a contact order under the Children Act 1989. A contact order is an order requiring the person with whom a child lives, or is to live, to allow the child to visit or stay with the person named in the order, or for that person and the child otherwise to have contact with each other (section 8). However, if the parents will not permit the applicant to see a child without a court order there is no guarantee that they will observe the order even if it is made.

4. References in this chapter to sections, Schedules and Parts are to the Children Act 1989 unless otherwise indicated.

5. Unless the grandparents belong to one of the categories of people entitled to apply for a residence or contact order. See section 10(5).

Whenever a court makes a decision about a child's upbringing, its paramount concern is the welfare of the child concerned.[6] A court must have regard to the general principle that delay in making a decision is likely to be prejudicial to the child's welfare[7] and must not make any order unless it considers that making the order would be better for the child than not making it.[8] When a court is determining a dispute between parents or considering whether it should make an order putting the child in the care of a local authority it must also have regard to a 'welfare checklist' before making its decision.[9]

The Children Act also introduced the concept of parental responsibility. This is the legal term for the rights and duties of a parent. The Act defines parental responsibility as 'all the rights, duties, powers, responsibilities and authority which by law a parent has in relation to the child and his property'.[10] Parental responsibility allows a person to make important decisions about children such as what their names should be, which school they should attend and whether they should receive certain types of medical treatment. Usually each person with parental responsibility can act independently but sometimes the law requires all the people with parental responsibility to consent to a course of action. Not all parents have parental responsibility. All mothers and any father married to the children's mother[11] have parental responsibility for their children. An unmarried father has parental responsibility if he has acquired it by formal agreement with the mother or by court order.[12] People who are not parents can acquire parental responsibility and keep it so long as certain court orders exist in their favour.

The usual order giving parental responsibility to non-parents is a residence order.[13] Local authorities obtain parental responsibility for children for whom they have a care order. Non-parents and local authorities with parental responsibility can make many of the same decisions as parents but they cannot agree to adoption or appoint a guardian.

Grandparents and Social Services

Grandparents may contact social services because they have worries about some aspect of their grandchildren's upbringing by their parents. It can be very hard for grandparents to report their own son or daughter's behaviour and this in itself can cause divisions in the family. What actions follow and the legal consequences depend on the seriousness of the allegations and social services' response to them. This kind of situation can lead to services being offered to the family or may result in the children being looked after by the local authority.[14] If the children have to leave their parents the grandparents may take on their care.

Grandparents' involvement with social services may come about because they are already caring for the grandchildren and need help or support. They may be able to receive this from their local authority because the Children Act places a duty on local authorities towards children in need in their area to safeguard and promote their welfare.[15] Where it would be consistent with that duty, local authorities must also promote the upbringing of the children by their families by providing a range and level of

---

6. Section 1(1).

7. Section 1(2).

8. Section 1(5).

9. When the court is considering making, varying or discharging a section 8 order that is opposed by one of the parties or an order under Part IV (care and supervision) it must have regard in particular to: (a) the ascertainable wishes and feelings of the child concerned (considered in the light of his age and understanding); (b) his physical, emotional and educational needs; (c) the likely effect on him of any change in his circumstances; (d) his age, sex, background and any characteristics of his which the court considers relevant; (e) any harm which he has suffered or is at risk of suffering; (f) how capable each of his parents, and any other person in relation to whom the court considers the question to be relevant, is of meeting his needs; (g) the range of powers available to the court under this Act in the proceedings in question (section 1(3)).

10. Section 3(1).

11. Section 2(1), (2) and (3). The section says married at the time of the child's birth but this is given a wide meaning by section 1 of the Family Law Reform Act 1987. Marriage after the birth gives the father parental responsibility too.

12. Section 4(1). An order may be made on the father's application. An agreement must be made and recorded in the prescribed manner (section 4(2)). See the Parental Responsibility Agreement Regulations 1991.

13. A residence order is an order settling the arrangements as to the person with whom a child is to live (section 8).

14. A child is looked after by a local authority if he is in its care or provided with accommodation in the exercise of its social services' functions (section 22(1)).

15. Section 17(1). Children in need are defined in section 17(10) and (11).

services appropriate to their needs.[16] These services can include assistance in kind or, in exceptional circumstances, in cash.[17] Examples of the kind of help that can be provided are nursery places, furniture and school uniforms. Where cash is given it may be in the form of a loan.[18]

Social services may already know the family and be working with them. They may approach the grandparents to see if they would be willing to provide the children with a home on a short-term or long-term basis. The Children Act encourages the placement of children with parents, persons who have or had parental responsibility, relatives, friends or other connected persons unless this is not reasonably practicable or consistent with their welfare.[19] This important provision means that the local authority should explore the options of care within the extended family.

Looked after children

Children are looked after if they are provided with accommodation by a local authority or are in local authority care under a care order.[20] Before making any decision about a looked after child, the local authority must try to find out the wishes and feelings of the child, his or her parents, anyone with parental responsibility, and anyone else who the local authority considers relevant.[21] The local authority must give these opinions due consideration along with the child's religious persuasion, racial origin, and cultural and linguistic background.[22] Grandparents with whom a looked after child is placed will be local authority foster parents unless they had a residence order immediately before a care order was made.[23] They will need to be approved as

foster carers but in their case approval is likely to be restricted to the particular grandchild or grandchildren. Approval should normally be given before placement but special rules apply to immediate placements.[24]

Accommodated children

A local authority has a duty to provide accommodation for children in need in their area if there is no one with parental responsibility for them, they are lost or abandoned, or if the person who has been caring for them cannot provide suitable accommodation or care.[25] It does not matter why the person cannot continue to provide care or accommodation or whether he or she is prevented from doing so for a short time or permanently. Although the local authority has duties towards accommodated children it does not have parental responsibility for them. Parental responsibility remains with the parents. The local authority is expressly forbidden to provide accommodation for children if a person with parental responsibility is willing and able to provide or arrange accommodation for them.[26] There are exceptions, for example, if a child of 16 agrees to be provided with accommodation.[27] If the parents want the children back they must be handed over. If the local authority fears for the children's safety or welfare and wishes to prevent the children returning to their parents it must apply to the court for an emergency protection order or care order.[28] In cases where grandparents have reported the parents to social services because of their conduct, or where there is hostility between the adults, the parents may effectively prevent social services placing the grandchildren with them by saying they will take them back.

---

16. Section 17(1).
17. Section 17(6). More specific duties and powers are set out in Part I of Schedule 2.
18. Section 17(7).
19. Section 23(4) and (6).
20. Section 22(1).
21. Section 22(4).
22. Section 22(5).
23. Section 23(3) and (4).
24. Regulation 11 of the Foster Placement (Children) Regulations 1991. Regulation 11(3) allows an immediate placement with a relative for a period up to six weeks.
25. Section 20(1). Accommodation means accommodation provided for a continuous period of more than 24 hours (section 22(2)).
26. Section 20(7).
27. Section 20(11).
28. Section 44(1) emergency protection order, section 31(1) care order.

Children in local authority care

A local authority can obtain a care order if it satisfies a court that the child is suffering, or is likely to suffer, significant harm. The harm, or likelihood of harm, must be attributable to the care given to the child, or likely to be given to the child, not being what is reasonable to expect from a parent or the child being beyond parental control.[29] The welfare test must also be satisfied and the court must have regard to the welfare checklist. Grandparents who wish to provide a home for their grandchildren should make this known to the local authority. It can be very difficult for them as they may perceive this as being disloyal to their own son or daughter who is resisting the care proceedings. If the local authority does not support them they may be able to be joined as parties to the care proceedings and apply for a residence order. It is essential that they try to be joined as parties if the application for a care order is combined with an application to free the children for adoption.

A local authority with a care order has parental responsibility for the child together with the parents.[30] The care order will discharge a residence order so any non-parents with parental responsibility will lose it. Although the local authority and parents share parental responsibility, the local authority has the power to determine the extent to which a parent can meet his or her parental responsibility.[31] However, the authority must allow parents, guardians and anyone who had parental responsibility before the care order was made, to have reasonable contact with the child.[32] Apart from a seven-day period in an emergency,[33] contact can only be refused if the authority obtains an order authorising refusal.[34] Grandparents may negotiate or be offered contact to grandchildren in care as the local authority has a duty to promote contact between the child and his or her relatives unless this is not reasonably practicable or consistent with the child's welfare.[35] Although grandparents do not have a right to contact[36] they may apply for leave to apply for contact.[37]

Discharge of care order/application for a residence order

Grandparents who are looking after their grandchildren in care may wish the care order to be discharged. They cannot apply directly to discharge the order because the court can only discharge an order on an application by a person with parental responsibility, the child or the local authority.[38] A local authority that supports the grandparents' wish to care for the children under a residence order cannot apply for a residence order on their behalf but it can apply to discharge the care order and invite the court to make a residence order in favour of the grandparents.[39] Alternatively, the grandparents can apply for a residence order. If the grandparents apply for a residence order they will normally have to pay the legal costs themselves unless they are eligible for means tested public funding. Sometimes the savings put aside for their retirement can mean grandparents fall just outside the criteria for help. They may receive some financial assistance from the local authority and some local authorities are willing to pay all of the grandparents' legal costs.

If the court makes a residence order the care order will automatically be discharged.

The grandparents will need to ask the court's leave to apply for the residence order unless they fall within one of the categories of people entitled to apply for a residence order. They will not need to obtain leave if the local authority consents to their application or if their grandchildren have

---

29. Section 31(2).
30. Section 33(3). A local authority acquires limited parental responsibility under an emergency protection order section 44(4) and (5).
31. Section 33(3).
32. Section 34(1).
33. Section 34(6).
34. Section 34(4).
35. Paragraph 15 of Part II of Schedule 2.
36. Unless they had a residence order before the care order was made (section 34(1)).
37. Section 34(3). See *Re M (Care: Contact: Grandmother's Application for Leave)* 1995 2 FLR 86 for the approach to a leave application.
38. Section 39(1).
39. Local authorities are forbidden to apply for a residence order (section 9(2)).

lived with them for at least three years.[40] The ban on local authority foster parents applying for leave to apply for a residence order does not affect relatives.[41] The Children Act provides that rules of court may prescribe categories of people entitled to apply for a residence order.[42] This would allow the court rules to be amended to extend the categories of people who can apply for a residence order without first seeking the court's leave. The Grandparents' Federation believes this power should be exercised in favour of grandparents as the requirement for them to obtain leave causes additional distress and unnecessary expense.

Residence orders in respect of a child in care

Deciding whether or not to apply for a residence order can be a very difficult decision. It is one that is often taken for the wrong reasons and without a full understanding of the legal implications. Some grandparents feel social services want the child 'off their books'.[43] Some say the social services do not agree with long term fostering. Some are fearful of what they perceive as veiled threats that the children will be removed from them and placed for adoption if they do not apply for a residence order. In *Re K (Care Order or Residence Order)*[44] the grandparents looking after the children wanted the care order to remain and the local authority wished it to be discharged. The children were suffering from a muscle wasting disease and the grandparents believed they would obtain more help if the children remained in care. The court refused to discharge the care order and make a residence order against the wishes of the grandparents.

Advantages of a residence order

The main advantages of obtaining a residence order are that the grandparents have parental responsibility and can care for the child without 'interference' from social workers. As they often tell the Grandparents' Federation, they are free to live their lives as a normal family. There are no more reviews. There is no need to get permission for activities like sleepovers and from the child's perspective he or she no longer has a corporate parent.

Disadvantages of a residence order

Finance

Perhaps the most obvious disincentive to obtaining a residence order is the financial position. Grandparents who are caring for grandchildren being looked after by the local authority are foster carers and will receive an allowance from the local authority. The amount paid varies and is often considerably less than is paid to non-relative foster carers but it can be an essential contribution to the family income. The allowance ceases when a residence order is made. Local authorities have a power to make a contribution towards the cost of accommodation and maintenance of a child who lives, or is to live, with a person under a residence order.[45] This payment is generally referred to as a residence order allowance. However, the residence order allowance surveys conducted by the Grandparents' Federation in England (1995/6) and in England and Wales (1997/8) show an alarming disparity in the criteria for determining whether or not an allowance should be paid and how much should be paid. Not all authorities had a written document about residence order allowances.[46] Some could not say whether they had ever paid a residence order allowance to a grandparent. Many restricted payments to cases where a child is looked after although some authorities paid an allowance where this would reduce the risk of the child being looked after and others operated more generous policies. The sum was invariably

---

40. Section 10(5). The period of three years need not be continuous but must not have begun more than five years before nor ended more than three months before the application (section 10(10)).

41. Section 9(3).

42. Section 10(7).

43. One grandparent carer said 'As soon as we got the Residence Order, you could hear them say "Bingo! That's finished".' Pitcher, D. (1999). *When Grandparents Care*, p27. Plymouth City Council Social Services.

44. [1995] 1FLR 675.

45. Paragraph 15 of Schedule 1. This provision does not apply where the residence order is made in favour of a parent or step parent.

46. One of the nine specific good practice suggestions in *The Children Act 1989 Residence Orders Study: A study of the experiences of local authorities of public law residence orders* (1995), Department of Health, was that local authorities should have policies about residence order allowances.

means-tested and subject to annual review but was often much less for relatives and sometimes time limited to as little as two to three years. This treatment can result in considerable hardship to the grandparents and to the children.

Even where long term provision is made a residence order ends when a child reaches 16 unless there are exceptional circumstances.[47] The power to extend the order is intended to cover a child who has learning difficulties and will need continued protection throughout his or her minority. The ending of a residence order at 16 will terminate any residence order allowance. It could be argued that the need to continue the allowance constitutes exceptional circumstances so that the residence order is extended until the child is 18. Enterprising local authorities are known to make use of cash for children in need in their areas to help out but this type of help is usually regarded as short-term or 'one-off' assistance. Where a grandparent has moved out of the local authority's area there would seem to be no power for the authority to continue to make payments for a child in need over 16.

Social work support

Once the children are subject to a residence order and no longer looked after, social work support is usually withdrawn. Some grandparents do not understand that this will happen or why. Grandparents who have parental responsibility cannot be obliged to receive support but a number would like it to continue and feel isolated and uncertain when support stops. Some complain of feeling left 'high and dry' with nobody to turn to, at a time when their grandchildren are unsettled.[48]

Conflicts with parents

A residence order decides with whom a child is to live and gives parental responsibility to the holder if he or she does not already have it. It does not take away anyone else's parental responsibility except that of the local authority. This can lead to difficulties for the grandparents who find they have no buffer between themselves and the parents as the local authority no longer controls the extent to which the parents can meet their parental responsibility. Some grandparents are afraid because they recognise that the parents could make their lives and their grandchildren's lives very difficult. Parents can meet their parental responsibility freely so long as this is not inconsistent with the residence order. However, there are some steps that can be taken to increase the stability of the placement where these will promote the child's welfare. Directions may be given about how the residence order is carried into effect and conditions can be imposed on the parents.[49] Additional orders can be made, for example, a prohibited steps order[50] preventing the parents from meeting some aspects of their parental responsibility without the court's consent or an order that the parents may not apply for certain types of order without leave.[51]

Appointment of a guardian

A problem that causes anxiety for older grandparents, or those who do not enjoy good health, is their inability to appoint a guardian to take their place if they should die before the children grow up. Even if they have a residence order they cannot appoint a guardian since only parents or guardians can do so.[52] If the children remain in care this is something that can be discussed with social workers and the carer's views recorded on the children's file. However, if there is a residence order and a sole grandparent dies only the parents have parental responsibility and the children may once again be at risk of suffering significant harm. Their inability to appoint a guardian may be one reason why some grandparents decide to apply to adopt their grandchildren.

---

47. Section 9(6).
48. *The Children Act 1989 Residence Orders Study: A study of the experiences of local authorities of public law residence orders* (1995), p38. Department of Health.
49. Section 11(7) provides that a section 8 order may contain directions about how it is to be carried into effect and may impose conditions on parents, those with parental responsibility and anyone with whom the child is living.
50. A prohibited steps order is an order that no step which could be taken by a parent in meeting his parental responsibility for a child, and which is of a kind specified in the order, shall be taken without the consent of the court (section 8).
51. Section 91(14) provides that the court may order that no order under the Act of any specified kind may be made with respect to the child concerned by any person named in the order without leave of the court.
52. Section 5(3) and (4).

Adoption

Neither the Adoption Act 1976 nor the Children Act 1989 imposes any restrictions on relatives applying to adopt. However, there are two main arguments against relative adoption. The first is that adoption distorts the biological relationships so that, for example, the grandmother becomes the adoptive mother and the mother becomes the adoptive sister. The second is that one side of the family is completely cut out. If the maternal grandparents adopt a grandchild, the whole of the father's side of the family ceases to be connected in law to the child. The need to introduce a new order that provides a feeling of greater security than a residence order and continues until adulthood without the disadvantages of adoption is widely recognised.[53]

If, exceptionally, an adoption agency wishes to place children with grandparents for adoption the placement will be an agency placement and the Adoption Agencies Regulations 1983 will apply. It will be necessary to go to the adoption panel for a 'best interests' recommendation and for the adopters to be approved and matched. If the grandparents were local authority foster carers the placement should change to an adoption placement on an identifiable date. The fostering allowance will stop but an adoption allowance might be payable.[54] The grandparents might decide to apply to adopt their grandchildren without support from the local authority. An adoption order cannot be made unless the grandparents have given notice of their intention to apply for an adoption order to their local authority.[55] The child becomes a protected child once notice has been given.[56] The application will proceed as a non agency placement and the local authority will investigate and prepare a schedule 2 report for the court. As in all adoption cases parents with parental responsibility must agree to the adoption or have their agreement dispensed with on one of the statutory grounds.[57]

The Private Law

Where the parents have died

Grandparents may be caring for their grandchildren because the parents have died. This may be an informal arrangement or they may have been appointed guardians by the court or by the parents[58] or the grandparents may have a residence order. Grandparents caring for a child informally without an order will have the same duties arising under the Children and Young Persons Act 1933 as any adult towards a child to protect him or her from harm. They will also be able to do whatever is reasonable in all the circumstances to safeguard and promote the child's welfare.[59] In practice they may manage very well without parental responsibility making decisions for the children without challenge. However, they may find it difficult if the school challenges their authority to consent to outings or trips or if a hospital wants a consent form signed for surgery. If a single issue needs to be resolved this can be achieved by applying for a specific issue order[60] but if it is necessary to go to court it will probably be more satisfactory to acquire an order that gives parental responsibility to the grandparents.

Where both parents have died it is likely that the grandparents will want to be guardians of their grandchildren until they grow up. There will be no need for the grandparents to apply for an order if a parent appointed them guardians under a valid will or signed document. The appointment will take effect immediately on the death of the surviving parent.[61]

The position is more complicated if one parent has died and the other survives. If the surviving parent has parental responsibility an appointment by the deceased parent will not take effect and the

---

53. See for example the *PIU Report on Adoption* (2000), Cabinet Office, recommendation 81.
54. Adoption Act section 57A and Adoption Allowance Regulations 1991.
55. Adoption Act 1976 section 22(1).
56. Adoption Act 1976 section 32(1).
57. Adoption Act 1976 section 16(2). The most usual ground, either alone or in combination with others, is that the parent is withholding agreement unreasonably.
58. Section 5(1) and (3).
59. Section 3(5).
60. A specific issue order gives directions for the purpose of determining a specific question which has arisen, or which may arise, in connection with any aspect of parental responsibility for a child (section 8).
61. Section 5(7).

court cannot appoint a guardian. The only exception is where the deceased parent had a residence order in his or her favour alone at the time of death. If the surviving father does not have parental responsibility or if the deceased parent had a residence order in his or her favour alone at the time of death, an appointment as guardian by the deceased parent will take effect.[62] If the deceased parent made no appointment the grandparents can apply to the court to be appointed as guardians.[63] Where it is not possible to become guardians the grandparents will need to apply for a residence order.

Where the parents are alive but are not providing care

Arrangements may be made privately between the parents and the grandparents for the grandparents to care for the children. This may be for all kinds of reasons, for example, if the parents' work takes them abroad at a crucial period in the child's education. In these circumstances the grandparents may do what is reasonable in all the circumstances to safeguard and promote the child's welfare.[64] However, the parents retain parental responsibility and the grandparents may only meet those aspects of parental responsibility that are delegated to them.[65] Modern communication methods mean that major decisions are still likely to be taken by the parents. The grandparents cannot keep the child against the will of a parent or other person with parental responsibility so if the parents want the child back he or she must be returned.

Sometimes grandparents are caring for their grandchildren not because of an agreement with the parents but because the parent just goes away. A single parent, perhaps with a mental health or drugs problem, might leave the child with the grandparents and not return to collect him or her. The child might be left on a number of occasions returning intermittently to the parent. In these circumstances the grandparents may simply get on with looking after the child. If they are concerned about the stability of the parent and the child's security they may apply to the court for a residence order. Grandparents normally need to get the leave of the court before they can apply for a residence order.[66] If leave is granted they must establish that the order will benefit the child.[67] The child's welfare will be the court's paramount concern and the court must be satisfied that making the order will be better for the child than not making the order or making a different order.[68] Although the parent and grandparents will share parental responsibility no one can act in breach of a court order.[69] Since a residence order determines with whom the child is to live this will prevent the parent from removing the child from the grandparents. If the grandparents obtain a residence order in these circumstances the Grandparents' Federation Residence Order Allowances surveys found that they would be unlikely to be able to obtain a residence order allowance. Local authorities regard these arrangements as private arrangements even though the children would have had to be accommodated if the grandparents had not provided on going care.

Where grandparents are caring for children without the involvement of social services, whether by agreement or otherwise, they are not private foster parents as they would be if they were not relatives.[70] The statutory regime covering private arrangements for fostering children does not apply to relatives.[71]

Human Rights Act 1998

No overview of the law would be complete without some reference to the recently implemented Human Rights Act 1998.[72] This allows applicants to enforce rights under the

---

62. Section 5(7).

63. Section 5(1).

64. Section 3(5).

65. Section 2(9).

66. Section 10(5). See too comments on the need to apply for leave above.

67. In *B v B (A Minor) (Residence Order)* [1992] 2 FLR 327 a residence order was made in favour of a grandparent because of practical difficulties in day-to-day decision-making and because the 11 year old child was disturbed about the apparent lack of stability in the legal arrangements for her.

68. Section 1(1) and (5).

69. Section 2(8).

70. Section 66(1).

71. Part IX.

72. Implemented October 2000.

European Convention for the Protection of Human Rights and Fundamental Freedoms (usually known as the European Convention on Human Rights) in the domestic courts rather than going to Strasbourg. Under the Act, the Government has a responsibility to ensure that new legislation is compatible with the rights under the Convention. If possible the courts must interpret existing legislation in a way that is consistent with the Convention rights. If this is not possible higher courts may make a declaration of incompatibility and Parliament must decide whether to amend the legislation. Public bodies, including local authorities, courts and adoption agencies, must not act in a way that is incompatible with Convention Rights unless forced to do so by legislation.

It is too soon to say how the courts will interpret the new provisions but it is widely accepted that among the articles most likely to be relevant in cases involving children are Articles 6 (the right to a fair hearing), Article 8 (the right to respect for a person's private and family life) and Article 14 (prohibition of discrimination).[73] Areas that are likely to see early challenges include care proceedings and proceedings for adoption and freeing to adopt. Local authorities will need to show good grounds to justify termination of contact with a child's family and permanent removal of a child from his or her family.[74]

Grandparents bringing up their grandchildren will be able to establish a family life and so will be entitled to protection. However, they will not be permitted to flout the rights of others. In *Hokkanen v Finland*[75] the persistent failure of the authorities to enforce the father's right of contact when the maternal grandparents continued to deny contact despite court orders was held to be a breach of the father's respect for family life. In other cases whether grandparents have a family life with their grandchildren is likely to depend on the quality of their relationship rather than the blood tie alone.

Conclusions

Some grandparents long to be carers of their grandchildren. Some face the sadness of losing contact because of family feuds, relationship breakdown or adoption from care of their grandchildren. Despite the special relationship that many grandparents have with their grandchildren, the Children Act does not give grandparents any rights to contact or to care but it does enable them to bring disputes before the courts (with leave) where the court will give the child's welfare paramount consideration.

Many grandparents who are caring for their grandchildren do not choose to do so but step in when circumstances demand it. This may be a purely private arrangement between them and the parents. It may be to prevent or end the children being looked after by a local authority or it may be as local authority foster parents of children who are being looked after. Sometimes grandparents are heavily penalised in terms of finance and lack of support for undertaking the care of their grandchildren and these issues need to be addressed.

Where the children are not looked after or will cease to be looked after there is a need for a legal order short of adoption that will give grandparents and grandchildren security of placement until the grandchildren's eighteenth birthdays and the holder the right to appoint a guardian.

Where grandparents take on care of children who would otherwise be looked after (whether or not they have in fact been looked after) careful consideration must be given to their financial situation. Local authorities cannot replace the social security system but grandparents should not be regarded as a cheap alternative to long term foster care. The payment of residence order allowances should be controlled by regulations and guidance and not depend on local authority discretion that ends up as a 'postcode lottery'. When allowances are paid they should continue as long as they are needed and not be arbitrarily time limited. Thought needs to be given to how payments can continue up to 18.

---

73. See for example Swindells, H., Neaves, A., Kushner, M., and Skilbeck, R. (1999). *Family Law and the Human Rights Act 1998.* Family Law.

74. Article 8(2) states: There shall be no interference by a public authority with the exercise of this right except such as is in accordance with the law and is necessary in a democratic society in the interests of national security, public safety or the economic well-being of the country, for the prevention of disorder or crime, for the protection of health or morals, or for the protection of the rights and freedoms of others.

75. [1996] 1 FLR 289.

It is vital that local authorities ensure that foster carer grandparents who agree to apply for a residence order fully understand the implications of this. They should not feel coerced into applying and if they decide not to apply should be supported in that decision. Where they do decide to apply their legal costs should be met in full. The current requirement to apply for leave to apply for a residence order is an added hurdle that should be removed by an amendment to the court rules.

Some grandparents are pleased to be free of social worker visits but others feel very vulnerable. Ongoing social work support should not be withdrawn from grandparents with a residence order but made available to families as long as it is needed.

2 Grandparents and the Care of Children: The Research Evidence

Lynda Clarke and Helen Cairns[1]

Introduction

Population ageing and the recent changes in family life in most developed countries are creating new challenges and opportunities for older people. People are living for longer and families have become more unstable and changed in nature: most notably with both parents working. This has resulted in changing intergenerational family relationships. For older people, the relationship with grandchildren is an important adjunct to their relationships with spouses and their children. Indeed relationships with grandchildren may become increasingly important for grandparents as they get older. Their spouse may die or disappear and relationships with children and grandchildren may be renegotiated as the balance or type of dependency changes. Conversely, grandparents may be expected to care for grandchildren or to contribute to their support in financial or emotional terms. As attitudes change towards older people's independence and autonomy this may, however, be at odds with their own desires to continue in paid employment or pursue other leisure interests.

Today, more older people are experiencing grandparenthood than ever before and yet this role, one of the main family roles for older people, has been largely ignored by social researchers and family policy specialists in Britain. Little is known about the extent of grandparental contact and involvement with grandchildren or the extent to which older people are satisfied with their role. This chapter will examine what we currently know about grandparents and the provision of childcare in Britain. Firstly we will review the research evidence to date and then present findings from a quantitative analysis of national sample survey data from Britain, the 1995 'Small Fortunes' (SF) survey. This will be used to map grandparental involvement with children from outside the household in terms of childcare and babysitting. Associations between grandparental care of children and their well-being will be measured in terms of educational achievement and behavioural problems. Finally, we shall suggest the current policy issues to be addressed, which we are considering in the light of our on-going research funded under the ESRC Growing Older programme of research.

What do we know about grandparents and childcare provision?

Very little research on grandparents and grand parenting has been conducted in this country. Conversely, in America there is a well established tradition of research on grandparents and furthermore, there are many support groups (600–700) for grandparents as well as strong grandparent lobbies at Washington DC and in individual states. The issues surrounding grandparenthood are, therefore, that much more advanced in the USA and this is from where much of the research emanates. The potential value of grandparents in this country has, however, been acknowledged by the Labour Government which has stated that it wants to encourage grandparents to play a more positive role in the lives of their families (The Home Office, 1998). Yet these recommendations have been made in the absence of evidence on the role of grandparents today. We know little about the diversity of the role of grand parenting in Britain, what they do for their families and how happy they are with their role.

Until recently, apart from the classic kinship studies of the 1950s and 1960s by Townsend and Young there has been very little research conducted specifically on grand parenting and grandparents in Britain. What we did know was drawn from a few qualitative studies focusing on specific issues and some quantitative work on older people and kin exchanges from a general perspective. Such studies included work on becoming a grandparent, negotiating the grandparental role in the family,

1. Part of this paper reports on research undertaken by Lynda Clarke and Nicola Shelton for the ESRC Award R00023776 *Kin Beyond the Household: Family Exchanges in a Changing Demographic Context.*

grandfatherhood and grandparents material help for families with young children. (Cunningham-Burley, 1984; 1985, 1986, 1987; Wilson, 1987). Finch and Mason (1993) also undertook both a survey and a qualitative examination of family obligations and responsibilities which included grandparents. These studies have all provided useful clues about specific facets of being a grandparent but were not designed to be generalised or, as in the latter case, were not aimed at exploring the grandparenthood role in particular. Other evidence of grandparental input into families can be gleaned from various surveys with questions on patterns of contact and support from extended family members. For example, the British Social Attitudes Survey (BSAS) kinship module of 1995 (McGlone *et al.*, 1998) revealed that grandparents play an important role in the lives of families with young dependent children. A small-scale qualitative study was also undertaken by Age Concern (Walsh, 1998) to explore the role grandparents felt they played in the lives of their grandchildren. Findings confirmed that this role was important for many older people. The interviewees also felt that today's generation of grandparents are more than twice as likely to act as child minders to their grandchildren than previous generations. The problem with such small-scale studies is that we cannot know whether their findings are generalisable, in other words whether they hold true for the entire population of grandparents.

The last few years, however, have seen growing interest in the topic of grandparenthood in Britain and a number of studies have recently been funded. The 1998 British Social Attitudes Survey (BSAS) (Dench *et al.*, 1999) represents a first look at grand parenting using a nationally representative sample. The survey asked grandparents about their relationship with one randomly selected grandchild and vice versa. From this we are able to glean valuable information, for the first time, about what grandparents do for their grandchildren. The survey found that levels of help with childcare provided by grandparents were fairly low. Only a quarter of grandparents with grandchildren under the age of six looked after them during the day and only 14 per cent took a grandchild under 13 years of age to or from school, at least once a week. Interestingly, it also found that mothers working part-time had slightly higher rates of help than mothers working full-time. 32 per cent of grandparents' where the mother worked part-

time looked after their grandchild (aged 12 or under) during the day at least once a week compared with 20 per cent if the mother worked full-time. Just 15 per cent of grandparents looked after their grandchild at least once a week if the mother was not in paid employment. The authors suggest that mothers working part-time are most likely to get family help with childcare probably because their needs are more consistent with the type and level of help that grandparents are willing to provide.

The survey also asked grandparents about their satisfaction with their role. The impact of family breakdown had quite a dramatic effect on grandparents' relationships with grandchildren, perhaps because grandparents felt obliged to provide greater help in such difficult circumstances. Indeed family breakdown was associated with the highest level of grandparental help and with high rates of dissatisfaction. While one third (32 per cent) of grandparents with grandchildren living with both of their natural parents and their mother worked full-time said they would like a life free of family duties, twice as many grandparents where the mother was separated from the grandchild's father (60 per cent) felt this way. High input in terms of childcare appeared to be combined with low satisfaction with the grandparental role (Dench *et al.*, 1999). Although the BSAS provides much needed and valuable information about what grandparents do for their grandchildren it is limited in that it only asked questions in relation to one chosen grandchild. It also only covered one year and as we do not have trend data it is impossible to know if any changes have taken place over time.

Custodial grandparents

Those grandparents who adopt a parental role undertake the most extreme form of childcare provision by grandparents. Unfortunately we know very little about the situation of custodial grandparents in Britain. The only information we have comes from small-scale qualitative research looking at grandparents who parent (Laws and Broad, 2000; Pitcher, 1999). In stark contrast this is an issue of increasing concern in the United States. The national census has been asking questions about grandparenthood in the US since 1970 and has shown a substantial increase in all types of households maintained by grandparents. Since the 1990s, however, the greatest growth by far has occurred in the number of grandchildren residing with their grandparents alone with neither parent present (Casper and Bryson, 1998). The main reasons given for grandparents adopting a parenting role are related to parental difficulties or inadequacies: increasing drug abuse, climbing divorce rates, teenage pregnancies, the rapid rise of single parent households, mental and physical illness, AIDS, crime, child abuse and neglect and incarceration.

In view of the increase in the number of grandchildren living with their grandparents in the US, it is not surprising that much research has been carried out in an attempt to understand the causes of this trend and also to document the effects on both grandparents and grandchildren. A number of studies have been undertaken in an attempt to profile grandparent-maintained households and document the relatively poor economic situation of these families. Studies that have focused on the economic well-being of grandparents living with their grandchildren have revealed the relative disadvantage of these families (Chalfie, 1994; Fuller-Thomson *et al.*, 1997; Casper and Bryson, 1998). These studies have shown also that: black grandparents are more likely to raise their grandchildren (Casper and Bryson, 1998; Fuller-Thomson, Minkler and Driver, 1997; Rutrough and Ofstedal, 1997); kin care is more common among black and Hispanic children (Harden, Clark and Maguire, 1997); and women are more likely than men to be caring for their grandchildren (Casper and Bryson, 1998; Chalfie, 1994; Fuller-Thomson, Minkler and Driver, 1997).

Despite the growing urgency of the situation in the USA we know little, if anything, about co-resident and custodial grandparents in Britain. Early indications from our ongoing study of grandparenting in Britain show, however, that the situation is not as extreme as in the USA. Only about 1 per cent of grandparents had grandchildren living with them, however as no trend data is available it is difficult to know if this has increased recently.

Perhaps of greater interest in the context of Britain is other USA research that has addressed the physical and mental health of grandparents who look after their grandchildren. The results of a number of these studies describe the health of these grandparents as poor compared to non-custodial grandparents. For example, using the Health and Retirement Study, Marx and Solomon (2000) compared the health and demographic characteristics of 123 custodial grandparents and 1152 non-custodial grandparents. They found

that custodial grandparents are more than 80 per cent more likely to report fair to poor physical health than non-custodial grandparents. Fuller-Thomson *et al.* (1997), using nationally representative data, also found that grandparents raising their grandchildren were twice as likely to be clinically depressed when compared to non-custodial grandparents. Smaller scale studies have had similar findings (Burton, 1992; Emick and Hayslip, 1999; Minkler *et al.*, 1992).

Not only can adopting this role have an impact on health, it can also have an enormous impact on the lifestyle of these grandparents. Custodial grandmothers often report having to make dramatic changes, for which they are unprepared, having assumed care of a grandchild (Fischer, 1983). Jendrek (1993) found that the majority of 114 grandparents caring for their grandchildren needed to: alter routines and plans; felt more physically tired; reported less time for oneself; and had less time to get things done. Many of the grandparents also reported less contact with friends and that they were less likely to do things for fun and recreation. Relationships with other grandchildren may also suffer. Custodial grandparents report not seeing grandchildren of whom they do not have guardianship less than they would like (Shore and Hayslip, 1994). Grandparents also report a concern that other grandchildren may be jealous of the attention they pay to live-in grandchildren (Kornhaber, 1996). In addition the relationship with the cared for grandchildren may also suffer. Grandparents in a position of authority tend to have a formal relationship with their grandchildren with less emphasis on indulging the grandchild in their care than traditional grandparents (Emick and Hayslip, 1999). Custodial grandparents are, therefore, unable to have the traditional usually care-free relationship with their grandchildren that others often report.

On the other side of the coin, however, positive benefits have also been found. Many studies of care giving grandparents report that despite any problems arising, care giving grandparents do feel useful and are happy to be able to 'rescue' their grandchildren (Minkler and Roe, 1993; Saltzman, 1992). Jendrek (1993) found that grandparents caring after grandchildren reported having more of a purpose for living. Thus raising a grandchild full-time can have mixed blessings. Although it has its problems, many grandparents also find it emotionally rewarding and recognise its energising benefits (Burton, 1992; Minkler and Roe, 1993).

The range and level of childcare that grandparents provide for their grandchildren can, therefore, vary quite dramatically from those who occasionally baby-sit to those who take on the full-time care of their grandchildren. In the next section we examine the level of childcare and babysitting from a nationally representative survey of grandparents and the effects of this on grandchild development.

Grandparents and daytime childcare

Recent government initiatives to encourage mothers to enter paid employment, specifically the Childcare Tax Credit in the Working Families Tax Credit, are targeted at poor and lone mothers (Family Policy Studies Centre, 1999). This covers 70 per cent of childcare costs subject to a maximum payment depending on family size. Such government action is a recognition of the changing demographic nature of families and the need to provide childcare to enable mothers to work.

There is limited availability and use of formal childcare facilities, such as day nurseries, in Britain and there is no statutory obligation on local authorities to provide childcare except where children are defined as 'in need' (Cohen, 1990; Moss, 1990; Meltzer, 1998). The arrangements that mothers make for childcare vary with the number of hours worked and type of employment (Corti *et al.*, 1994). The cost of childcare relative to women's wages for part-time work may act as a disincentive to use paid childcare. In this scenario informal care by grandparents and other relatives or friends plays an important role in caring for children when mothers work (Martin and Roberts, 1984; Corti *et al.*, 1994).

How far grandparents are involved in childcare and whether this varies by the child's family type is the question examined here. The data analysed are from the *Small Fortunes* (SF) Survey, undertaken in 1995 by the Centre for Research in Social Policy, Loughborough University for the Joseph Rowntree Foundation. This survey was a nationally representative sample survey of 1239 children, stratified by age, birth order and family type.

It can be seen that over half (59 per cent) of the sample children were not looked after by anyone apart from their mother, and a further fifth (22 per cent) were not looked after by a grandparent (Table 1). In total, one fifth (19 per cent) of children were looked after in the daytime by grandparents. This is slightly lower than the estimate found in the BSAS survey (Dench *et al.*, 1999). Grandparents were more likely to be looking after younger than older children and to be looking after them for more hours per week (Table 1). The fact that grandparents were most likely to care for children under the age of five is related to the fact that they are not at school.

Table 1: Grandparent daytime care by age of child

| Hours per week | percentage | | | |
| | Age of child | | | |
	0–4 years	5–9 years	10–16 years	All ages
Parent only care	42.6	58.4	70.5	58.8
No care by grandparent	26.8	20.2	19.1	21.6
1–4 hours	10.6	12.6	3.7	8.5
5–14 hours	8.1	5.3	5.0	6.0
15–39 hours	9.0	2.1	1.2	3.7
40+ hours	1.8	0.3		0.6
Base-weighted 100%	2938	3368	4182	10488

Children under five years old who were at school were less likely to be looked after by grandparents for 15 hours or more per week (results not shown).

Children with mothers who worked full time were most likely to be looked after by grandparents and for long periods; nearly one third (30 per cent) were looked after by grandparents, 8 per cent for between 15 and 39 hours per week and 3 per cent for 40 or more hours per week. One quarter (25 per cent) of children whose mothers worked part time were looked after by grandparents also but only 5.4 per cent for 15 hours or more.

Daytime care by grandparents was related to family resources in a positive relationship. Grandparents were more likely to look after children who lived in owner occupied housing (23 per cent) than those who lived in local authority (10 per cent) or privately rented housing (13 per cent). They were more likely to look after children whose mothers had qualifications (21 per cent) than those whose mothers had no qualifications (12 per cent). Children in families with the highest incomes were more likely to be looked after by grandparents than those with the lowest incomes: 9 per cent in the bottom gross family income quartile (under £154 per week) and 15 per cent in the second quartile (£155–£289) compared with 29 per cent in the third quartile (£290–£420) and 25 per cent in the top quartile (£443 or more per week).

Family size was inversely related to being looked after by a grandparent. Over one quarter (27 per cent) of only children were looked after by grandparents compared with one fifth (19 per cent) of children with one sibling, one eighth (12 per cent) of children with two other siblings, and only 8 per cent and 6 per cent of children with three and four or more other siblings respectively. The model below shows the relative importance of the explanatory factors which we investigated to explain whether or not a grandparent provides daytime care for the target child in the Small Fortunes Survey. It can be seen that this model explains a considerable amount of the variance in daytime care by grandparents. This model includes only the variables found to contain explanatory power once other variables were included. Our initial model included whether the mother had qualifications or not, marital status of mother and receipt of income support.

Family type and mother's working status are the most important influences on whether or not

the child is looked after by grandparents in the day. Children in two parent families where both parents work are the most likely to receive daytime care from a grandparent. The chance of care is reduced by 78 per cent for those children in two parent families where only the father works. Children in lone mother families were 70 per cent less likely to be looked after by a grandparent and children in couple families where neither parent worked 22 per cent less likely.

The age of the child is important in deciding the chance of childcare. The older children, aged 11 to 16 years, were significantly less likely to receive care from grandparents, which is presumably related to the fact that they do not need care or can be cared for by an elder sibling.

Grandparents and babysitting

Little is known about the provision of babysitting for children when parents go out in the evenings for both social or work reasons. However, this is one important way in which grandparents might be involved in providing help for their children and grandchildren. In fact one in four grandparents did baby-sit for children in this study. Babysitting by grandparents was particularly high for younger children, over one third of children under five years (35 per cent) and just under one third (29 per cent) of children aged between 5 years and 10 years old had been looked after by a grandparent in the last month. Babysitting by grandparents was even fairly common for the oldest children; nearly 15 per cent of children aged 10 years to 16 years had been babysat by grandparents in the last month.

A surprisingly large proportion of the parents of the children in the survey reported that they never went out without their child: more than one in four (28.9 per cent). The reasons that parents gave for not going out included not being able to afford to go out or afford a babysitter, not wanting to leave the child, not having anyone to trust to baby-sit and not wanting to go out or interested in going out. One in three children (33 per cent) whose parents did go out were never babysat by their grandparents. This was higher for the older children (Table 3) because one in ten of children aged between 10 and 16 years looked after themselves if their parents were out.

In the same way as daytime care by grandparents, babysitting was related to family resources in a positive manner. Babysitting by

Table 2: Logistic regression model of daytime care by grandparent

Explanatory variables	Odds ratio	Significance level	Confidence interval
Child's age:			
0–5	1.0		
6–10	0.71	0.110	0.47–1.08
11–16	0.32	0.000	0.20–0.51
Other children in family:			
One	1.0		
Two or more	0.51	0.006	0.32–0.82
None	1.14	0.525	0.76–1.69
Family type			
Two parents:			
—both work	1.0		
—only man works	0.22	0.000	0.14–0.36
—only mother works	0.27	0.025	0.08–0.85
—neither work	0.89	0.000	0.03–0.24
Lone mother:			
—not work	0.31	0.000	0.16–0.58
—works	1.32	0.293	0.78–2.24
Parent:			
Under 40 years	1.0		
40 years or older	0.53	0.112	0.25–1.16
Tenure:			
Owner occupied	1.0		
LA rent	0.54	0.017	0.32–0.89
Private rent	0.57	0.335	0.18–1.79

Number of observations: 1199
Prob>chi2: 0.000
Pseudo R2: 0.1514
Log likelihood: -577.62154

grandparents was more common for children living in owner occupied housing than children living in rented housing. Nearly half of children in owner occupation were babysat by grandparents and nearly one in three (29.3 per cent) had been babysat in the last month by grandparents. This compares with one quarter (27 per cent) at all and 16 per cent in the last month of children in local authority rented housing and just under one third (30.2 per cent) at all and 8 per cent in the last month for children in privately rented housing. Children whose mothers had qualifications were more likely to be babysat by grandparents (43.3 per cent) than

Table 3: Babysitting by grandparent by age of child

	percentage			
	Age of child			
	0–4 years	*5–9 years*	*10–16 years*	*All ages*
Never goes out alone	27.2	29.2	29.8	28.9
Never babysitting by grandparent	22.2	29.4	33.1	28.9
Child looks after self	0.2		10.1	4.1
Not this month	15.0	12.4	12.2	13.1
1–5 evenings last month	33.2	27.4	12.1	22.9
6–10 evenings last month	1.8	1.6	2.5	2.1
More than 10 evenings last month	0.3		0.1	0.1
Base-weighted 100%	2938	3368	4182	10488

those who did not have qualifications (24 per cent). Children in families with the highest incomes were more likely than those in the lower income groups to be babysat by grandparents. One half (50.6 per cent) of children in the top income quartile were babysat by grandparents and one third (33.8 per cent) had been babysat in the last month. This compares with one quarter (27.7 per cent) and one fifth (19.9 per cent) respectively for the lowest income quartile.

The employment status of the mother was not related in the same way to babysitting as daytime care by grandparents. Mothers who were not working were more likely not to go out in the evening than those who were working but there was little difference in the proportions of children who were babysat by grandparents in the last month by mothers working status.

Grandparental input and the well-being of grandchildren

The relationship between grandparental support and measures of child well-being is an overlooked topic of study. For this exercise we used data from the children of the 1958 National Child Development Study (NCDS).[2] We modelled the reading, verbal and behaviour scores of these children who were aged 5–17 years. We included the predictors found to be significant in the previous work as well as grandparental support. We measured grandparental input from three main sources. First, a number of responses by the mother as to whom she would turn for support—advice about an important change in her life, help if she was sick, borrowing money, if she was upset by a problem with a spouse, and if she felt depressed and needed to talk or merely needed help with domestic chores. Second, from data on regular payments from someone outside the household and third from regular or usual childcare arrangements. The items on whom the mother would turn to for support and regular money payments showed no association with any of the measures of child development or behaviour.

Grandparental input, in the form of childcare, showed no association with the child's reading or verbal skills. The only significant results were for the models including grandparental childcare and children's behaviour. Children who received grandparental childcare and were living in a lone parent family where the mother was

2. Lynda Clarke and Ian Timaeus developed work undertaken by Joshi, Clarke and Wiggins for the ESRC Award L 129 251 027 *The Changing Home: Outcomes for Children* in order to examine the input of grandparents and child well-being.

economically inactive were significantly more likely to have bad behaviour. This is difficult to interpret but may reflect grandparents stepping in to help with problematic children or may reflect a poor parenting situation. The problem with such analysis of secondary data is that the measures of input from grandparents are indirect and the other factors that one would suspect to be of import for child well-being (material affluence, emotional security, input from other family members, etc.) are unlikely to be known or measured in detail.

Concluding comments and future policy priorities

Family life has changed dramatically in the last three decades. Demographic, social and economic changes have affected the living arrangements and lifestyles of children. Children are being born into more diverse family situations than in past decades and their risk of both losing co-residence with one parent, usually their father, living in a lone parent family and gaining a 'step-parent' have increased. Family life has changed for children in a number of ways other than living without one natural parent. There are important changes in domestic life and the role of families that are having major influences on the young today. Family life has become less gender segregated, mothers are more likely to be working and shared care of children by mothers and fathers is more common than in the past. The role of fathers and parenting are being examined and the importance of the family articulated in official policies

Family interaction and support can be central to the well-being of both adults and children. Support can take the form of economic contributions of cash or in kind, providing meals, clothes or holidays for example, as well as emotional or practical help. The level and type of such family support is changing as a result of both demographic and social changes. It could be argued that population ageing and increasing family break-up, lone parenthood and the increasing employment of mothers mean that support for children by kin from outside the household, especially by grandparents, may become increasingly important for modern families. On the other hand, it could be

postulated that the desire for autonomy among older people, and higher ages at first birth and the use of domestic aids and formal childcare by mothers, mean that grandparents will not be available or needed to provide childcare for grandchildren. We do not know whether either of these scenarios are true as little is known about family exchanges beyond the household.

The Government may wish to encourage grandparents to play a more active role in their families, for example by urging local housing authorities to ensure that wider family members are able to live near each other wherever possible (The Home Office, 1998). Nevertheless, we know little about the role played by grandparents in family support and the care of grandchildren in Britain today. In addition, we know little about how important being a grandparent is to older people themselves and whether they are prepared to look after grandchildren. Grandparents are now becoming a fashionable topic of conversation and research. We shall know more in the near future when current research being undertaken by the authors[3] reaches its conclusions. The need for policy in this direction, in terms of grandparental rights of access to grandchildren, is clear but we do not know how many grandparents are prepared and willing to lend more support to grandchildren and actively care for them on a regular basis. The evidence to date suggests that the story is one of great variation.

References

Burton, L. (1992). Black Grandparents Rearing Children of Drug-addicted Parents: Stressors, Outcomes and Social Services Needs. *The Gerontologist,* 32(6): pp. 744–751.

Casper, L.M., and Bryson, K.R. (1998). *Co-resident Grandparents and their Grandchildren: Grandparent Maintained Families.*

Chalfie, D. (1994). *Going it Alone: A Closer Look at Grandparents Parenting Grandchildren.* Washington DC: American Association of Retired Persons.

Cohen, B. (1988). *Caring for Children: Report for the European Commission's Childcare Network.* London: Commission of the European Communities.

Corti, L., Laurie, S., and Dex, S. (1994). *Caring and Employment.* Employment Department Research Series 39. The Stationery Office.

Corti, L., and Dex, S. (1995). Informal Carers and Employment. *Employment Gazette,* March.

---

3. ESRC project *Grandparenthood: Its Meaning and Contribution to Older People's Quality of Life.* Part of the *Growing Older* Programme of research.

Cunningham-Burley, S. (1984). 'We Don't Talk About it...' Issues of Gender and Method in the Portrayal of Grand Fatherhood. *Sociology*, 18(3): pp. 325–338.

Cunningham-Burley, S. (1985). Constructing Grandparenthood: Anticipating Appropriate Action. *Sociology*, 19(3): pp. 421–436.

Cunningham-Burley, S. (1986). Becoming a Grandparent. *Ageing and Society*, 6: pp. 453–470.

Cunningham-Burley, S. (1987). The Experience of Grandfatherhood. In Lewis, C., and O'Brien, M. (Eds.). *Reassessing Fatherhood: New Observations on Fathers and the Modern Family*. London: Sage.

Dench, G., Ogg, J., and Thomson, K. (1999). The Role of Grandparents. In Jowell, R., Curtice, J., Park, A., and Thomson, K. (Eds.). *British Social Attitudes: the 16th Report*. Ashgate Publishing Ltd.

Emick, M.A., and Hayslip, B. (1999). Custodial Grandparenting: Stresses, Coping Skills and Relationships with Grandchildren. *International Journal of Ageing and Human Development*, 48(1): pp. 35–61.

Family Policy Studies Centre (1999). *Supporting Families*. Family Briefing Paper 11. London: Family Policy Studies Centre.

Finch, J., and Mason, J. (1993). *Negotiating Family Responsibilities*. London: Routledge.

Fischer, L.R. (1983). Transition to Grandmotherhood. *International Journal of Ageing and Human Development*, 16: pp. 67–78.

Fuller-Thomson, E., Minkler, M., and Driver, D. (1997). A Profile of Grandparents Raising Grandchildren in the United States. *The Gerontologist*, 37(3): pp. 406–411.

Harden, A.W., Clark, R.L., and Maguire, K. (1997). *Informal and Formal Kinship Care*. Washington DC: US Department of Health and Human Services.

Home Office (1998). *Supporting Families: A Consultation Document*. London: The Stationery Office.

Jendrek, M.P. (1993). Grandparents who Parent their Grandchildren: Effects on Lifestyle. *Journal of Marriage and the Family*, 55: pp. 609–621.

Kornhaber, A. (1996). *Contemporary Grandparenting*. California: Sage Publications.

Laws, S., and Broad, B. (2000). *Looking After Children Within the Extended Family: Carers' Views*. Leicester: De Montfort University.

Martin, J., and Roberts, C. (1984). *Women and Employment: A Lifetime Perspective*. London: HMSO.

Marx, J., and Solomon J.C. (2000). Physical Health of Custodial Grandparents. In Cox, C.B. (Ed.). *To Grandmother's House we go and Stay: Perspectives on Custodial Grandparents*. Springer Publishing Company.

McGlone, F., Park, A., and Smith, K. (1998). *Families and Kinship*. London: FPSC.

Meltzer, H. (1995). *Day Care Services for Children*. Office of Population, Censuses and Surveys. London: HMSO.

Minkler, M., and Roe, K. (1993). *Grandmothers as Caregivers*. Newbury Park, CA: Sage.

Minkler, M., Roe, K., and Price, M. (1992). The Physical and Emotional Health of Grandmothers Raising Grandchildren in the Crack Cocaine Epidemic. *The Gerontologist*, 32: pp. 752–761.

Moss, P. (1990). Work, Family and the Care of Children: Issues of Equality and Responsibility. *Children and Society*, 4(2).

Pitcher, D. (1999). *Grandparents who Care for their Grandchildren: Issues for Children, Families, and those Working with them*. Social Services, Plymouth City Council.

Rutrough, T.S., and Ofstedal, M.B. (1997). Grandparents Living with Grandchildren: A Metropolitan/Non-Metropolitan Comparison. In Casper, L.M., and Bryson, K.R. (1998). *Co-resident Grandparents and their Grandchildren: Grandparent Maintained Families*.

Saltzman, G.A. (1992). Grandparents Raising Grandchildren. *Creative Grandparenting*, 2(4): pp. 2–3.

Shore, R.J., and Hayslip, B. (1994). Custodial Grandparenting: Implications for Children's Development. In Gottfried, A., and Gottfried, A. (Eds.). *Redefining Families: Implications for Children's Development*. New York: Plenum.

Walsh, J. (1998). *Across the Generations*. England: Age Concern.

Wilson, G. (1987). Women's Work: The Role of Grandparents in Intergenerational Transfers. *Sociological Review*, 35(4).

3 Family and Friends who are Carers: A Framework for Success

Ann Wheal

Introduction

The principle argument put here is that the use of Family and Friends As Carers (FFAC) is critical in maintaining family unity. Anecdotal evidence and the NFCA research (1999) strongly suggest that wherever possible the placement choice of most children and young people is with their family.

Kosensen in her Scottish study (1993) and research in America (Child Welfare League of America, 1994) also suggest that this type of care is likely to be more successful than when a child is placed with stranger carers. This is because the child will be staying within its own community, have the same friends and health care support, and often attend the same school. In most cases FFAC should be considered as the first option, not just for these reasons but because it will often prevent the break up of the family. The religious and cultural rituals and traditions will continue to be part of the child's life and the chance of a successful return home to the child's parent(s) is greater.

During 1997 I carried out a piece of research with Julia Waldman for the National Foster Care Association on behalf of the Department of Health (*Friends and Family who are Carers: Identifying the Training Needs of Carers and Social Workers*. NFCA, Wheal and Waldman, 1997). During the research we contacted and visited three local authorities, who from the Waterhouse research (NFCA, 1997) appeared to have different levels of use of FFAC: an inner city authority, an urban one and an inner London borough. The aim of the research was to identify the training needs of both carers and workers for this type of care. As part of the research we also looked at what policies were available and how these were implemented. The outcome of the research was a working document to enable training materials to be produced (see Flynn's chapter—Ed.). However, we acquired a huge amount of qualitative materials, to date unpublished, some of which is referred to throughout this chapter.

This chapter looks at the way this type of care might develop in order to meet the needs of children and young people. It is in four parts.

The first part looks at the background of this type of care. Part Two offers some suggestions for developing a coherent and structured framework as a way of meeting most children's desire to be cared for by their family or close family friends rather than with a stranger carer (NFCA, 1999). The third part tells Terry's story of being cared for by his aunt after his mother's death and of his anxieties, guilt and regrets when he lived with his father's new wife. Part Three also looks at other issues around this type of care. In conclusion, the chapter suggests a way forward.

This chapter does not seek to pass judgement on current or previous practice, more it attempts to highlight some of the prejudices and commitments to FFAC, and to suggest ways of putting a structure around an often subjective and emotive subject.

Background

Families and neighbours have always sought to support each other and this still occurs today, particularly within black and ethnic minority communities as well as other family structures. Yet, especially with the mobility of labour and the greater proportion of women making up the work force, even compared with twenty years ago, providing family support for other family members is not as viable as before, and furthermore, when it does occur, it often involves far greater sacrifices made by carers.

There have also been differences of opinions, and continue to be (note the 'permanency' and, more recently, adoption discussions) as to what is best for children. For example, the following advertisement for recruiting foster carers by Camden Social Services, published in *Fostering*, Special Newsletter (Camden, 1974):

> ...if this also includes brothers, sisters, grandparents, aunts and uncles, so much the better.

At the same time as Camden were advertising for family carers, other local authorities and organisations such as Barnardos were sending children to other parts of the country because parents (and by implication possible family carers) 'don't know the right answer' and children need to be brought up properly (Barnardos, 1974).

The spasmodic and varied use of FFAC has continued to this day. Practice varies not just from local authority to local authority but sometimes within an individual local authority itself (Wheal and Waldman, 1997). When referring to her research, Waterhouse (NFCA, 1997) also notes that:

> There were marked differences in practice between authorities in their use of relatives and friends as approved carers. Metropolitan boroughs were most likely to use related carers, while county councils were least likely. However, some authorities might be using alternative legal frameworks for such placements, such as Section 17 payments and residence orders. This is an area for further exploration.

FFAC today still lurches from one approach to another. Clearly, what is needed is an overall strategic plan for children to ensure that wherever possible children should be cared for in their placement choice, that is, with a family member or a family friend wherever possible.

A Framework

Diagram A suggests a set of guidelines for professionals when considering what is best for the child. This fits within the framework of The Children Act 1989, The Children Act (Scotland) 1995 and the Children (Northern Ireland) Order, all of which state that wherever possible children should be looked after within their own family.

We must now address the basic fundamentals of caring for children. If, after all possible help and support, a child cannot live with their parent(s), then living with friends or family, either full time, or part time, should be the first option considered by social workers. Policies must be in place to facilitate this. The following is a model that could be adopted. It is based around a paper presented to the Department of Health, Quality Protects, Placement Choice Project Group, February 2000. For this type of care to work effectively and well:

- There must be a formalised acceptance that this type of care is, in most cases, in the best interests of the child and should be the first option considered wherever possible.
- One name and definition for this type of care must be chosen and become universally accepted to avoid confusion. Until one name and one criterion is set and nationally agreed,

some children will fall through the net; some will receive inappropriate care and the wide differences in allowances paid will never be resolved. Examples of names currently in use are kinship care, de facto care, district vetted, child specific, self presenting carers, network care, named carers, specified carers, grey area carers and in Australia 'kith and kin care'. The Department of Health recommendation is that family and friends as carers (FFAC) should become the universally accepted term.

- Good interagency working is essential so that local authorities know when a child is no longer with their own parent(s).
- Changes in the attitude of professionals are needed so that they consider the placement choice of the child first. FFAC should not be considered second best. Everything should be done to ensure that the child and the family receive appropriate support and advice.
- Changes in procedures are required to ensure a service that has the best interests of the child at heart and not as a means of saving money. A manager of an inner London Borough announced, quite proudly at a meeting, that the allowance paid by her authority to FFAC was one and a half times the current government's family support allowance. As one who has cared for my grandchildren I can say that not only is this totally inadequate, it does not take into consideration loss of earnings, extra equipment necessary and other costs such as visiting the parent.
- Clear guidelines and support must be produced for staff and appropriate training provided.

  I am sure we must have some procedures somewhere but I can't say I've actually seen them.

  (social worker when being interviewed for FFAC research, 1997)

- The diversity amongst relative/friend carers must be acknowledged: aunts, uncles, parents, neighbours, friends of carer, friends of family, teacher of child, friend of mother, step-father, older sister but most often, grandparents.
- The concept of transition and the contexts in which relatives or friends manage the change from a private and personal relationship with a child and their primary carer(s) to one which is framed by a statutory duty of care must be recognised.

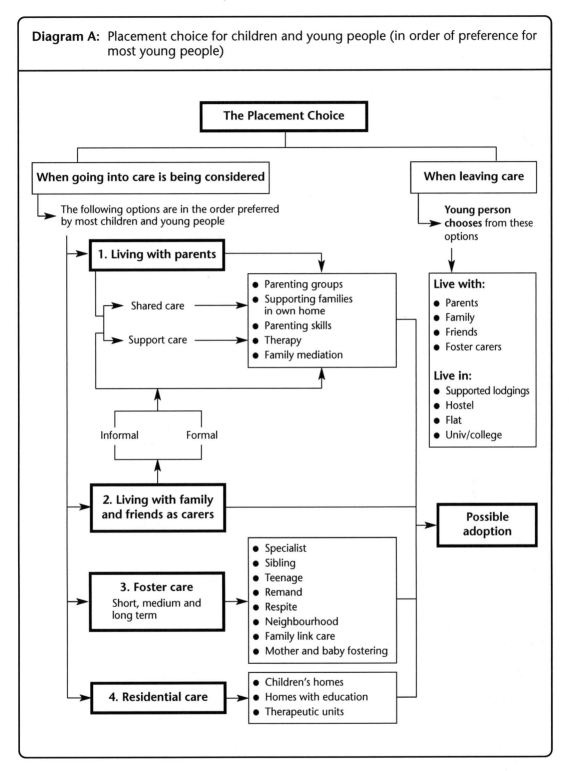

Diagram A: Placement choice for children and young people (in order of preference for most young people)

The Placement Choice

When going into care is being considered

When leaving care

The following options are in the order preferred by most children and young people

Young person **chooses** from these options

1. Living with parents

Shared care

Support care

- Parenting groups
- Supporting families in own home
- Parenting skills
- Therapy
- Family mediation

Informal   Formal

2. Living with family and friends as carers

3. Foster care
Short, medium and long term

- Specialist
- Sibling
- Teenage
- Remand
- Respite
- Neighbourhood
- Family link care
- Mother and baby fostering

4. Residential care

- Children's homes
- Homes with education
- Therapeutic units

Live with:

- Parents
- Family
- Friends
- Foster carers

Live in:

- Supported lodgings
- Hostel
- Flat
- Univ/college

Possible adoption

To enable clear policies to be defined and to put some form of order into a very ad hoc, but most important, system of caring for children, I believe these groupings should be considered.

Group A: where the state is involved

This group contains all children who are the responsibility of a local authority or where the local authority has become involved, regardless of whether the child is the subject of a court order or not.

Kinship carers looking after children in this group should be subject to all the *same regulations and support* as for stranger carers: including similar support for the kinship carers' children if required. They should also get the same *financial reward* as stranger carers.

The only differences might be:

- A less stringent recruitment criteria may apply than for other carers where the benefits to the child of being cared for in this way may be greater than the possible risk. However the criteria must be clearly defined and followed and appropriate checks made.

- Type of training necessary for the carers and for the social workers (see chapter 13).

- Support care should be offered as and when appropriate especially if care is to be long term.

- Consultation regarding the issuing of court order should involve these carers.

Important issues to consider are:

- If family or friend carers subsequently wish to become stranger carers (having successfully looked after a child(ren)) what additional training etc. will be needed for them to become approved foster carers? This is a very sensitive issue from the carer's perspective.

- The type of court order issued must be in the best interest of the child and not in order to save money, for example residence orders.

Group B: private intervention

This category will include:

- A child being cared for as a result of family crisis.

- A child rejected by its mother: for example when the child is born severely disabled.

- Cases where it is part of family culture to share the upbringing of the child.

- Private fostering where parent(s) may be studying, working or have returned to their country of origin for example:

Private fostering often slips through the net of statutory scrutiny and remains unmonitored. If private fostering were placed within this group then appropriate checks would automatically be made if appropriate.

- Shared/support care provided by the family to assist a parent who is unable to totally care for the child, thus preventing child being 'looked after'.

In order to prevent the groups of children in section B entering 'care', support both short term, long term, emotional, practical, financial and technical should be offered to the family or friend carer. In some cultures it would be inappropriate for families to be offered or to accept financial support to help them care for the children of someone in their family and this must be acknowledged, understood and respected. The fact that different forms of support are available should be made known to the carers, possibly through the health or education services.

Criteria for safety checks, both practical within the home, and in the quality of care, should be drawn up. Health visitors and schools will, in most cases, be aware of who is bringing up the child and this information should be collated on a database and made available as appropriate (restricted circulation—carer informed who has access) in order to monitor the well-being of the child and ensure his/her safety.

Group C: neighbourhood fostering

In this category will be those who are recruited within the home location of a specific child, for example when it is known that a mother who is incapable of looking after a child is pregnant again and suitable plans need to be made to care for the new child. These carers, once trained, would become available as stranger carers in the future.

Neighbourhood fostering is a scheme that specifically targets prospective carers in areas of potential high need of foster carers i.e. within the neighbourhood where many looked after children live. In this way carers will come from similar backgrounds, religions, race and class. The children will go the same school, have the same friends, doctor etc. There will often be similar family expectations and in some cases the carer will be known to the family. As one parent said:

> *I know that we're not capable of looking after our baby, but it's so important that she is only a few streets away and we know she is happy.*

(*Working with Parents*, p. 84)

In most cases the local authority will only be directly involved with Groups A and C. However, if appropriate support were provided as necessary for families in Group B then the chances of the child / family moving to Group A are considerably reduced.

Having clearly defined the different groups that might be included within the umbrella term of family and friends who are carers, policies will need to be developed for each group. Before any decisions can be made the important issues need to be identified:

Issues

The next part of this chapter looks at Terry's story and then discusses some of the issues of his particular case. It shows how difficult it is to make the appropriate decisions which are in the best interest of the child whilst still maintaining family unity. This section then looks at more specific issues that must be resolved before clear policies and guidelines can be produced.

Terry's story

My Mother died when I was three years old, leaving my father with three boys. For about a year I believe we remained as a family unit with the assistance of a home help. One of my brothers attended a special boarding school so he was away a lot of the time.

My father was then away for approximately a year or just over and the family was dispersed: his departure was sudden and I am told that my uncle (my father's younger brother) picked me up from the street and took me home. He was a sick man. My aunt, his wife, had to look after him, her eight-year-old daughter, run a small haberdashery shop and look after me.

Although not a blood relative my aunt formed a strong attachment to me. She comes from a large family and has numerous nephews and nieces, but it is probably fair to say that I remain her favourite.

I remained with my aunt and uncle for approximately eighteen months to two years: my father re-appearing and re-marrying during the latter part of that time. Throughout the time with my aunt I had regular contact with both my father's and mother's extended families. I do not have clear memories of those early years but I do remember episodes. I was, I am sure, basically happy. My relationship with my cousin was close and my only memories of my mother are of her ill in bed: I have no image of her.

My step-mother insisted from the outset on bringing the family together. This was initially resisted by my aunt but I joined my father and brothers and step-mother. Subsequently when I visited my aunt she found it difficult to let me go. Thus a very little boy was pulled in two different directions, with shouting and arguing
between aunt and step-mother and anger all round. I must have been very insecure at the time.

With the benefit of hindsight it is apparent that my step-mother was a control freak. My brothers and I were totally cut-off from both my mother's and father's families, mainly because they showed us photographs of my mother and wanted to remind us of her. My eldest brother left home when he was sixteen as the relationship with my step-mother was non-existent. My second brother is mentally handicapped and was institutionalised from a very young age. It is very much to my step-mother's credit that one of her first actions was to bring him home. He stayed with us for approximately 10 years and then was institutionalised again: but there has been a happy ending.

My dependency and loyalty to my step-mother grew throughout those early years. Everything I ever achieved was always seen by her as a result of her input. Any step out of line by me resulted in physical punishment to the closest part of my anatomy be it body or face. My nose was made to bleed on a number of occasions. My father although extremely strong physically never hit me and never interposed himself.

My dependency on my step-mother precluded me from making any real friends and also meant that I was reluctant to go on any school trips which would take me away over night. Not surprisingly with this amount of control at home I was mischievous at school and constantly in trouble for talking in class.

I have memories of seeing both my grandmothers at certain times and of my guilt that they were unable to see more of me. No contact was maintained with any of my cousins.

One particular incident concerned the wedding of my cousin with whom I lived as a child. I was about sixteen and the family was invited. My father insisted that he would go and my step-mother that she would not. I remember agonising as to where my loyalty lay: I did not go and bitterly regret this even today.

This account of Terry's childhood shows how difficult it is to decide exactly what is in the child's best interest.

Some of the issues in this case seem to be:

- Had the father received any social services support following the death of his wife, or in fact, had the aunt received any advice or help?

- How come that Terry was picked up from the street? During the NFCA (1997) research a carer reported a similar event of finding a little girl outside her home. On this occasion it transpired that the girl's mother had been imprisoned and none of the agencies had made provision for the girl.

- Throughout his story, Terry continually mentions the lack of contact with the rest of his family. He also mentions that he has no image of his mother.

- Child protection issues of both physical and mental abuse by his step-mother are apparent.

- The difficulties of 'letting-go' cannot be over-emphasised as my own experience confirms (*The RHP Companion to Foster Care*, 1999). This can cause the child, as well as the family, huge problems.

  ...we thought he was ours, and then he was gone.
  (Sarah)

- Certainly it seems that interagency working did not occur within education, the police, health, and social services.

There is a school of thought that believes in the sanctity of the family, with families solving their own problems without outside interference. In essence this is what happened to Terry but at what cost to his childhood happiness?

Specific Issues

Placements: A senior manager in the NFCA research noted that:

> They have tended to evolve these placements, rather than being thought through and it is time now to sit and think about it and how we're going to deal with them in the future, because as I say, I think there is going to be far more of them.

Clearly, with the shortage of stranger foster carers this prediction is likely to be true. What then is needed is for a clear structure, such as the one suggested above, to be in place nationally, and then issues such as those discussed in this section to be considered and appropriate local policies developed.

Quality of care: For many social workers the burning issue is 'Can poor parents become 'good' or 'good enough' parents?'. The answer is, we do not really know. However, evidence in the United States (Child Welfare League of America, 1994) and in the UK (Kosenen, 1993), suggest that placement with kith and kin does work as far as the children are concerned. What is needed is a flexible and adaptable approach from the authorities providing that all necessary safety checks are implemented.

Assessments: Another difficulty for the social worker is the fact that in the majority of situations, the children are in situ, often staying with a relative or friend as a result of a crisis. Assessment procedures usually happen after the child has been placed:

> *...as far as doing any work or any sort of assessment I didn't do very well there at all. The children were always well cared for and happy when I saw them.*
> (social worker)

Financial reward: Many carers only contact the local authority because they need access to financial support in order to maintain the same family lifestyle with one or more additional children for whom they are caring. For these families the local authority involvement should be on using the strengths and values of the extended family and on providing financial support to assist this.

The whole vexed question of payment and allowances must be resolved and clear guidelines produced for all groups of carers within this framework:

> *I think this type of care is an interest free loan or very low interest loan!*
> (manager)

This type of care is far too widespread and likely to increase in use in the future for it to be left to the whim of the local area manager. Our research highlighted (Wheal and Waldman, 1997) the wide disparity of payment of allowances for what appeared to be very similar circumstances. In one case a family was paid the same amount for a week as another family was paid for a month for caring for two apparently similar groups of children.

The children of the carers: As with stranger foster carers, the children of FFAC should also be considered:

> *...it was very disruptive for the other children and it upset them...because they knew the family they were knowing what was happening and I had to explain an awful lot more than I would have done normally, stuff that you don't really want an eight or nine year old knowing about.*
> (carer)

What do these children think? What help were they given to come to terms with the situation? What did they tell their friends?

Conversely, knowing that one of their own children has failed in their parenting role or adult life may make the carer possessive towards other children still living at home. A local family was bringing up their grandchild because their eldest daughter, aged 18 years, had a baby after refusing to have an abortion because of religious beliefs. Immediately the baby was born the young girl totally rejected the child. The parents then became overly strict towards their younger children, restricting their freedom and preventing them enjoying normal teenage pleasures. This type of behaviour may also occur if drug abuse is involved for example.

Jealousy is also another problem that may occur within families where not only does a child come into a family, often uninvited but out of necessity, but because of their childhood experiences these children need additional care and attention to that which is given to the existing family members.

Changing family relationships: Other family difficulties that need to be addressed are the whole question of emotions and changing family relationships (see Greeff and O'Brien chapters on this critical area—Ed.). The parent(s) who cannot bring up their child must feel jealousy towards the carers. If the children return home they will also feel jealousy when they see the special bond that has developed between the child and the carer. The children may not understand their own mixed emotions or know where their loyalties lie. The carers on the other hand will feel torn between 'letting go' and wanting to maintain the close relationship with the child that has developed over time. It may also not be possible for the same relationships to exist that were previously in existence before the child was cared for by FFAC, for example knowing how the child had been treated; the previous priorities of the parent(s) or how easily the parent may be influenced by others.

Clearly there is a need for such families to receive support and counselling to enable the rest of their family to get on with their lives. Children's views, both the carer's children and the child being cared for, should be canvassed at appropriate times.

Adoption: Adoption is another issue. The same family mentioned above, decided after several years of total rejection by the child's mother that the best option for the child would be for them to adopt him. Intense pressure by the social worker was put on the child's mother to make contact with the child which she refused. It took several more years of fighting their case before it was finally agreed that the couple who had been bringing the child up for 6 years should be allowed to adopt. This couple are articulate and in a financially secure position so were able to fight their case but what of other less fortunate carers who might wish to adopt the child for whom they are caring? It does not take account of the emotional stress for everyone of such a long and drawn out process. It is imperative that clear guidelines are set down so that although each case must be assessed on its merits the whim of particular groups or individuals should not be allowed to get in the way of the best interest of the child.

Access to support: Waterhouse (1997, p. 83) highlights another important area in the use of relatives and friends as approved carers to ensure the needs of carer and child is reflected rather than any 'blanket' policy by agencies:

> *In the case of relative/friend carers approved as foster carers, a different level of service is provided by many local authorities, with less access to specialist family advice, support and training. Identification of varying policies and practices about the approval and use of friends and relatives as carers needs further exploration, especially given the potential of this group to provide placements for specific children.*

Other sensitive areas which also need to be managed are:

Carer's role:

> *Grandparents don't want to be seen as respite carers but grandparents.* (social worker)

Contact with parents:

> *Contact with parents varies from case to case but it's very difficult to manage. It's a very sensitive issue that certainly requires a lot of careful monitoring. There are no guidelines on this, this would be a good thing to put in some training for professionals.* (social worker)

Staff training and support: Without staff being given specialist training to handle such issues, the carers and other family members will always have problems. If this type of care is to be extended then some of the current pressures on social workers need to be alleviated:

> *...a very good long term outcome for the three children but absolutely huge amounts of work for the social worker to undertake.* (social work manager)

> *...I'm there for the children and the pressure is on for a residence order, private arrangement, close it and get on the with the next case, that's the pressure upon us.* (social worker)

Government initiatives: The present government has issued many new initiatives under the banner of 'family support', such as Sure Start Schemes, Early Excellence Centres, Parenting Programmes. Clearly there is a need for creative thinking and 'joined up' working to ensure that FFAC and also parents are able to avail themselves of these and other schemes that are available to ensure the child receives the best possible quality of care.

Conclusion

The above section on issues has not mentioned the differences between the carers in Group A and Group B as many of the issues will be the same or similar. What is needed is clear guidelines set out for social workers so they know when they should be looking to these carers to be substitute carers similar to stranger carers and when they should be offering particular types of support to the families to enable them to stay together.

Creative use of the different sources of funding needs to be made such as social inclusion money, family support, benefit allowances, attendance allowances, respite care money and looked after children funding as well as creative use of resources such as family group conferences, support care, shared care and respite care.

A Director of Social Services, when seeing the suggestions made for this framework said 'but if you start supporting all these families it will cost a fortune'.

In fact, if these families were supported, many children would not need to go into public care with all the stigmas, problems and financial costs that involves. If we are really serious about supporting all children to enable them to achieve their potential and have success in life, there needs to be a change of mindset in all areas of social policy and social work.

In the year when the Human Rights Act was implemented it is time to ensure the rights of children to be cared for in the best possible circumstances when they cannot live with their parents. In many cases this care will be undertaken by family and friends of the child or of the parent.

- Carers have a right to be appropriately trained and supported.
- Social workers have a right to be suitably trained and supported to enable them to carry out the specialised role of this type of care in a professional manner.
- Both groups have the right to have in place, and know of, the policies which will enable the rights and needs of the child to be met in the best possible way.
- Children have a right to a placement of their choice; to remain within their family and friend network if at all possible and to be enabled to live happy and successful lives.

References

Barnardos (1974). *Night and Day*. Essex: Barnardos.

Camden Association of Foster Parents (1974). *Fostering: Special Newsletter*, May edition. London: Camden Association of Foster Parents.

Child Welfare League of America (1994). *Kinship Care: A Natural Bridge*. Washington DC: CWLA.

Department of Health (1999). *National Standards for Foster Care*. Peterborough: HMSO.

Kosensen, M. (1993). Descriptive Study of Foster and Adoptive Care Services in a Scottish Agency. *Community Alternative*, 5(2): pp. 126–128.

National Foster Care Association (1999). *Survey of Children and Young People's Views of the Fostering Service to Inform the National Standards for Foster Care*. London: National Foster Care Association.

Waterhouse, S. (1997). *The Organisation of Fostering Services, A Study of the Arrangements for Delivery of Fostering Services by Local Authorities in England*. London: National Foster Care Association.

Wheal, A., Waldman, J. (1997). *Friends and Family as Carers: Identifying the Training Needs of Carers and Social Workers*. London: National Foster Care Association.

Wheal, A. (Ed.) (1999). *The RHP Companion to Foster Care*. Lyme Regis: Russell House Publishing.

Wheal, A. (Ed.) (2000). *Working with Parents, Learning from Other People's Experience*. Lyme Regis: Russell House Publishing.

Wheal, A. (2000). *Kinship Care: Discussion Document Quality Protects, Placement Choice Project Group*. Southampton: Department of Social Work Studies, University of Southampton.

4 Kinship Care, Child Protection and the Courts

Joan Hunt

Introduction

The importance of the extended family to children who cannot remain with their birth parents is a key theme in the 1989 Children Act (Mackay, 1989). The legislation requires courts, as well as local authorities, to look at kin as a primary resource, (Section 23(6)), provides new opportunities for relatives to intervene in court proceedings (Section 10) and new legal orders, in the form of Residence Orders (Section 8), by which they might acquire parental responsibility.

This chapter draws on the findings of two linked research projects to examine the effect of these changes on children whose futures have to be decided by the courts because they are deemed to have suffered, or to be at risk of suffering, significant harm. The first study, *The Last Resort: Child Protection, the Courts and the 1989 Children Act* (Hunt et al., 1999a) compared court proceedings in the two years preceding and following implementation of the Act, looking in detail at a sample of 83 post-Act cases from three local authorities, in which application was made in care proceedings under s31 of the Act. The second study, *The Best-Laid Plans: Outcomes of Judicial Decisions in Child Protection Cases* (Hunt et al., 1999b) followed up 131 of the 133 children in the earlier sample, charting what happened to them for between two and four years after the court proceedings had ended. Since neither study specifically focused on the issue of kinship, they can only offer a glimpse of what happens to this most needy group of children. As yet, however, there appears to be very little else available in this very under-researched area.

Local authority consideration of kinship care prior to proceedings

In a small study of out-of-home placements in Oxfordshire Thomas (Thomas and Beckett, 1994) concluded that since the Children Act much greater attention was being given to the option of a kinship placement. Nonetheless it was only fully explored in 18 of 31 cases and there were still too many cases where discussion had taken place only with parents, other relatives not being contacted directly. The *Last Resort* study similarly suggested that, post-Act, social workers were taking the kinship network more thoroughly into account. In some cases placements had already been tried and in most there was evidence that contact had been made with relatives. For instance in all but three of the 20 cases in which there was a clear plan to place the child in permanent substitute care the kinship option had been explored. At the other end of the spectrum, where proceedings started as the result of a crisis and little was known of the family, the wider family had been investigated in all but five of 14 cases. Nonetheless, as these figures show, the possibility of a kinship placement was not routinely investigated. Occasionally it was even clear that had the extended family been more fully explored the trauma of care proceedings could have been avoided. Relatives were rarely invited to pre-court case conferences, there only being three examples of this happening. Nor were relatives frequently used for short-term protection: of the 41 cases involving emergency measures there were only seven in which a kinship placement was used.

Participation in care proceedings

In the dying years of the legislation which preceded the Children Act, grandparents achieved a special legal status, being the only people, other than the child, the parents and the local authority, entitled to participate in care proceedings (Children and Young Persons (Amendment) Act, 1986). Controversially, the new law did not preserve this hard-won position. Instead, there was to be a new 'open-door' policy (DoH, 1989: p. 23), under which 'anyone interested in, or affected by, proceedings' could seek the leave of the court to be joined. It was argued that 'leave will scarcely be a hurdle at all to close relatives…who wish to care for, or visit the child'. (Law Commission, quoted in DoH, 1989: p. 23). Further, guardians ad litem (independent social workers who represent children in certain court proceedings, including care) were given the specific duty to advise the court on the existence of anyone with an interest in the child who should be informed of proceedings (Family Proceedings Courts (Children Act 1989) Rules, 1991 r1 (6)(c)). Thus it would be expected that the extended family would have a higher profile within the court proceedings than hitherto.

Evidence from the *Last Resort* study indicated that in the early years of the Act this was certainly the case. Legal and social work practitioners reported greater involvement of relatives in proceedings generally and analysis of the sample cases confirmed this general perception. In 37 cases (45 per cent) non-parent adults (almost all relatives) were either joined to proceedings (30) or participated without being parties. This was higher even than in pre-Act wardship cases (24 per cent) in which the courts, unfettered by statute, were already able to grant party status to anyone with a legitimate interest in the child. This suggests that the Act had changed more than just the legal position of relatives.

It was notable, however, that relatives were rarely parties from the beginning of proceedings. On occasions this was unavoidable, dictated by developments in the case, with the need for care away from the birth family not becoming apparent until proceedings were well advanced. Typically relatives would wait until it was clear that the child would not be returning home before stepping in. In one case of physical abuse, for instance, the local authority worked to rehabilitate the child, first with mother and her partner, then with mother alone. It was only after proceedings had been going for six months and both strategies had failed that an aunt offered to care. In some instances, however, more strenuous efforts by social services might have brought relatives into the picture earlier and avoided delay. It was also evident that the ability of the extended family to participate effectively in proceedings could be limited by the restrictions on publicly funded legal representation. Although anyone joined to care proceedings was entitled to non-merits-tested legal aid, unlike parents and children, they were subject to a means-test. Several practitioners raised this issue while two of the small number of grandparents we interviewed told us that they had not been able to afford legal representation. Given that all the other parties to the case will be represented this is clearly discriminatory and undermines the much-vaunted 'open-door' principle.

Placement with relatives during proceedings

In 69 of the 83 cases in the *Last Resort* sample the children spent at least some time away from their birth parents during proceedings. In 16 cases, interim care was provided for all, or more usually, some of the time, by relative carers (23 per cent). In seven, emergency placements had been made, while in an eighth of cases the child remained with the grandparents with whom she and her mother had been living prior to mother's decision to return to a partner suspected of sexual abuse. A further eight placements were made in the course of proceedings. This included one case in which Social Services had rejected the parents' proposal for an aunt to provide care while injuries were investigated. At the first hearing, on the advice of the guardian ad litem, the court awarded interim residence to the aunt.

The 'success' rate for these 16 interim placements was high, only two breakdowns being recorded and none of the children being put at risk. Of the eight cases in which the children were with relatives from the start one broke down, three placements became long-term, and four ended with the children being rehabilitated. Five of the placements made during proceedings became long-term, one broke down, and two provided the basis for a gradual rehabilitation.

Kinship care as a long-term placement option

In the course of proceedings kinship care was considered as a long-term placement option for at least one child in 20 cases. There was little variation across the three sample authorities in the proportion of cases in which this was an issue. By the end of proceedings there were five cases in which kinship care remained an option, to be explored alongside adoption, foster care or rehabilitation and 11 in which there were firm plans for placement. The 15 children in these latter cases represent 25 per cent of those whose futures, it had been decided, lay in permanent substitute care, the proportions per authority varying between 18, 25 and 31 per cent. These figures are echoed in a more recent study (Waterhouse, 1999) in which 26 per cent of children placed away from home following care proceedings went to relatives, one authority placing 21 per cent, the other 31 per cent. The majority of children for whom kinship care was the firm plan were already living with their relatives by the time of the final hearing. Three of the 13 'sets'[1] of children had been cared for by these relatives throughout proceedings and five moved there between three to 12 weeks before the final hearing. Plans were in hand for all the remaining children to be placed.

In general, placement plans had evolved in the course of proceedings, sometimes quite late in the day. There were only two 'sets' in which kinship care had been the intention from the start; in three the original plan had been to seek permanent substitute care outside the family altogether. In the remainder, a typical feature of care cases (Hunt, 1998) there was no clear plan at the outset, proceedings being used to provide a safe forum within which the children could be protected while the various options, including rehabilitation to parents, were assessed. For the most part, even if the local authority was not the prime mover in formulating plans for relative care, where this became the firm plan they agreed that this was the way forward. However there was one case in which they evidently had serious reservations and two in which they had essentially 'caved in'.

Opposition to kinship placements, however, was more likely to come from the parents. In eight of the 13 'sets' at least one parent formally contested the final hearing and in a further two there had been considerable opposition at an earlier stage. Thus in addition to taking on children with damaging early experiences, many relative carers were likely to have to cope with parental hostility and need to devise strategies for protecting the children from the consequences of being in the middle of warring adults. One of the most worrying of these cases was that of a 10-year-old boy who shall be described here as 'Marcus', who went to live with his aunt 'Patience' but only after both his mother 'Constance' and Social Services had been persuaded to shift their positions.

Case example: 'Marcus' (aged 10 years)

Proceedings on Marcus were brought because of physical abuse. Social Services' plan was for long term care, although the difficulties of finding a culturally matched placement were acknowledged. Although originally accommodated with his aunt, Patience, Marcus's mother, Constance, had insisted on his removal and because of the animosity between the sisters and other practical and cultural difficulties, re-placement had not been considered feasible.

Under pressure from Marcus, this possibility was re-opened and with the prodding of the guardian, became the local authority's care plan. By the substantive hearing, Constance was still contesting the Care Order, the assessment of Patience was not finished and the guardian was sceptical about Social Services' commitment to the plan. The case was adjourned. Constance 'accepted' the plan as the lesser of two evils and Marcus went to Patience five weeks before the final hearing.

A Care Order was considered essential in this case because of the conflict between the two sisters. Care Orders were also made on four other 'sets' of children for whom kinship care was the firm plan, the remaining eight being covered with Residence Orders, four accompanied with Supervision Orders. All the children for whom kinship care was still only an option were subject to Care Orders.

There was no evidence that relative carers were strongly averse to orders which gave some power to Social Services, indeed in some the potential support this offered was clearly positively welcomed. For others it was also a question of financial support. Residence Order Allowances are discretionary and their use varies across the country (Grandparents' Federation, 1996; Social Services Inspectorate, 1995). At the time only one of the sample authorities made such allowances and it was clear that some relatives had been advised by solicitors to opt for a Care Order for that reason. None of the Care Orders were made in cases where relatives were seeking Residence orders. Ancillary orders in relation to parental contact were made in all but three cases. Of the ones accompanying Care Orders only one (relating to Marcus's contact with his mother) actually defined contact. The rest allowed contact at the discretion of the local

---

1. Usually the placement plan was the same for all children in the family. However this was not invariably the case. In one family of four children, for example, only one went to relatives, the rest being placed with their divorced father. In order to deal with this problem the term 'set' has been used to apply to children from the same family for whom the plan was the same.

authority. The orders accompanying Residence Orders (both Contact and Prohibited Steps Orders) tended to be more specific, often reflecting Social Services' concern about contact with one or both parents.

The children and their prospective carers

The ages of the children for whom kinship care was planned or considered reflects the overall sample, 13 of the 20 (65 per cent) being no more than six years old and 11 under five. The gender balance (60 per cent girls, compared to 53 per cent overall) somewhat over-represents girls, but not substantially so. However there was a significantly higher proportion of children from ethnic minority or mixed heritage backgrounds (14; 70 per cent of all such children, compared to 48 per cent). Two more recent studies (Harwin *et al.*, forthcoming; Waterhouse, 1999) also report over-representation.

The concerns leading to proceedings spanned the whole range though with a predominance of physical abuse and/or neglect. In addition to these experiences of poor parenting many children had also spent a period in care. Few were moving directly from parents to relatives and in addition to time in care during proceedings several were either already accommodated at the point court action was taken or had previous lengthy care episodes. In the *firm plan* group, for instance, four children had been fostered for more than a year prior to proceedings and a further two had twice spent lengthy periods in care previously. So it was by no means the case that these children presented less problematic issues to their potential carers.

Although it was more often maternal relatives contemplating taking on these troubled children this was not invariably so. In one case, for instance, two half-siblings were separated, each going to live with their respective paternal grandparents. Two other studies have also commented on the involvement of paternal relatives, Waterhouse (1999) finding equal involvement and Harwin *et al.* (forthcoming) greater. It was also somewhat surprising that prospective carers were slightly more likely to be aunts and uncles than grandparents (11 of 18 'sets'). This is also in line with the findings of both Waterhouse (1999) and Harwin *et al.* (forthcoming).

Outcomes: were placements made?

All the children for whom kinship care was a firm plan at the end of proceedings were placed, usually within days, the longest interval being six weeks. In contrast only one of the children for whom kinship care was only an option was actually placed. Bizarrely, moreover, this placement was not with the (paternal) relatives who had been involved in the proceedings, but with maternal relatives who had not even been aware of the child's existence. This was one of two cases in which Social Services decided not to proceed; in the others the relatives changed their minds. In both the former cases, however, the evidence suggests that the relatives had good cause to be dissatisfied with the decision-making processes. If the decision had been made in the context of on-going legal proceedings, while the outcome might have been the same, the process would undoubtedly have been perceived as fairer and more open.

Outcomes: did placements last?

By the end of the research all but four of the 15 children (9 of 13 sets) were still in placement although plans were being made in anticipation of another placement ending. Three placements had terminated at 3, 9 and 17 months respectively, the other two had lasted for almost three years. Although it is possible that further breakdowns could be expected, since only two of the remaining placements had been tested for such a long period, there was no indication that any were as yet that fragile. Harwin *et al.* (forthcoming) also reports a continuation rate of two in three children.

A comparison of the 'discontinued' and 'continuing' groups showed that it was girls rather than boys, younger, rather than older children, and white children who were more likely to be still in placement. Only three of the six boys were still placed compared to seven of the nine girls. Six of the seven children aged six or less were in continuing placements whereas four of the seven aged ten or more had experienced placement breakdown. Four of the seven placements involving children from ethnic minority groups broke down, compared to only one of the six others. (This contrasts with Harwin's study in which all the breakdowns concerned white children, although the findings with regard to age are similar).

Placements which were originally protected with Care Orders had the highest rate of breakdown: three of five compared to two of the four with Supervision Orders and none of those with only Residence Orders. This may only indicate which placements were perceived to be the most vulnerable and in this respect validate the original assessment. It is important to note that analysis of the circumstances in which breakdown occurred shows it does not merely reflect differences in the ease with which Social Services could terminate placements.

It is noteworthy that all three 'sets' about which Social Services had significant reservations broke down, compared to two of the ten in which they were relatively confident. In comparison parental opposition seemed to have no discernible effect on breakdown rates: although three of those eight placements ended, so did two of the five which parents supported. That is not to say that conflict had no effect, particularly on the children caught in the middle, but in itself it was not a good predictor of placement failure.

Three of the cases which broke down were given poor prognoses at the outset and in two the reasons for breakdown were as predicted. In both the original placements the children had essentially 'driven' the decision, with Social Services having significant reservations. In one case it could be argued that a more thorough assessment of the carer's family situation would have identified the obstacles and in another that the capacity of ageing grandparents to care long term for a child with considerable special needs was not realistically assessed. Thus in all but one case it could be argued that the original decision was insecurely based. However a breakdown rate of one in three children, five of 13 sets, though regrettable, is not high, given that relatives were usually taking on children with poor early parenting, disrupted care experiences and in many cases, having to deal with the active hostility of their parents. It also compares favourably with the 54 per cent breakdown rate for children placed in long-term foster care.

Given the problems these placements were likely to face, the support available from Social Services could have been crucial. In line with other research (Tunnard and Thoburn, 1997), however, it was found that the support offered to these kinship placements varied tremendously, from the impressively assiduous to the disgracefully negligent. Nor did the legal status of the case guarantee a particular level of input: the most neglected case was a child on a Care Order, the most well served on a Supervision Order.

Case example: 'Marcus'

The potential difficulties in Marcus's placement were manifest. As the Social Services' file noted, it was 'beset with cultural complications'; the 'rift between the sisters has left a residue of bitterness'. Despite this Social Services did not provide even a minimum level of service. The social worker left within a month. Her strong recommendation that Patience have her own support worker was not implemented. Moreover, due to staff shortages, the case was not transferred to the long-term team and remained unallocated for the next year. A formal complaint lodged by the guardian ad litem appointed in subsequent discharge proceedings included a formidable list of service and management failures including a totally inadequate response to expressions of concern from the school and Constance and pleas for help from both Patience and Marcus.

By the time a social worker was allocated the situation was reaching crisis point with Patience asking for Marcus to be removed, Marcus producing a range of challenging behaviour and Constance threatening to apply for discharge of the Care Order. Although initially matters were put on hold while an assessment was conducted, Marcus took matters into his own hands, went back home and steadfastly refused to move. The care order was subsequently discharged.

Although this case was extreme, service deficiencies were identified in a further three cases. However, even if more help had been available it is doubtful that these placements could have been saved, while in Marcus' case this must be regarded as at least a possibility. The fact that placements ended prematurely does not, of course, necessarily mean that the experience was entirely negative. None of the placements were terminated because the children were not being adequately cared for and in two they were doing well. However in the other three it did appear that the placement had not worked in the children's interests. In two the children complained about the way they had been treated, two were affected by conflict among their adult relatives, in all three the carers seemed unable to manage the child's behaviour, which deteriorated during placement. There were also concerns in two cases about the carers' ability to protect the children from their parents, with Social Services suspecting that unauthorised contact was taking place, placing the children at risk.

Outcomes—continuing placements

The duration of Social Services' involvement post proceedings in the continuing cases was very varied. One case, where the child was placed abroad on a Residence Order, was closed immediately, three 'sets' were formally closed within eight months and another two were 'de facto' closures, with no contact recorded after 14 and 22 months respectively. Social Services were still working with the remaining two sets between 18 and 26 months later. Only one of the closed cases re-opened, closing again after a period of intensive family therapy had eased the problems grandparents were experiencing in dealing with the behaviour of their adolescent charge. All the continuing cases originally governed by Care Orders were still open, all those with Residence Orders, even accompanied by Supervision Orders, were closed. While Supervision Orders were not a sine qua non for active involvement, neither did they guarantee it. In one case no visits to the family had been made for the last 10 months of the order.

Closure did usually reflect the achievement of satisfactory arrangements and even in cases which were still open, the trajectory was towards improvement. None of the placements appeared to be on the verge of breakdown and only one was still experiencing significant difficulties. This child was also the only one to suffer renewed abuse and to be subject to further care proceedings. One of the children originally on a Care Order was now subject to Residence and Supervision Orders and a second was to be adopted by her grandparents. Although there appeared to be no plans to discharge the remaining two Care Orders they were not being kept in place because of local authority concerns about the placement, rather, it seems, because the carers wished to be assured of continuing support.

In addition to these 'hard' measures of success, qualitative assessments of the placements, variously obtained from Social Services' records, court reports and practitioners, attested to generally good, even excellent placements in which most children were seen to be thriving. Typical comments included 'the grandparents have coped well' and 'the placement has had a very positive effect'.

This is not to say that placements had been plain sailing, or that all the children were doing well. By the end of the research there were still concerns about four children two years or more after placement. Two siblings who had previously spent lengthy periods in foster care were displaying many symptoms of disturbed behaviour, enuresis, tantrums, sleeping and eating problems, although it was generally considered that 'there has been an enormous improvement'. Another child was described as 'defiant', 'sometimes difficult to manage' and 'disruptive in school' although his aunt had done 'an exceptionally good job in caring for him'. The third placement, however, had been particularly fragile, and although exceptional in this sample, the severity of the problems described is a salutary example of how badly things can go wrong, even when the placement has not broken down.

Case: 'Cheryl' (aged two years)

Social Services intervention in relation to two year-old Cheryl was the direct result of concerns expressed by her aunt, Sonia, who cared for her throughout the investigation and subsequent proceedings. Family relationships deteriorated significantly during proceedings, and both parents opposed the application for a residence order. In her report the guardian wrote:

(The case) has been plagued with recriminations between family members. Cheryl has suffered from this and all family members are to blame…A lot of work is required with the family as a whole…It would be tragic if this remains a matter of strong dispute.

Sadly these fears were realised, the relationship between the two families continuing to be marked by hostility, overt aggression, mutual recriminations and allegations. Increased welfare input had little effect and Social Services were proposing to return to court when Cheryl's father assaulted one of her siblings. Care proceedings were initiated on all the children.

Subsequently concerns arose over possible sexual abuse and although Cheryl's carers were exonerated it was pointed out that her needs had often become subsumed for them beneath the agenda of beating her parents and that Cheryl had had to become 'two children for the two families'.

More than three years after placement the relationship between the two families was described as 'appalling, lots of distress, anger, jealousy and one-upmanship'. Cheryl is living with carers who have nothing good to say about her birth parents and is estranged from both them and her siblings in care, all attempts to set up sibling contact having been rebuffed.

The difficulties in this case call into question the wisdom of the original decisions. Would a Care Order have been more helpful? It would have given Social Services the authority to insist on contact being maintained and more radically, to terminate the placement when the conflict did not abate. Would Cheryl have been better off being placed in foster-care in the first place, at least until there had been a thorough assessment of the family dynamics? Should the level of hostility between the two families have ruled out the relatives as long-term carers? None of the social workers familiar with the case were prepared to gainsay the original decision, considering that the advantages outweighed the disadvantages. Others might beg to differ.

Cheryl was the only child still placed with relatives who was not in contact with at least one of her birth parents. This apparently satisfactory finding, however, is somewhat misleading, in that seven 'sets' of children had lost touch with one parent, including previously significant figures and for at least three contact had been highly conflictual.

The loss of maternal contact was the most noticeable. Mothers had been the key figures in the lives of all these children and by the close of proceedings all but one were still in touch. By the end of the research, however, this had dropped to four and contact was likely to be terminated in another. In contrast most of the fathers had previously occupied a peripheral role, but six of the eight who had had contact at the end of proceedings were still seeing their children.

Mothers were more likely to retain links with children placed with their own side of the family, contact continuing in four of the six maternal family placements but in none of the five paternal ones. This seemed to be less important for fathers with contact continuing in four of the five paternal placements and two of the three maternal ones.

Mothers were also more likely to be involved in overt conflict.

Case example: 'Jolian' aged 6 years

Contact between Jolian, placed under a Care Order with his aunt Leila, and his mother Pamela was initially both supervised and at a neutral venue, reflecting the high level of conflict there had been during proceedings. As relationships between Pamela and Leila improved contact became more frequent and informal and plans were made for rehabilitation.

After this plan failed the unreliability of Pamela's contact led to renewed hostility and a return to formalised and supervised contact outside the home. After Leila was persuaded by Social Services to apply for a Residence Order relationships deteriorated even further, leading on one occasion to a literal 'tug-of-love' when Pamela tried to pull Jolian from Leila's arms. All attempts to resolve the contact issues during the residence proceedings failed, and even though Pamela eventually decided not to contest she continued to seek a defined contact order, distrusting anything less specific, because:

…although my sister has convinced everybody that she has an open minded and helpful approach to contact that is not the case. She has a grudge against me…She convinces everyone that she will let me have good contact but she won't…

No order was made on contact, although the local authority undertook to ensure it took place at least four times a year.

Two months later Pamela snatched Jolian. Although she returned him, ten days later she again threatened to remove him. According to the latest information available, almost four years after placement, Leila was trying to move house because of Pamela's harassment and all contact had been suspended.

In all, three continuing placements were characterised by serious chronic conflict between parents and carers and in each by the end of the research maternal contact had either ceased or was likely to do so. In two the children had actually been snatched and were living under threat of repetition. Carers described children cowering terrified as they witnessed these angry confrontations and their confusion and insecurity caused by prolonged adult conflicts. As Leila expressed it: 'Jolian is in two worlds; he doesn't know whether he is coming or going'.

Supporting placements

The difficulties which parents experience in maintaining contact with children in foster care are well-attested (Millham *et al.*, 1986). This research suggests that these can be just as marked where children are placed with kin and that a higher proportion of children might have been able to remain in touch if parents had been given sustained help, both to sort out their own lives and to manage the inevitable emotional turmoil occasioned by losing their children to other members of their families.

The research also suggests that more support was needed for the carers. The only carer we were able to interview in this group, whose charge was on a Care Order, was full of praise for Social Services and for individual social workers. Even so she said she would have welcomed more help in taking on the caring role. Jolian's aunt only applied for a Residence Order under severe, and it would appear quite unfair, pressure from Social Services to demonstrate her commitment to him by doing so or risk having him placed outside the family.

In this case Social Services gave a commitment to remaining involved. On the whole, however, carers with Residence Orders tended to be more left to their own devices, with cases either closing quite early or remaining open largely on paper. One such carer, who actually contacted the guardian ad litem for advice, is reported as saying 'I don't know why Social Services bothered with a Supervision Order, I haven't seen a social worker.' Even in Cheryl's case, where there was some social work involvement, her carers told a case conference three months after proceedings had ended that they had not had as much help from Social Services as they could have done. The fact that the social worker was advised to step up visiting is perhaps some confirmation of the truth of this claim.

According to the case conference record, the social worker's response to the complaint was that she was Cheryl's social worker, not theirs, a somewhat insensitive comment, even if accurate. In the field of public foster care this issue is often dealt with by providing support workers for foster parents. However even where relatives were acting as local authority fosterparents this did not seem to happen, even if, as in Marcus's case, it was seen to be plainly necessary.

Providing every relative carer with a support worker would probably neither be affordable nor necessary. The research suggests, however, that there is a case for offering a support worker for at least a limited period; particularly one with expertise in dealing with the particular issues that kinship placements present. If such a specialist was available in every authority

relatives could be offered the opportunity of a follow-up visit or at least advised how to seek help if the need arose. At the moment, if the social worker who previously dealt with their case has left, relatives may not know how to access help.

Setting up links with other relative carers might be an additional or for some a more acceptable option, given that relationships with Social Services might be somewhat strained and/or ambivalent. There was evidence, for example, that relatives found it difficult to acknowledge the difficulties they were experiencing, fearing they would be seen as failing and that social workers felt diffident and uncertain about interfering.

Conclusion

The generally positive outcomes of the kinship placements considered in this chapter should provide encouragement for the professionals involved in child protection cases to give serious consideration to this option. While the extended family now appears to enjoy a higher profile both before and during court proceedings there is much that remains to be done to ensure that the resources available within the child's network are fully exploited and relatives can play an active part in decision-making. However it is also vital that kinship care is not seen as an easy option, absolving Social Service departments of their responsibilities. Capitalising on the potential of kinship placements requires recognition of their unique characteristics and their individual strengths and weaknesses, assessment of the needs of all the parties to the arrangements and the provision of appropriately tailored services. It is only in this way that the laudable intentions of the Children Act will be realised.

References

Department of Health (1989). *An Introduction to the Children Act*. HMSO.

Grandparents' Federation (1996). *Residence Order Allowance Survey*. Grandparents' Federation.

Harwin, J., Owen, M., Locke, R., and Forrester, D. (forthcoming). *A Study to Investigate the Implementation of Care Orders Under the Children Act 1989*.

Hunt, J. (1998). A Moving Target: Care Proceedings as a Dynamic Process. *Child & Family Law Quarterly*, 10(3): pp. 281–289.

Hunt, J., Macleod, A., and Thomas, C. (1999a). *The Last*

Resort: Child Protection: The Courts and the 1989 Children Act. The Stationery Office.

Hunt, J., and Macleod, A. (1999b). *The Best Laid Plans: Outcomes of Judicial Decisions in Child Protection Cases.* The Stationery Office.

Lord Mackay of Clashfern, Lord Chancellor (1989). In debates on the Children Bill, House of Lords, 7th February, col. 1439.

Millham, S., Bullock, R., Hosie, K.. and Haak, M. (1986). *Lost in Care. The Problems of Maintaining Links between Children in Care and their Families.* Gower.

Social Services Inspectorate (1995). *The Children Act 1989 Residence Orders Study: A Study of the Experiences of Local Authorities of Public Law Residence Orders.* DoH.

Thomas, N., and Beckett, C. (1994). Are Children Still Waiting? Recent Developments and the Impact of the Children Act 1989. *Adoption and Fostering,* 18 1 Spring.

Tunnard, J., and Thoburn, J. (1997). *The Grandparents Supporters Project: An Independent Evaluation.* Grandparents' Federation.

Waterhouse, S. (1999). The Use of Kinship Placements in Court Proceedings. *Seen and Heard,* 9(4): pp. 27–36.

5 Keeping Children in Kinship Placements within Court Proceedings

Suzette Waterhouse

Introduction

Relatives of children subject to care proceedings in England and Wales now have an increasing profile when considering placement options for children who cannot remain with a birth parent. Kinship care has been prioritised as the placement of choice under Section 23(2) of the Children Act 1989 enabling the child's extended family, when appropriate, to become active parties in court proceedings involving the child. This legal change has been coupled with greater recognition of the strengths of such extended family placements for children ('kinship carers'), and the inherent instability and lack of choice often involved in 'stranger' foster care placements arranged by the local authority.

Placement within the wider family has been further strengthened under Article 8 of the Human Rights Act 1998, where the child has 'a right to respect for his private and family life, his home and his correspondence'. International case law has established that extended family relationships fall within the definition of family life.

In the USA, kinship care is the fastest growing service provided by the child welfare system. The proportion of children in such placements has risen from 3% in 1986 to over 45% in 1990 (Meyer and Link, 1990; Gleeson and Craig, 1990). There are indications that certain local authorities in England are making much more extensive use of such placements (Waterhouse, 1997) although in the UK this falls short of that reported in the USA.

Research in both the USA and UK indicate that kinship placements are very enduring and have a high level of stability and satisfaction. Indeed they are more stable placements than those made with traditional foster carers (Scannapieco, Hegar and McAlpine, 1997; Meyer and Link, 1990; Rowe, 1984; Berridge and Cleaver, 1987). However, such placements are often less effectively monitored and supported than traditional foster care despite their complexity often requiring additional supports (Scannapieco et al., 1997; Everett, 1995). For example, the arrangements for contact may require more rather than less support and may require the local authority to mediate or implement plans.

Recent research of care leavers further reinforces the enduring nature of family ties, and emphasises that, in the longer term, it is their extended family, not the local authority, to whom young people look to for support as they move out of the care system (Marsh, 1999).

In England and Wales, the Children Act 1989 ensures that children who become the subject of care proceedings have the most thorough assessment made of placement alternatives for their future care. The Children and Family Court Advisory and Support Service (CAFCASS, incorporating from 31.3.01 the Guardian ad litem and Reporting Officer Panels) should ensure that all options are properly investigated. For those children unable to remain with a parent, the court arena provides an opportunity to look carefully at the option of an extended family placement, supported if necessary by legal order.

Court care proceedings have a clear time frame and a specific outcome for a child at their finish. Clear information is required to be collected about case outcomes, which can be usefully collated for research purposes.

This chapter considers key findings from a research study (first stage reported as Waterhouse, S. (1999). The Use of Kinship Placements in Court Proceedings. *Seen and Heard*, Volume 9, Issue 4.), that considered this data in relation to the use of kinship placements as an outcome of court care proceedings. It then identifies and discusses issues relating to the use of kinship care within a family proceedings framework.

Research Study

The data reported upon in this chapter is gathered from a sample of 650 children who were the subjects of applications for care and supervision orders in Midshire and Southshire during a four-year period ending 30.9.99. The author is a panel member for these two authorities, which are considered comparable ones by the Audit Commission (Audit Commission, 1999).

All applications for care or supervision orders that had been *concluded* in courts in these two counties between the four-year period 1.10.95 and 30.9.99 were included in the study. Children whose proceedings had been eventually withdrawn at a final hearing were also included. As can be seen below, 650 children were identified as meeting these criteria for inclusion in the study.

One application to court could involve more than one child, i.e. a sibling group, although obviously children could have siblings not involved in the proceedings. Sibling groups were not homogeneous in terms of sharing a placement outcome. A different outcome for each child was quite possible. Therefore, data was collected individually for each child. The same child could occur more than once in the sample if

he or she had been the subject of more than one set of proceedings over the study years.

Information was collected from Guardian ad litem record sheets of case closures, and related to:

- Profile information for all the children e.g. age, ethnicity.

- Information as to where the child was placed at the end of the proceedings.

- If the placement was with a kinship carer, further information was sought including details about the relationship of the carer to the child and type of order.

The results that follow are based on a maximum cohort of 650 children. However, in respect of each variable, sometimes information was incomplete and the number of children is slightly smaller.

Table 1: Number of care proceedings children by year

	Child numbers Midshire	Child numbers Southshire	Total no. children
Year 1: 1.10.98 to 30.9.99	92	93	185
Year 2: 1.10.97 to 30.9.98	50	84	134
Year 3: 1.10.96 to 30.9.97	80	105	185
Year 4: 1.10.95 to 30.9.96	77	69	146
Total	299	351	650

Of the 650 children, approximately half of the children (46%) were Midshire court proceedings and a half Southshire (54%). One third of the children were singly involved in proceedings, while approximately two thirds of the children formed part of a sibling group. This figure concurs with other research emphasising, that for

the majority of children, their care experience is shared with siblings (Mullender, 1999). Siblings could be half-siblings or stepsiblings and often had different surnames. Sometimes proceedings relating to siblings would start at different times but would be consolidated together with a shared final hearing. Both the single and sibling children could have other siblings not involved in the proceedings who might live either at the subject child's home or elsewhere.

Placement outcomes

Three possible outcomes for the children at the point that the final hearing was concluded were identified:

1. Child with a birth parent (referred to subsequently as a *parental placement*).

2. Children placed with unrelated local authority carers (*stranger placement*).

3. Children placed with a relative or a friend of the child (*kinship placement*).

The results that follow are based on a 'snapshot' of the location of the child at the point the proceedings ended, rather than the care plan, actual or intended. For the majority of children, this was likely to be their intended permanent placement. However for a small number of

children this would be temporary e.g. they could be in a stranger placement, awaiting the parent's release from prison.

For 646 children their location at the point the proceedings ended was clearly stated in the records (see Table 2 below). Overall, *slightly less than a half (45%) of children were placed with one or both parents* at the point the proceedings had ended. This emphasises that for many children care proceedings do not result in permanent removal from the care of a parent. Of the remaining children, a similar percentage (43%) was in stranger placements, while 12% of children (81) were in a kinship placement. Therefore, *for 57% of the children, restoration to the birth family in some form had been achieved.*

These percentages are very similar to the 47% of children in parental placements and 12% in kinship placements noted by Hunt and Macleod (1998) who followed up placement outcomes for 131 children involved in care proceedings some years earlier.

Table 2: Child numbers by type of placement (Information available for 646 children)				
	No. children in parental placements	No. of children in stranger placements	No. of children in kinship placements	Total
Midshire	126 (42%)	132 (44%)	38 (13%)	296
Southshire	163 (47%)	144 (41%)	43 (12%)	350
Total	289 (45%)	276 (43%)	81 (12%)	646

However, as a return to a birth parent is usually the first and preferred option to pursue for a child, a kinship placement is only a real alternative for those children for whom return to a parent cannot be achieved. The kinship group therefore needs to be considered as a proportion of those children not in a parental placement (276 plus 81), rather than in relation to the whole sample of children (646). *The percentage of children in a kinship placement rose to a more significant 21%*

when only the group of children who were *not* in a parental placement (in total 357) at the end point of the proceedings was considered. This is an increased figure to that found by Hunt and Macleod's research using earlier data, where the plan for 17% of children not in a parent placement was a kinship placement.

The use of kinship placements appeared to be increasing even within the four years of this study, as Table 3 (overleaf) illustrates:

Table 3: Placement outcomes for 645 children over the period 1995–1999				
	1998/99	1997/98	1996/97	1995/96
(1) **Children in parental placement**	43%	49%	42%	46%
(2) **Children in stranger placements**	42%	37%	47%	44%
(3) **Children in kinship placements**	16%	13%	11%	10%
(4) *Total children*	*100%* *(n=185)*	*100%* *(n=133)*	*100%* *(n=184)*	*100%* *(n=143)*
(5) **Children in kinship placement as %** **of all children not with a parent**	27%	26%	19%	18%

While the percentage of parental placements varied between 42% and 49% over the four year period without any particular trend, for those children not in a parental placement, kinship placements rose consistently from 18% to 27%, so that for the most recent year data was collected, *over one in four of the children placed away from a parent were with a relative or friend.*

Variations between the two authorities regarding the proportion of children not with a parent who were placed with kin were apparent. Most significant were the figures for the last year data was collected, which showed that, of the children not with parents at the end of proceedings, 33% of Midshire children were placed with kin compared with 21% of Southshire children. However, the situation is a complex one to explain. Undoubtedly during this period, Midshire has been under pressure from a shortage of short term foster carers in a way that Southshire has not (SSI, July, 2000). This could, for pragmatic reasons, lead increasingly to looking to family and friends to provide child care. However, differing professional practices at fieldwork level could also account for this.

Age and ethnicity of the children

Information regarding child age, ethnicity, order type and relationship of child to kinship carer was collated for the three years (1.10.96 to 30.9.98). The majority of the children involved in

the care proceedings were young, with just over half (53%) being below five years old.

The children in kinship placements were more likely to be very young children than older children. Twenty four per cent of under fives who were *not* in a parent placement were in a kinship placement, as were 20% of 5–9 year-olds and 14% of 10–14 year-olds. None of the nine children aged over 15 who were placed away from their parents was in a kinship placement. This seemed surprising as it is logical that older children might be more likely to be in kinship care if they cannot be with their parents, having more established links with extended family members, and requiring a shorter commitment to their care given their age. It is likely, however, that many such placements for older children are being made outside of care proceedings.

Information regarding ethnic origin was available in respect of 437 of the children. The considerable majority of the children in the sample were white European (84%), with 16% of children coming from minority ethnic groups. Asian and African Caribbean children represented 3% and 1% of the cohort respectively. However, the number of children from mixed parentage groups was notable. Overall, *11% of the children were of mixed parentage* (15% Southshire, 8% Midshire). This figure may reflect national estimates that children of mixed parentage are about two and a half times more likely to be looked after by local authorities than white children (NFCA, 1997). Nineteen of the mixed parentage children were Black Caribbean/white, eight were Asian/white, five were mixed parentage/white, four were Black African/white, four were Portuguese/white, and one was Mexican/white. In the other cases details were not available. Therefore the *mixed parentage group of children was very diverse ethnically and culturally.*

For each year that the study covered, *children from mixed parentage groups had increased.* It is surprising and concerning that this was not only an increase in terms of absolute numbers but also in terms of proportion, representing a rise from 9% in 1995/96 to 17% in 1997/8 of all the children.

Similar percentages of children from white European and mixed parentage backgrounds were in parental placements at the time the proceedings ended (45% and 44% respectively). Most of the children from Black Caribbean and Asian ethnic backgrounds were placed with a parent (75% and 86% respectively) but the numbers of children in each of these groups was very small. Of those children not in a parental placement when the proceedings ended, 18% of white European children and 24% of mixed parentage children were in a kinship placement. Both of the two Asian children were placed with extended family, but the single Black Caribbean child was in a stranger placement. Therefore, proportionately, the mixed parentage group of children were slightly more likely to be in a kinship placement if they were not placed with a parent, but the numbers are obviously small.

Kinship placements and orders

Information was collected in respect of the kinship placement children as to whether the court made a care order or residence order when the proceedings ended. It did not prove possible to collect additional information regarding the making of supervision orders alongside residence orders (as such outcome information was not universally available) nor regarding the payment of residence allowances with residence orders, (as this information was not contained in panel records nor even known to the Guardian).

Of the 52 children in total who were in a kinship placement for the three-year period 1.10.95 to 30.9.98, *42% were placed on residence orders and 58% on care orders.* Southshire courts had made an equal number of residence and care orders in respect of the 32 children in kinship placements in that county, while *Midshire courts had made twice as many care orders* as residence

orders for the 18 children where information was available.

This differing practice could reflect agency, Guardian ad litem or family preferences although the numbers here are small. The possibility of agency preferences operating is interesting. Care orders require the approval of the relative of the child as a foster carer under the Family Placement Regulations 1991 and as such, make greater demands on local authorities in terms of supporting, financing and reviewing placements. It would be interesting to know more regarding the basis upon which orders are made.

Kinship placements and relationship of the carers

Given the fact that fathers of children can often be marginalised in care proceedings, it was surprising and encouraging to find that *not only were maternal relatives active in providing kinship care for a child, paternal relatives played an active part also in providing substitute care for children,* particularly in the case of older children. Of the children aged under five years in kinship placements, 64% (n=18) went to maternal relatives, 31% to paternal relatives and the remainder to friends of the child's family. For children aged 5–9 years, these figures were reversed, with 36% (n=5) going to maternal relatives, 57% (n=8) to paternal relatives and one child to a friend. All the children aged over 10 years old were placed with paternal relatives.

Grandparents were as active as uncles and aunts in providing kinship care for the under fives. There was no suggestion that they took more of a 'backseat' role in respect of young children and babies. Twenty-nine of the 52 placements were with maternal or paternal grandparents.

The other notable feature was *the range of different relatives who offered substitute care*: 44% were individuals other than a grandparent of the child and more than one in ten had no blood relationship to the child. This range of relatives reflects other research findings (Marsh, 1999) where care leavers identified a variety of wider family members from whom support was sought when they ceased to be looked after by the local authority. It is important therefore when considering the kinship option for children to *look to a wider range of relatives and friends* of a child than only to grandparents.

Advantages of kinship placements for care proceedings children

All children have extended families and, in many respects, that only one in four children finds their way into a kinship placement at the end of care proceedings is a low figure. Even the rising figure of 27% of children in kinship placements identified in this study falls short of the 45% kinship placements reported in certain American states (Meyer and Link, 1990; Gleeson and Craig, 1990). If it were possible to include in the figures those children not involved in care proceedings but needing accommodation away from parents, a higher overall percentage is likely to be apparent. Nevertheless, there seems scope for trying to improve the kinship placement rate, even, and particularly, within care proceedings cases. Such placements have real benefits both short-term and long-term for care proceedings children.

In the shorter term, over a half of children who are subject to care proceedings are likely to have lengthy periods in care while an outcome to the legal process is determined and a permanent outcome decided upon. Kinship placements during this period are likely to enhance placement stability for a child during a time when a child is at risk of sequential moves between local authority foster carers. Nationally, there is a real shortage of short-term foster carers and inherent instability of placements because of this. This was highlighted by a survey carried out in June 1998 which showed that children who were the subject of care proceedings and who did not remain at home with parents throughout the proceedings had an *average of 2.5 moves during the course of six months* of the proceedings (Northamptonshire Panel of Guardians ad litem and Reporting Officers 1998). Such a high level of placement instability has persisted as a difficulty in this county and is a concern for many local authorities (SSI, 2000). Placement within the extended family therefore provides the child with enhanced stability during a period of great stress, change and uncertainty.

In the longer term, care proceedings children are likely to have a lower rate of restoration to a birth parent than those children who are voluntarily accommodated. The only alternative to a kinship placement may be the drastic measure of stranger adoption. There are advantages for a child in being brought up within their family in terms of identity, maintenance of family links and a sense of 'connectedness' or belonging. Such placements

inevitably are likely to be culturally a better match than stranger adoptive placements.

Assessment thresholds

There undoubtedly are factors particular to the care proceedings setting which operate as barriers to and militate against the making of such kinship placements. Care proceedings demand a complex balancing act between the child's need for protection and family life (Human Rights Act, 1998) and the welfare principle of the Children Act 1989.

Care cases raise fundamental issues about what thresholds relatives have to cross to keep children within the wider family where parents may have failed to keep a child from harm. How competent does a relative have to be in order to be permitted by the local authority and court to care for a child of the family? If a parent became unable to care through a fatal accident or illness, a relative in all likelihood would step in to take over responsibility for the child without any need to be assessed as suitable by the state. Certainly there would not be a requirement for a substitute relative to be approved by a local authority permanency panel in such circumstances.

This is not the situation once a child is involved in care proceedings, as the court and involved professionals are obliged to consider the child's best interests and the welfare principle. However, this still leaves a dilemma as to what threshold relatives have to cross to secure a child's placement with them. Is it sufficient that the relative's parenting does not expose the child to the likelihood of significant harm (i.e. is just good enough all right?) or does the relative have to cross a higher threshold than this? Certainly there have been difficulties in getting the approval of permanency panels to endorse relative placements as fostering situations in care proceedings. Difficulties persuading panels to approve relatives have arisen where proposed kinship carers have criminal convictions for e.g. fraud or handling stolen goods, or medical histories or age profiles that make panels respond negatively to such placements. But it is precisely these placements that need the support of the local authority with access to training and financing.

Where there are concerns about age or ill health profiles on the part of kinship carers, clear contingency plans for the child can be a constructive way forward to endorse such placements. A plan can be drawn up formally to allow for circumstances where a grandparent or other relative may become incapacitated and therefore unable to care. There is great value in using family group conferences to address such issues so that the family themselves can devise a written plan that can be made available to court and permanency panels.

In other circumstances, concern about possible parental harassment of the child's placement with relatives can be a major worry for agencies. For example, a parent may have mental health problems or misuse drugs or alcohol. This can make their behaviour unpredictable, aggressive or violent. Again, using a family group conference structure, a family safety plan can be written. If necessary, professional advice including involvement from police domestic violence officers can provide a very helpful input into the plan.

A model of kinship care often prevails in care proceedings where relatives have to prove their ability through assessment to take on the care of the child. Emphasis should move from 'approving' towards 'enabling' relatives to care for children in such circumstances.

Relatives can have great difficulty participating in the court process if they do not agree with the local authority's placement plans for a child. There is a considerable financial cost for relatives in becoming involved in care proceedings if the relative falls outside the qualifying limits for legal aid. If a relative is not eligible for legal aid and has no legal parental responsibility, they will have to finance their own legal representation. To take on the local authority in such circumstances is not an even playing field. In one authority a family took out a loan of £5000 to pay their legal costs and had to spend £800 on first witness statements before the local authority agreed to the long-term placement of a child with them. For a family to end up with a debt of this size at the start of taking on the extra cost of an additional child must be very counter productive.

If a relative is approved as a foster carer for a child, the financing, support and training available to such carers is often set at a lower and inferior standard to that of local authority foster carers. There is an urgent need to address this issue as relatives can find themselves just as much in need of resourcing as other carers. Loss of earnings, loss of future plans, plus the extra costs of taking on an additional child need to be taken into account by local authorities in considering how to enable such placements to be successful.

There remains scope for local authorities to be more proactive in the recruitment of relatives to care for children in care proceedings. At an early stage family networks need to be mapped out and family members made aware of the need for a placement for a child. Agencies should have positive policies and practices to address how to promote such care, by identifying and approaching relatives and others within the child's network regarding support which is available if they take on the care of a child. Dedicated family placement officers specialising in kinship placements should be considered as a way forward. There is a need to tailor training to the needs of kinship carers, who may find themselves suddenly caring for a relative's child in advance of any full assessment of their strengths and needs. If the kinship carer needs support and training in respect of, for example, behavioural difficulties, mental health issues or contact difficulties, training and support needs to be responsive to this.

The placement embarked on for a child at the outset of any care proceedings is pivotal. This can set the scene for a whole host of subsequent decisions. Often decisions about whether or not to place with relatives are made almost instantly at the point of emergency removal of a child on very summary information. For other children, such placements may have to await very detailed scrutiny of the relative's situation. Practice in this respect may reflect the views of the social worker dealing with the crisis and there appear certainly to be inconsistencies of approach between workers.

Children who have been studied while in kinship care have significantly better levels of functioning compared with those placed in stranger foster care and, once adults, those who have enjoyed kinship childhood placements do equally as well in terms of adult functioning as those who have been brought up by stranger carers (Benedict, Zuravin and Stallings, 1996). Fein, Maluccio, Hamilton and Ward (1983) commented at the end of their large permanency planning study that children whose out-of-home care experience had been with relatives seemed to do better after exit from care. Therefore it seems crucial to maximise for children their opportunity to be placed at an early stage both temporarily and permanently within their extended family if they cannot live with a birth parent.

References

Audit Commission (1999). *Report of the Review of Social Services in Northamptonshire County Council.* Department of Health.

Barn, R., Sinclair, R. and Ferdinand, D. (1997). *Acting on Principle: An Examination of Race and Ethnicity in Social Services Provision for Children and Families.* London: BAAF.

Benedict, M.I., Zuravin, S., and Stallings, R. (1996). Adult Functioning of Children who Lived in Kin Versus Non-relative Family Foster Homes. *Child Welfare*, 75: pp. 529–549.

Berridge, D., and Cleaver, H. (1987). *Foster Home Breakdown.* Oxford: Blackwell.

Everett, J. (1995). Relative Foster Care. *Smith College Studies in Social Work*, June: p. 235.

Fein, E., Maluccio, A., Hamilton, J., and Ward, D. (1983). After Foster Care: Outcomes of Permanency Planning for Children. *Child Welfare*, 62: pp. 485–562.

Gleeson, J., and Craig, L. (1990). Kinship Care in Child Welfare: An Analysis of States' Policies. *Children and Youth Services Review*, 16(2): pp. 7–21.

Hunt, J., and Macleod, A. (1998). *The Best Laid Plans, Outcomes of Judicial Decisions in Child Protection Cases.* Centre for Socio-Legal Studies, University of Bristol.

Marsh, P. (1999). Leaving Care and Extended Families. *Adoption and Fostering*, winter, 22: p. 4.

Meyer, B., and Link, M. (1990). *Kinship Foster Care, The Double Edged Dilemma.* Rochester, NY: Task Force on Permanent Planning for Foster Children.

Mullender, A. (1999). *We are Family: Sibling Relationships in Placement and Beyond.* London: BAAF.

National Foster Care Association (1997). *Foster Care Facts 1997.* London: NFCA.

Northamptonshire Panel of Guardians ad litem and Reporting Officers (1998). *Children the Subject of Care Proceedings in June 1998.* Unpublished survey.

Rowe, J., Hundleby, M., and Garnett, L. (1989). *Child Care Now.* London: BAAF.

Scannapieco, M., Hegar, R., and McAlpine, C. (1997). Kinship Care and Foster Care: A Comparison of Characteristics and Outcomes. Families in Society: *The Journal of Contemporary Human Services*, pp. 480–488.

Social Services Inspectorate (2000). *Inspection of Children's Services: Northamptonshire, 5th–20th July 2000.* Department of Health.

Social Services Inspectorate (2000). *Social Services Performance in 1999–2000.* Department of Health.

Waterhouse, S., and Brocklesby, E. (forthcoming). *Placement Choices for Children in Temporary Foster Care.* London: NFCA.

Waterhouse, S. (1999). The Use of Kinship Placements in Court Proceedings. *Seen and Heard*, 9: p. 4.

Waterhouse, S. (1997). *The Organisation of Fostering Services: A Study of the Arrangements for Delivery of Fostering Services in England.* London: NFCA.

6 Family Dynamics in Kinship Foster Care

Roger Greeff

Introduction

Kinship care of children is a practical expression of the pattern of relationships within the extended family: in most cases it will express the warmth and commitment between family members, a sense of solidarity and mutual support, and a shared sense of care and responsibility for the child. In some other families, by contrast, the offer to care for a child may be resonant of competition, criticism and condemnation, or of dutiful obligation within the extended family. In extreme cases, the offer to take responsibility for the child may itself be a manifestation of a widely established pattern of child abuse within the family.

This chapter will aim to explore some of the ways in which social workers may use an understanding of family dynamics to make better sense of the strengths and risks within a kinship care arrangement, and to work with the family dynamics as the placement progresses. It will also try to locate these placements within the overall social context of the families concerned; this, for families in contact with social workers will probably mean some level of poverty and social deprivation (Thornton, 1991; Berrick *et al.*, 1994). This emphasis on the 'ecological' context of families has recently been highlighted in the *Framework for the Assessment of Children in Need and their Families* issued by the Department of Health (DoH, 2000a).

In a range of communities, the fact of relatives caring for children may be entirely 'normal'—it is precisely how extended families operate to care for their children in an everyday pattern. Thankfully, in these communities there is still a strong feeling that the child is the responsibility of the whole family. Interestingly, these communities appear to be those which retain a distinctive ethnic identity, and communities excluded from embourgoisement: oppression reinforces the need for solidarity. Equally, we must take care not to generalise about families within a particular community or culture (Ahmad, 1990; Dutt and Phillips, 2000). For instance Chamba *et al.* (1999) report that at least some Asian parents with a disabled child felt that the responsibility lay entirely with them, and

therefore resisted seeking support from their wider family. In their sample, too, Asian and African-Caribbean parents received less support from relatives than white families.

One key factor will be in identifying what 'the family' actually means to this particular family: 'account must be taken of the diversity of family styles and structures, particularly who counts as family and who is important to the child' (DoH, 2000a: 2.15). An early use of a genogram may prove helpful: Portengen and van der Neut (1999) have suggested that, as well as identifying the extent of the network, working at the genogram with the family can identify:

- the strength, intensity and degree of reciprocity in particular relationships
- the roles of specific individuals within the family
- something of the patterns, norms and culture within the family

We need of course to be aware that the 'family' may include 'fictive kin,' people who the family thinks of as members even though they have no formal link.

While the phenomenon of kinship care is very widespread, the main focus of this chapter will be upon those situations where social workers are involved, and on *kinship fostering* in particular. This focus inevitably narrows onto those situations where families have experienced particular hardship, crisis and difficulty. As shorthand, I have chosen to refer to the carers as 'grandparents' (they very often are), and to people as 'she' as a small gesture of anti-sexism.

Empowerment and Partnership

It is of course fundamental that social workers need to ensure that they avoid problematising a situation which may have many strengths: the *Framework for the Assessment of Children in Need and their Families* (DoH, 2000a) has made this very clear. Portengen and van der Neut (1999) have pointed out that social workers can tend to focus on *individuals* and their *problems*, whereas family work needs a wider view of a *network of relationships*, not just the individual, and on *strengths*, not just difficulties. Our primary impulse, they argue, should be to empower families, not to problematise them.

Motivation

One early question to ask is about the *motivation to care*. We are exploring what Titmuss (1970: 212) called 'the reciprocal rights and obligations of family and kinship'. For most family carers, the offer to care for a child will be 'natural' - an expression of their existing commitment to the child, and a feeling, in a positive sense, of a responsibility for her. This might be termed 'abundance' motivation: what sociologists have called 'expressive' support. Pitcher (1999) found that 40% of the grandparents caring for a grandchild in his survey described their prior relationship with the child as a strong, normal one: this clearly provides a basis of enjoyment and commitment to the child as a strong platform for the uptake of care.

In systems terms, we see an inclusive, active extended family system, with an existing sense of shared care and responsibility for the child. This pattern will probably have involved distinct roles, however: grandparents will have been fulfilling the role of grandparent, not acting as primary carers. It is for this reason that even where the background is entirely positive, the process of adjustment may still be demanding, as new roles are adopted and relationships therefore change.

The immediate spur to taking over the care of the child may be a sense of *necessity*: the carers could not contemplate the child going into care, be that a foster home or residential care. This may be accentuated when the family is Black: a sense that continuing care within the family is one key way to ensure that the child continues to be integrated within her own (Black) community.

Another pattern of motivation may be explained by the notion of '*family accounts*' developed by Boszormenyi-Nagy and Spark (1984): over time, family members build up a sense of who 'owes' whom. These 'accounts' may then influence how an individual responds to requests or pressure from another member of the family: 'I owe them, so I had best agree to what they want.'

This sense of *obligation* may be at a level of genuine affection and gratitude for help offered by the parent in the past, and as such is not negative. However, this motivation is in the nature of a transaction between the carer and the parent. There may be some concern that the focus of this motivation is towards the parent rather than the child, and as such lacks the child-centred commitment which is the real strength of kinship care. This question, how far the response is to the child rather than the parent or the crisis, may be a central and crucial one for social workers to ask in assessing the strengths of new kinship care arrangements.

For some carers, there seems to be very little real choice: they are the obvious, or only, relatives available, so they have to undertake this responsibility towards the child. This very generalised sense of *moral duty* is essentially depersonalised and, without a sense of personal commitment either to the child or her parent, it thus has real possibilities of generating a 'Cinderella' situation. The child is looked after dutifully; their basic needs are met, but there is no real emotional closeness or commitment: at best they will be aware that they are a second class member of the household: at worst it will be quite clear that the carers would be happier without them. This situation appears, thankfully, to be quite rare: 1 of 55 placements examined by Rowe *et al.* (1984). However, carers themselves do point up the need for social workers to avoid exploiting feelings of obligation and applying excessive pressure on carers to take up the responsibility of care, or to persevere when pressures are becoming unbearable (Wheal, 1999).

Finally, for some carers, especially grandparents, their motivation may be driven at least in part by *guilt*. They may have a feeling that their child's failure as a parent may represent their own failure to adequately parent her. In this light, there may be an impulse to expiate the past, or to redeem it by showing that this time they can make a good job of child rearing.

Motivations:		
Motivation	**Mode**	**Focus**
commitment	care	child
necessity	rescue	child
family accounts	payback	parent
duty	moral obligation	depersonalised
guilt	expiation	self

A new role for the parent

The continuing role and level of involvement of the parent is clearly crucial in any substitute care placement. It is here that the concept of family systems as having *boundaries* is important. The boundary separating family members within a system or sub-system may be more or less permeable, and more or less clear. If the boundary is *diffuse*, 'fuzzy', then it is never quite clear who belongs and who doesn't: members of the family can be drawn in or drop

out without a clear sense of what is happening. Alternatively, the boundary may be *rigid* and unbending, locking current members in and permanently excluding all others. The ideal pattern is of a system with *clear but permeable boundaries*, so that it is clear who belongs, but it is also possible for members to leave or join smoothly (Burnham, 1991). Is the parent included or excluded from the primary network for the child, and is there some flexibility, so that she can re-work her relationship with her child?

Figure 1: Diffuse, unclear system boundaries

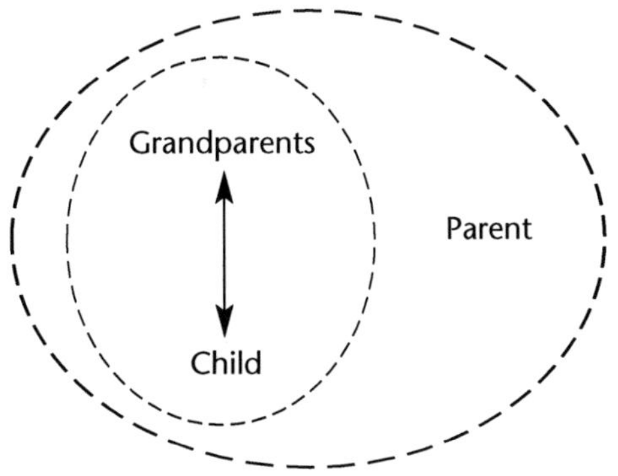

Figure 2: Closed system, parent excluded

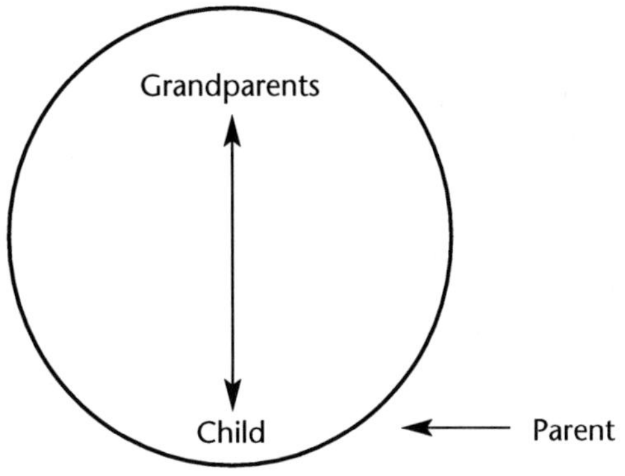

Key to figures

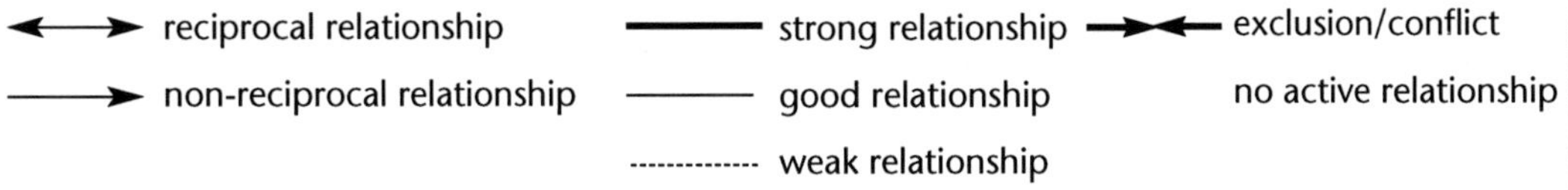

◄——► reciprocal relationship ——— strong relationship ➤◄ exclusion/conflict

——➤ non-reciprocal relationship ——— good relationship   no active relationship

------------ weak relationship

The evidence suggests that the predominant pattern in kinship foster care is one where the child has regular contact with her parent, but will stay with her grandparents more or less indefinitely. This seems to suggest that very often the system boundaries are clear, not ambiguous, and that the system is stable. Perhaps it is this clarity which allows the parent to continue involvement without bringing threat or anxiety to the situation. It has been observed that kinship carers often value having some court order to frame the situation—this may represent a

recognition of the importance of clear, reliable boundaries.

In systems terms, a key question is who comprises the *new parenting sub-system* (Minuchin, 1974). Does the take-up of care by the new carer feel to the child's parent like something that will hold them in place as a parent, or as a change which will take away that sense of parenthood, marginalising her or returning her to a role as (failed) child? Will she see herself (and be seen by their child and the grandparents) as continuing to parent her child, or will her status as parent be temporarily or permanently suspended?

There is a range of roles available to her. She may continue parenting within a shared care arrangement: within this, she may share very evenly with the caring activity and in responsibility for the child. Alternatively, the grandparents may see themselves as parenting on her behalf, delegated care, and look to her for guidance and decision making. More frequently she may become the junior, and occasional, partner in the care of her child.

Another aspect at the inception of the new care arrangement, an equivalent to the motivation of the new carers, is the *attitude of the parent*. Is she encouraging? Does she at least give her permission, if not her blessing? Similarly, it will be crucial to the future of the arrangement whether the new relationship between parent and grandparents is oppositional or co-operative in nature. This may be an important factor in influencing how far the arrangement becomes something in the way of 'shared parenting' rather than a take-over. It will also be central to the child's experience: we know the importance for children of 'parents' who can work together (Howe, 1995). It is one of the advantages of kinship foster care that parents often seem more able to accept substitute care within the family compared with care by strangers.

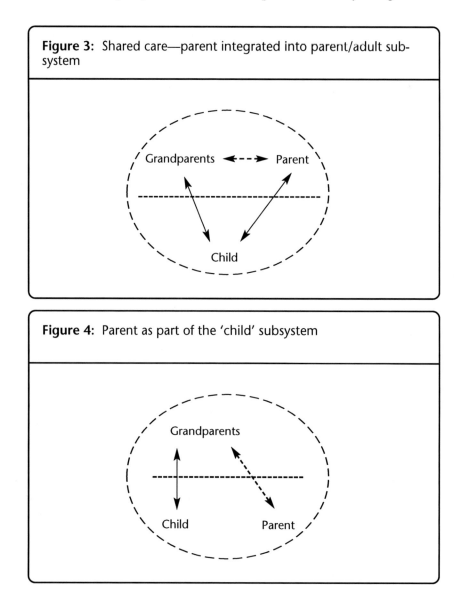

Figure 3: Shared care—parent integrated into parent/adult sub-system

Figure 4: Parent as part of the 'child' subsystem

Family history: making sense of the dynamics

Gorrell Barnes points out the need to hear 'the story within which (the current situation is) embedded' (1998: p. 173). *Family history* may help to explain how the current situation has arisen, and whether there are significant aspects of the family's shared past that will influence the proposed care arrangements. A family systems perspective also suggests that the worker should accept that there is no one objective story of a family's life: there will be a 'plurality of truths' (Gorrell Barnes, 1998: p. 41). She suggests that workers may learn important lessons about the family by detecting which explanations and 'discourses' are dominant, and which are silenced or marginalised.

Worrall (1999: p. 188) refers to the influence of the 'historical roles, power relationships and expectations that exist within the kin family group.' In some cases, there might be a pattern over the years where the grandparents have always tended to 'put down' the parent, their child, and so the parent's difficulty (seen as failure) will be seen as predictable, consistent with her life script, and thus, that it is only 'natural' that the grandparents eventually take over from their 'inadequate' daughter. It is here that a systems understanding may be important in recognising that an explanation which loads the blame onto one person's inadequacy is almost certainly an over-simplification.

A systems perspective will point up that a breakdown in parenting will almost always have been compounded by factors in the family's exosystem: poverty, unemployment, isolation and so on. 'The care and upbringing of children does not take place in a vacuum. All family members are influenced both positively and negatively by the wider family, the neighbourhood and social networks in which they live' (DoH, 2000a: 2.13).

A systems perspective will also suggest that a 'uni-causal moralistic' explanation, that she's to blame, she's a bad parent, it's all her fault, is far too simple. However, thinking of family systems, we must ask what function does this 'disappointing child' (the parent) play in the dynamics of the wider family. It could be that the grandparents and others in the family bolster their own self-esteem by patronising and looking down on the parent. This process will only be eased when they are able to gain a sense of self-worth from a more appropriate and genuine

source. A systems-informed intervention by the social worker may be able to achieve this, with the result that the parent is relieved of the emotional burden of that role. She may then be able to resume a more positive role within the family, and in particular as parent to her child.

At a more extreme level, the 'put down' imposed upon the parent may amount to *scapegoating*, the process whereby facets that other members find it impossible to acknowledge within themselves and their relationships are loaded onto one individual. She is apparently the one, the only one, who experiences depression, or has sexual affairs, or behaves irresponsibly. This is a dangerous pattern, in that the exclusion, the separation and isolation of this family member, is precisely what is meeting the needs of other family members. In this situation, it is unlikely that the parent will, without professional help within the family, be able to recover or redefine her position; the family needs her to continue to fail. There is some danger in this scenario that, freed from their child care responsibilities, she will distance herself effectively from the family: 'do a bunk'. If this is successful, the family may still need someone to fulfil the scapegoat role, and the individual chosen for this role may be her child; 'she's just like her mother'. Any child caught in this script will be unable to develop her own sense of identity, as her needs are subordinated to the dominant theme within the family.

This example highlights the established patterns of behaviour and relationship within the family. There will already be a range of roles, many of them extremely helpful for the new placement. Family members may have well-established roles as supporters, mediators, advisers, advocates, rescuers and so on, and there will be well-established alliances which can offer support in the face of difficulty.

Planning for care—support or isolation

The Children in Need Assessment Framework (DoH, 2000a) has reminded social workers of the importance of a clear understanding of the child's specific needs and the carers capacity, and to assess the support or stress within the wider family and community environment. It specifically points workers to community resources:

- social integration
- income
- employment

- housing
- wider family
- family history

Systems thinking about the 'ecology' of a family can help in assessing the strengths and vulnerabilities of the kinship care plan. What are the relationships within and beyond the family which will have the potential to support the carers and the placement? Is this arrangement an expression of an *open system* with flexible boundaries, responsive to feedback and with a range of other support available within the extended family and the community, or a *closed system*, seeking to contain a difficult situation within a tightly closed intimate circle? This links with Holman's helpful distinction between 'inclusive' and 'exclusive' foster families, and consequent attitudes to the child's history and to partnership working with the agency (Holman, 1975).

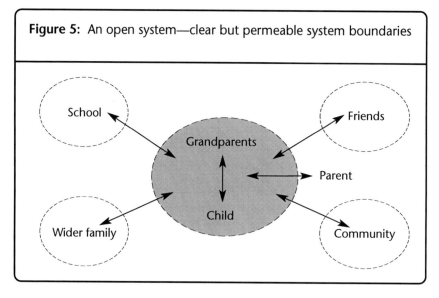

Figure 5: An open system—clear but permeable system boundaries

Family Group Conferences are, of course, a direct activation of family dynamics, seeking to identify a shared sense of commitment to this child. The success of most Family Group Conferences suggests that the wider family does see the child as part of their network of relationships, and as their shared responsibility. As with other issues within families, however, workers need to be aware of the gendered nature of some of this negotiation and decision making: the key discussion within the conference and the family may be essentially between women, and focused on *which* woman should take up this caring role. As Gorrell Barnes (1998: p. 13) puts it: 'Gender…is often one of the vital discourses that affect the mental health and emotional well-being of (specific) individuals in the family.'

Another perspective that sometimes needs acknowledging is that the new (female) carer may well already support other family members as a key part of her script as 'carer' within the family. It is not that unusual for her to be caring already for someone in an older generation as she assumes care of the child. As the wider family

and the worker breathe a collective sigh of relief that the child is safely placed, the possibility of carer overload and burnout must not be ignored.

As Worrall says, 'When family links are numerous, strong, emotionally positive, have common goals, and information is shared, risk potential is minimised' (1999: p. 187). This is amply evidenced by some of the examples given by Pemberton (1999) in her review of her work with Irish Travellers. On occasion, the extended family made it very clear that the responsibility for this child was being taken on, not by one member of the family, but by all of them.

In contrast, Worrall (1999) suggests that members of the extended family will often make offers of support at the planning stage, but that once the placement is effected, the wider family may tend to withdraw and stand back from the placement. She emphasises the importance of support from neighbours and friends beyond the family. This wider network of support may be crucial for children with a disability; Marchant and Jones (DoH, 2000b) point out the significant number of people, unpaid and paid, who may be needed to contribute to a successful pattern of care and support.

Gorrell Barnes suggests that any clear understanding of family situations must be based on looking not just at the family system, but also at the social system in which it is embedded, and at the overall 'ecostructural' system. Thus the worker needs an awareness not only of the support systems available to the family within their community and neighbourhood, but also how far there is poverty and exclusion from opportunity in education and employment. Further, she will also need to know whether this family has to face racism, or a disabling environment for a family member with physical or mental impairment. Of course, we cannot ever ignore the fact that these families are often at the margins of poverty (Laws and Broad, 2000). Individual families will have developed their own particular pattern of family life, derived from cultural values, their social experience, and economic reality (Hartman, 1979).

Adjustment

Changes in family membership, arrivals or departures, 'all involve the development of new patterns and the loss of old ones' (Gorrell Barnes, 1998: p. 3). As with any change of placement for a child, adjustment is a crucial initial stage in the placement, and this will be true even when the placement is a natural development out of previous shared care.

One of the main arguments in favour of kinship care is that it minimises the disruption and discontinuity for the child: the people and the way of life in the new placement are familiar and probably consistent with their previous experience. This is not, however, a panacea: Worrall (1999: p. 189) points out that in her sample 'the fact that the children were in the care of extended family members, who were known to them and totally committed, did not prevent severe behavioural and emotional problems.' These may prove a major challenge for the carers, though Pitcher's sample reported that one of their major encouragements was the improvement they saw in the child's behaviour (Pitcher, 1999).

For many children moving into a new family, it may well seem to them that the task of fitting in to the new family is one which they must try to work out for themselves, their responsibility:

I have tried the whole year to fit in with your family. I just want to be your daughter.

(Worrall, 1999: p. 190)

Pitcher reports that almost 1 in 5 of the children missed their parent, or had to deal with feelings of being rejected by them. They also needed help with understanding what had happened to them, and why: the essential need for life story understanding. It is important that they are helped to ask for support with these issues from their carers. Equally, as with all children separated from their parents, it is vital that they are allowed to maintain a sense of loyalty to their parent. It is potentially very damaging if the child is caught in a triangulated conflict between her carers and her parent (Carter and McGoldrick, 1989).

At the interface between the family system and the outside world, it is a major strength of kinship care that it is far easier for a child to explain that they are now living with their granny than why they are living with unrelated foster carers 'in Care'. None the less, some explanation will be expected by school friends and others: we should not neglect the fact that an important part of the child's successful negotiation of this boundary with the outside world will, like all new placements, involve some thought about the need for a 'cover story.' This will not call for a falsified account, but will question how much of the situation people need to know about, and how to frame the explanation offered. The cover story may also need to have different versions for different audiences.

For the child, one of the key benefits of a placement with kin is that there are a range of adjustments they will *not* have to make. There is evidence that children in kinship foster care feel more secure than in other forms of foster care: 'fewer...feared having to leave the foster home' and they had a 'basic feeling of security and lack of anxiety about their present status and future plans' (Rowe *et al.*, 1984: p. 180, 185). They are also more likely to be placed with their siblings (Berrick *et al.*, 1994), and to have contact with their parents (Rowe *et al.*, 1984; Berrick *et al.*, 1994). The importance of this continuity of relationship cannot be over-emphasised.

It goes without saying that there will be major adjustments for the *carers*, in particular major restrictions on life outside the home. They may find that they are not as able to pursue leisure and educational opportunities; some carers are forced to leave work.

My life has been put on hold...it's a full time job.

(Laws and Broad, 2000)

One of the most widespread comments from carers is the financial cost of assuming care for the extra child or children. This is a major issue for social policy, and for social work agencies supporting (and relying on) these placements. Equally, these effects may lead to an increased isolation of the family unit from outside relationships and support, just as the need for support may be increasing.

The motivation to care for the child may, or may not, be equally shared between the partners.

> *My husband blames me for taking on x but he's very patient and understanding.*
>
> (Waldman and Wheal, 1999: p. 39)

Taking on the care of the child may lead to an increase in love and respect between the partners sustained by their shared commitment to the child. It can also lead to strain on the marital relationship because of the stress of dealing with the child's difficult behaviour and reduced time together to nurture and enjoy their own relationship (Pitcher, 1999). Ultimately it may lead to a breakdown in the relationship between the partners in some cases (Worrall, 1999).

One of the key concepts in systems thinking is that one change within a system will have 'knock-on' effects on all other members of the system. Thus the adjustments will involve not only the carers, the parent and the child, but the *birth children* of the carers. The National Standards for Foster Care (NFCA, 2000) have highlighted the need for attention and support for this group. It may be here that the ambiguity of the situation is most clearly expressed:

> *One of our children refers to her as 'my sister', and one as 'my cousin'*
>
> (Worrall, 1999: p. 190)

In addition to possible confusion and ambiguity, there may well be jealousy and resentment from the carers' children: they will now be sharing their parents' time and attention, perhaps their own bedroom, with the 'newcomer' (Laws and Broad, 2000).

> *You can't call her 'Mum'…She's not your mum! You've taken everything of mine, you're not taking my Mum.*
>
> (Worrall, 1999: p. 194)

These reactions may even be felt by those who have already left home, but are still an active part of the family system. It is noteworthy that the carers in Waldman and Wheal's survey mentioned managing the changes in their relationship with their own children as one area where they felt that help would be valuable (Wheal, 1999).

Acknowledging abuse and neglect

Part of the relevant family history may be that there have been long term concerns about the child within the family, including in some cases, the grandparents making referrals to the authorities. This may obviously have confirmed an oppositional relationship between the grandparents and the parent. Nonetheless, it may come as a relief for the parent when the change of care occurs. Interestingly 80% of the grandparents in Pitcher's survey reported that their son or daughter seemed pleased that the child was with the grandparents now it had happened (Pitcher, 1999).

Equally, Pitcher found that a quarter of grandparents knew nothing of the difficulties until the crisis - and rightly argues that social workers must take care to distinguish the shock experienced by these grandparents, and the time they need to come to terms with the situation, from the very different and obviously worrying phenomenon of denial. As Foulds says, 'Denial is common, and is an understandable human response but it can be dangerous' (1999: p. 72). In some situations the social worker will be asking the grandparents to monitor the relationship between parent and child or to supervise contact. In any case it will be vital that the grandparents are able to acknowledge the abuse or neglect.

In a situation where one of the main strengths is family loyalty, social workers should perhaps not be surprised if, as outsiders, they meet with grandparents who don't want to fully acknowledge 'in public' how badly their own child has failed to provide for or protect their grandchild. It will, none the less, be crucial that an open working relationship proves possible between the worker and the carers. 'Closure' of the family to the outside world is a serious warning sign (Reder *et al.*, 1993).

The Worker and the Agency

As the new arrangement rolls out, the two key questions may well be, where does the child's parent fit in, and in the case of kinship foster care, what kind of working relationship will there be between the family and the worker ? In viewing these issues, the notion of *systems boundary* may prove very helpful, as will the concepts of *alliance, coalition and exclusion*. An *alliance* within a family occurs when two or more members identify a common purpose: ideally, this will characterise the relationship between grandparents and parent in sharing their concern for the child's upbringing. By contrast, a *coalition* involves an element of conflict; here we are seeing two or more members of the family uniting in opposition to some other family member. This could be the situation where the grandparent carers continue to see the parent as a threat, and effectively unite to exclude her from the parenting role.

O'Brien (1999) has developed a framework for analysis of the developing three-way relationship between the carers, the parent, and the worker. She suggests persuasively, on the basis of her research, that although the ideal pattern will be one of open, mutual co-operation and agreement about what is best for the child, the reality can also be one of conflict and exclusion. I will offer a brief and simplified account of her work.

The ideal pattern is one typified by a 'high level of consensus…characterised by partnership, collaboration…mutuality and co-ordination' (O'Brien, 1999: p. 119). O'Brien's research suggests that in a triangular set of relationships

between carer, parent and worker, there is a strong tendency for two of the partners to form an alliance, more or less marginalising the third party. She finds that these sets of relationships fall into two main categories, *co-operative networks* and *conflictual networks*.

Within the overall category of 'co-operative networks,' O'Brien identifies two models, '*shared care*' and '*quasi-adoption*.' In '*shared care*' the parent, grandparents and worker are all initially agreed that this arrangement is the ideal for the child, and the relationship between the carers and the parent is strong, stable and co-operative. O'Brien suggests that as this situation continues over time, the strength of the carer-parent relationship and the fact that the agency is relaxed about the care of the child can lead to the agency taking more and more of a back seat, while the carers and parent feel that this is essentially an arrangement between themselves, and are happy to marginalise the worker, and to minimise her role and level of involvement.

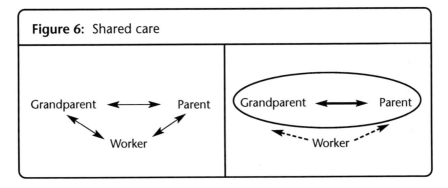

Figure 6: Shared care

The second pattern identified by O'Brien is that of a '*quasi-adoption*'; here, there is concensus that the long-term future of the child lies with the grandparents, and the parent is in agreement or is absent. As time goes by, the grandparents play

the key role, supported, perhaps distantly by the worker, and the parent is increasingly excluded. There is no great conflict because the key axis between worker and carers is not challenged by the acquiescence or absence of the parent.

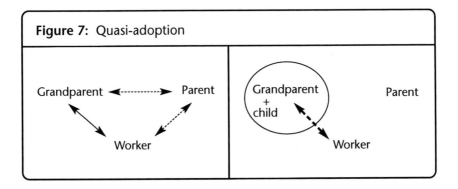

Figure 7: Quasi-adoption

By contrast with these basically co-operative networks, O'Brien goes on to identify *conflictual* networks, 'characterised by high levels of tension and conflict between the participants' (1999: p. 124). The first category of conflictual network identified in her sample was ambivalent or *oscillating* networks. Here, the family carers and the parent are initially agreed that they want to limit the interference of the agency, and therefore create a coalition to marginalise the worker. This tends to intensify the worker's anxiety about the situation, so that there is a growing sense of antagonism between the worker and the family. The oscillation may occur when at some stage the parent develops a wish to resume the care of her child. The carers may now re-align with the worker in challenging how realistic this plan for restitution actually is, and in arguing for the child to stay with them.

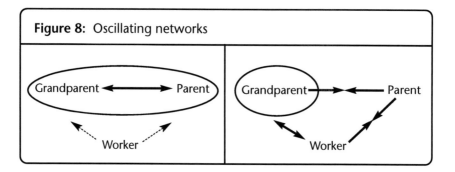

Figure 8: Oscillating networks

The second category of conflictual networks, O'Brien terms *distressed networks*. Here the parent's relationship with the carers and with the worker is 'characterised by high levels of disagreement,' and as the placement goes on, she becomes increasingly marginalised (1999: p. 128). These placements, O'Brien observes, may frequently be those where the child has been removed by court order, so the notion of partnership with the parent may already have proved elusive. It is in these placements that conflict over contact between the parent and her child may be a key, and endemic feature.

It may be interesting to speculate whether it is a reflection of these dynamics that the social worker offers a potentially important ally within the overall dynamics that results in many kin foster carers valuing their relationship with the worker more than many non-relative foster carers seem to do (Berrick *et al.*, 1994). It may be that the relationship with the worker in 'standard' foster care is essentially a functional one, and does not have this additional, emotionally-charged element.

Conclusion

This chapter has aimed to outline the ways in which a family systems perspective can cast light on kinship care situations. Some of the ideas highlighted have been:

- The question of membership (who belongs to this family or network?).
- Boundaries (are roles, relationships and membership fixed or flexible?).
- Subsystems (is it clear who is playing the adult or parenting roles?).
- The significance of family history in explaining the behaviour and potential of today.
- The pattern of rules and expectations, and the distribution of power.
- The importance of the ecology of the family, and support systems in its community network.

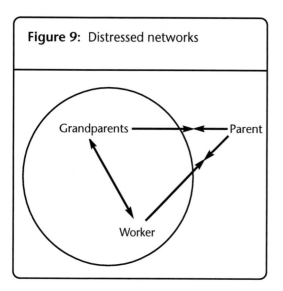

Figure 9: Distressed networks

- The processes of adjustment necessitated by a new child within the family.
- The dynamic nature of the relationship with the worker, and the danger of marginalisation.

Perhaps the critical importance of a systems analysis lies in the view that family systems are dynamic, open to change, and in fact probably in some degree of change and evolution all the time. With clear understanding and assessment, workers should be able to intervene to help the process of change in a direction which will benefit the child who is our ultimate concern.

References

Ahmad, B. (1990). *Black Perspectives in Social Work.* Birmingham: Venture.

Berrick, J., Barth, R., and Needell, B. (1994). A Comparison of Kinship Foster Homes and Foster Family Homes. *Children and Youth Services Review,* 16: pp. 1–2.

Boszormenyi-Nagy, I., and Spark, G. (1984). *Invisible Loyalties: Reciprocity in Intergenerational Family Therapy.* Brunner/Mazel.

Burnham, J. (1991). *Family Therapy.* London: Routledge.

Carter, B., and McGoldrick, M. (1989). *The Changing Family Life Cycle* (2nd edn.). Boston: Allyn and Bacon.

Chamba, R., Ahmad, W., Hirst, M., Lawton, D., and Beresford, B. (1999). *On The Edge: Minority Ethnic Families Caring for a Severely Disabled Child.* London: Policy Press.

DoH (2000a). *Framework for the Assessment of Children in Need and their Families.* London: HMSO.

DoH (2000b). *Assessing Children in Need and their Families: Practice Guidance.* London: HMSO.

Dutt, R., and Phillips, M. (2000). Assessing Black Children in Need and their Families. In DoH. *Assessing Children in Need and their Families: Practice Guidance.* London: HMSO.

Foulds, J. (1999). Kinship Fostering and Child Protection. In Greeff, R. (Ed.). *Fostering Kinship.* Aldershot: Ashgate.

Gorrell Barnes, G. (1998). *Family Therapy in Changing Times.* London: Macmillan   .

Hartman, A. (1979). *Finding Families: An Ecological Approach to Family Assessment in Adoption.* London: Sage.

Holman, R. (1975). Exclusive and Inclusive Concepts in Fostering. *British Journal of Social Work,* 5(1).

Howe, D. (1995). *Attachment Theory for Social Work Practice.* London: Macmillan.

Laws, S., and Broad, B. (2000). *Looking After Children in the Extended Family: Carers' Views.* Leicester: De Montfort University.

Minuchin, S. (1974). *Families and Family Therapy.* London: Tavistock.

NFCA (2000). *National Standards for Foster Care.* London: NFCA.

O'Brien, V. (1999). Evolving Networks in Relative Care: Alliance and Exclusion. In Greeff, R. (Ed.). *Fostering Kinship.* Aldershot: Ashgate.

Pemberton, D. (1999). Fostering in a Minority Community. In Greeff, R. (Ed.). *Fostering Kinship.* Aldershot: Ashgate.

Pitcher, D. (1999). *When Grandparents Care.* Plymouth: Plymouth City Council.

Portengen, R., and van der Neut, B. (1999). Assessing Family Strengths. In Greeff, R. (Ed.). *Fostering Kinship.* Aldershot: Ashgate.

Reder, P., Duncan, S., and Gray, M. (1993). *Beyond Blame: Child Abuse Tragedies Revisited.* London: Routledge.

Rowe, J., Cain, H., Hundleby, M., and Keane, A. (1984). *Long Term Foster Care.* London: Batsford.

Thornton, J. (1991). Permanency Planning for Children in Kinship Foster Homes. *Child Welfare,* 70.

Titmuss, R.M. (1970). *The Gift Relationship.* London: Allen and Unwin.

Stelmaszuk, Z.W. (1999). The Continuing Role of Kinship Care in a Changing Society. In Greeff, R. (Ed.). *Fostering Kinship.* Aldershot: Ashgate.

Waldman, J., and Wheal, A. (1999). Training Needs of Families who are Foster Carers. In Greeff, R. (Ed.). *Fostering Kinship.* Aldershot: Ashgate.

Wheal, A. (1999). Family and Friends who are Carers. In Wheal, A. (Ed.). *RHP Companion to Foster Care.* Lyme Regis: Russell House.

Worrall, J. (1999). Kinship Care in New Zealand. In Greeff, R. (Ed.). *Fostering Kinship.* Aldershot: Ashgate.

7 Contributions from an Irish Study: Understanding and Managing Relative Care

Valerie O'Brien

Introduction

This chapter is drawn from a PhD research study conducted in Ireland between 1993–97 (O'Brien, 1997) and further developments arising in the field since that date. The study is the only one of its type conducted to date in Ireland and has contributed significantly to an understanding of this care option for children. This chapter is divided into two sections. Section one outlines the aims of the study, the development of relative care in Ireland and key findings in relation to the children's and relatives' biographical details, and the care career of the children. Section two describes and traces the processes involved at the decision-making, assessment and post-assessment stages. The chapter concludes with a discussion of the implications for practice and puts forward a model that may assist future practices.

Section One

The study had four specific aims. It aimed to establish a profile of children and the families involved in relative care. The second aim was to examine familial and professional viewpoints which obtain when the child is placed in the relatives home prior to a formal assessment being completed, drawing on the experiences of the multiple participants involved. The third aim was to examine the extent to which a systemic framework (using the fifth province approach) provides a conceptual frame for understanding evolving networks (O'Brien, 1999). A systemic framework refers to a mode of practice in which context; relationship, interaction and meaning are central. The fifth province conceptual approach was developed in Ireland in the early 1980s as a systemic clinical model for use in the area of child sexual abuse (Kearney et al., 1989; Colgon, 1991; Byrne, 1995). The fourth aim was to establish how an understanding of the networks could lead to improved case management practice, and a model of working

which will benefit the participants. This chapter focuses predominantly on key findings arising at different junctures of decision making, assessment, support and access and makes references to other key findings arising from the other research aims.

Research design

The quantitative aspect of the study was based on examining file data pertaining to 92 children in relative care (relative based on a blood or marriage relationship). This provided baseline data to examine general trends and assisted the development of a sampling frame aimed at examining the different types of networks in existence. Qualitative data was collected on six networks arising from the sampling frame developed. In each network, the birth parents, relatives, children and social workers involved were all interviewed. The study aimed to address the hypothesis that intra-familial relationship determined the family/state relationship and that different networks of relationships evolved over time (O'Brien, 1999). It is outside the brief of this chapter to address the in-depth findings related to the different networks that were identified. The typology of networks, the key factors giving rise to their evolution, and the practice implications are discussed in O'Brien (1999). Decision-making, assessment, access, support and planning were examined as key junctures in the evolving networks.

Relative care in Ireland: setting the scene

The development of formal relative care in Ireland is traced in part to the Child Care Act 1991. Relative care was introduced as a viable care option, alongside foster care, residential care and adoption. Different options are needed to meet the care needs of the approximately 3600 children in state care at any one time in Ireland.[1] The numbers of children in care have not

---

1. The Department of Health and Children took the last snapshot of the total number of children in care on the 31st December 1996. Prior to this, the total number of children in the care system was taken in the 1992 snapshot.

changed dramatically in the last thirty years, but the use of individual care options has changed.[2] Foster care has become the dominant placement of the care system. In Ireland, the percentage of children who are in foster care rose from 50 to 75 per cent of the total care population between 1977 and 1997 (Kelly and Gilligan, 2000). Prior to the publication of the child care regulations in 1995 (Dept. of Health, 1995a) it was not possible to distinguish between children placed in foster care as distinct from relative care, as both groups of children were recorded as being in the foster care system. This lack of separation of information on the use of relative care was also a feature of many international child welfare systems, (Gleeson, 1996) and made it difficult to track precisely the rate at which change was taking place. Currently, approximately one quarter of all children entering care are placed in relative care though variation exists amongst regional areas (Dept. of Health, 1999).

The emergence of relative care in Ireland has been traced to the preference for foster care over residential care as outlined above, a shortage of traditional foster parents, greater emphasis on family connection as a means to enhance children's identity, the emergence of partnership as a key principle in child care, and positive research outcomes. However, it may be argued that its early development reflected a value system among individual workers which reflected an ideological preference for family unity, and a placement crisis which left little choice but to use this care option rather than a coherently formulated policy that provided specific guidance and regulation for the developing practice.

It is also important to stress that, as relative care has expanded, it has been developing within the existing foster care system, which in itself is characterised by multiple challenges in terms of meeting children's needs, recruitment and retention of foster carers, role confusion, and placement breakdown (IFCA, 2000).

Profile of children, their care careers and relatives

The biographical information on birth families reflects a population that is characterised by

poverty, as indicated by high dependency rates on social welfare, housing status and lives blighted by addiction and inability to cope. These findings show many characteristics which are similar to children in the general care population in Ireland (Richardson, 1985; O'Higgins, 1996).

The childrens' care careers show that, for over half the children in relative care, the current placement was their first experience with the care system (57.6%). Of the remaining children who had previous care experience, the majority were moved from within the care system to the relatives. The high percentage (63%) of children in relative care on the basis of court orders reflects national trends (Dept. of Health, 1992) and known international trends (Rowe et al., 1984; Dubowitz et al., 1990; Thornton, 1987; Berrick, Barth and Needell, 1994; Iglehart, 1994). The longer period of time that children stay in relative care was identified in the literature as a key issue with policy and practice implications. The study showed that four out of every ten children (39%) were in relative care for longer than three years. This information would be more meaningful if it had been possible to compare the length of time in the placement with the initial care plan, and placement decision-making.

One of the advantages cited in the literature for relative care, is the greater opportunity it provides to keep siblings together (Johnson, 1995). The study showed that two-thirds of the children had siblings placed with them, or within the extended family network. Only four children were placed with relatives who also fostered non-related children, and this gives a picture of relative carers as principally fostering children from their own families. While relatives are an important resource to the agency in facilitating sibling unity, the study also points to the resource implications required to support multiple placements. This was especially the case in light of the trend identified whereby a significant number of the children were placed within a two year age difference of existing children in the relative's family.

Over half the children (58.7%) were living in relatives' homes where the assessment process had been completed. The length of time to approval was generally between seven and

---

2. In 1988, 2,614 children were in care (Dept. of Health, 1990). In 1996, 3,688 children were in care (Dept. of Health, 1999). This reflects an increase in the care population, a trend that is also identified between 1982 and 1988. The total number of children in care increased by 10% between 1982 and 1988. When a longer view is taken, there is a decrease in the number of children in care. In 1968 there were 4,834 in public care (Gilligan, 1991: p. 85).

twelve months. The failure to achieve the approval in the regulated twelve week period has implications for both the agencies, and also seriously impacts on the relatives who were unable to avail themselves of the full fostering allowance until the assessment is completed. A new regulation, which provides for payment from the time an emergency placement is made, has changed this situation. At the time it was a particularly acute issue given the socio-economic status of some relatives.

The profile of the relatives in the study was similar to international studies in terms of low income levels. While slight variation existed in the age structure of relatives compared to international trends (Rowe *et al.*, 1984; Berrick *et al.*, 1994; Iglehart, 1994), the relatives were on average older than the traditional foster parents approved by the agency. The children were predominantly cared for by relatives on the maternal side of the family, with maternal aunts providing care in the greatest number of instances.

Section Two

In this section, the main findings arising from the process orientated analysis at the different junctures of decision making, assessment, support and access are summarised. The richness of the findings emerges from the multiple participants' views, and shows how conflict, familial obligations and necessity propel the networks. The five principal concerns in relative care (O'Brien, 2000), protection needs, service provision, reunification rates, financial equity and applicability of the traditional foster care system, are addressed as part of this discussion.

Decision-making

The principal issues which the study addressed at the decision-making stage concerned the route by which children enter relative care, the interests of the relatives, and the impact of the current case management system on the subsequent developing network. The study found that the children were moved to the relatives' home from their own home, or were already being cared for informally by relatives, or were already in the care system. This is similar to the available research findings (Berrick *et al.*, 1994; Rowe *et al.*, 1984).

It was found that families who become relative foster parents are motivated to care for the children by the wish to either rescue the child in the event of the child being in the care system already, or to keep the child from entering an anonymous care system, which is a finding similar to Thornton (1987, 1991) and Berrick *et al.* (1994). The level of caution among relatives, informally caring for children, to agreeing to become foster parents for the agency, was shown. Many had little alternative options to secure adequate financial help, or to protect the child in the event of a deteriorating relationship between the relatives and the birth parents. At the decision-making stage a high degree of co-operation and agreement generally existed for the care plan at the outset of placements in all the networks, although variations were evident in the extent to which the birth parents welcomed the state services' intervention. Nonetheless, all birth parents expressed a preference to have their children placed with relatives at this stage, rather than placing them outside the family.

Tensions were evident at the decision-making stage which need to be considered, namely the difficulties for the relatives in approaching the agency, the hesitancy of the social workers about the risk assessment model used, and the birth parents annoyance at the relatives for contacting the agency. Certain factors also contribute to difficulties not being identified or articulated. These include the speed of placement, the lack of opportunity or commitment to network with other relatives, or to address the concerns and make plans with the family as a group, the lack of specific skills among front-line workers to assess or to conduct network and family meetings, and to manage conflictual relationships. These factors are all identified as contributing to the difficulties which unfold later.

Assessment

The study has shown that the assessment of relatives challenges many of the theoretical, professional and organisational bases on which assessments are currently organised. In the process, the agency is confronted with many practical and ethical difficulties. At a practice level, much of the confusion surrounding relative assessments can be traced to the fact that the process is occurring in a context of competing ideologies. The values of partnership and empowerment, on which the self-selection model of assessment practice is built and which social workers aspire to, are somewhat at variance with practices and values underlying the social control function of child protection practice, which results in a paradoxical situation for both worker and relative. Furthermore the study shows how the protracted nature of the process, and the co-existence of multiple roles and tasks during the assessment stage is a particular characteristic of relative placements, and is compounding the difficulties for both the social workers and relatives. In summary, it was shown that the model currently used to assess relatives is a replica of the assessment model and approach used with traditional foster parents. Superimposing this model of assessment in relative care is causing problems, as the process by which the relatives become connected with the agency, the different demographic profile of the relatives, the fact that the placement is already made, and the family connection between relatives, birth parents and children, are not provided for in the traditional model. The traditional framework was developed to prepare stranger foster parents for a hypothetical child at an imagined future date, which is very different from the characteristics of the relative placement.

A further finding at this stage shows that the birth parents distance during the assessment process reflects the start of an increasingly peripheral position, which occurred dramatically in a number of the networks, and caused high levels of pain and distress for many of the participants, and not just the birth parents. Inclusion of birth parents at this stage of the process is necessary to safeguard against an increasing peripheral position.

Support: service provision and protection

Support services were examined against a backdrop of literature which pointed to the lower level of monitoring and service provision for relatives and children in a number of studies carried out in the USA (Berrick *et al.*, 1994; Dubowitz *et al.*, 1993; Iglehart, 1994; LeProhn, 1994; Task Force, 1990; and Thornton, 1987, 1991). It was outside the scope of the study to establish if the participants in relative care received significantly lower levels of services and monitoring/supervision than those in traditional foster care.

The study shows that the family members did not make a distinction between support and supervision, and tended to see the agency in a monitoring role rather than a supportive one. Some difference existed between the networks, but there was confusion throughout. The lower level of

contact by the agency after the initial phase was welcomed by the relatives, and perceived as showing agency satisfaction with their work. However, the relatives who welcomed the limited contact showed a lack of understanding of the availability of services, and expressed a high level of ambivalence about asking for help in case their motivations were misinterpreted. Interpreting the lack of contact from the agency as a belief that they were expected to manage independently undoubtedly influenced the way the participants negotiated service requirements.

The principal findings arising in the study in respect of support in relative care are:

- Support in relative care is a broad concept, and refers to the range of services designed to meet the financial, emotional, and practical needs of the different participants.

- The participants need for support varies over time according to their position and relationships in the network.

- Support is of crucial importance, being the most significant issue in bringing families who are already caring informally into contact with the agency. The demographic profile of the relative networks, and the tendency towards multiple placements, point to the high level of support needs.

- Confusion existed between support and supervision/protection needs, and was evident at multiple levels and in a range of relationships.

(O'Brien, 1997; O'Brien, 2000 pp. 201–202)

Protection and safety

The main hypothesis of the study was that the intra-familial relationship determines the family/state relationship. The study confirms this. However, the intra-familial relationship, and subsequent development in the network of relationships, was also directly affected by the extent to which the agency was satisfied that the protection needs of the children were met in the relative home. The literature suggests that concerns about the welfare of the child in relative care arises in a context where there is (a) a lack of rigorous pre-placement assessment and less monitoring of relative placements (Kusserow, 1992); (b) confusion regarding assessment frameworks to determine suitability of relative homes (Killackey, 1992); and (c) an implicit agenda among professionals about the relatives' inability to protect the child in light of the difficulties of the birth parents (Thornton, 1987, 1991). It is perceived that establishing adequate levels of protection for children in relative care is part of a wider discourse, which is shaped by the uncertain relationship between the private domain of family and the public domain of child abuse.

In this ambivalent space, protection and supervision of the relative home remains a recurring theme at all stages of the evolution of the network. It was seen to be particularly acute at the decision-making and assessment stage. The study shows that the diversity of family types and lifestyles, the continued influence / impact of the dysfunctional family theory, and the current emphasis on child abuse and protection were juxtaposed by the social workers with the perceived benefits of relative care, such as family connections being important for children's identity, and relative care offering children greater continuity of placement and sibling unity. As the placements proceeded, the social workers clearly saw the benefit of many relative home placements for the children, and even in the most distressed networks many of the previous concerns were dissipated. The confusion about what constitutes adequate protection, and what level of support, assessment and supervision is necessary, is at the heart of many of the difficulties in relative care, and reflects the fact that a specific model for working with relative care has not been developed to date. This confusion is compounded where the care plan for the child is unclear, or where major differences in participants' views of the plan have never been adequately articulated.

Access

In the study, it was shown that access is seen as the barometer by which the level of tensions in the network of relationships is evident. The themes of competence and incompetence, loyalty and disloyalty, affection and anger, control and loss of control are played out in the arena of access in the network. If cordial / harmonious relationships exist between the family members, and the agency is satisfied that the child protection needs are safeguarded, the family members are given a clear mandate and encouraged to organise access themselves, with the agency providing an overseeing role.

In the networks where access was problematic, the difficulties were seen to evolve over time, but were not in existence when the placements commenced. The difficulties reflected disagreements over the care plan and conditions imposed on access, and were connected with the fundamental questions of 'who owns the child' and 'who is in control'. The stories surrounding access in the networks highlighted many difficulties that hindered trouble-free access. The principal difficulties for the birth parents were associated with not fully understanding or agreeing with the plan / system in place. The birth parents showed limited appreciation / insight about the way their addictions and mental health problems impacted on the negotiations. They felt increasingly marginalised, shut out and distanced from their children, as problems arose. Where access was difficult, the relatives found that their patience was seriously tested, and many felt their tolerance of the birth parents had reached breaking point. The relatives expected the agency to invoke controls to safeguard the placement and to exert control when this point was reached. The children generally felt that the relatives were supportive of their wishes. The agency intervened with more rigorous access conditions in an attempt to ameliorate growing conflict. These restrictions sometimes further compounded the difficulties, leading to a system fraught with distance, conflict, exclusion and unhappiness.

Future plans

In comparing the literature of relative care with traditional foster care, the major issues which emerge are that placements last longer, and reunification rates are lower (Dubowitz *et al.*, 1993; Link, 1996; Ingram, 1996). The majority of relatives also show an unwillingness to adopt (Thornton, 1991; CWLA, 1994) and relatives were resigned to rearing the children in their care to adulthood, as they were committed to the children. In the relatives' discussion of the future, they knew that the children had a preference for growing up with their own parents, but they were realistic that this was not a possibility in many of the networks. Sometimes this was at a huge cost to themselves, but they were prepared nonetheless to keep going. This motivation, which is undoubtedly connected with a sense of obligation and loyalty associated with being 'family', is one of the great strengths of relative care, and perhaps accounts for the greater stability of relative care compared to other care options.

The participants' views of the future in the study were shaped by two particular context markers, which must be considered in light of the research findings on reunification rates and permanency planning in relative care. The first relates to the existence of only two categories of foster care in the agency, i.e. short term and long term. This limited categorisation can result in a lack of consensus among the participants as to the type of placement in existence, as short-term placements can become long-term because of unfolding events, rather than being explicitly planned for. An intermediate care category could help workers retain a time-limited perspective. The second important context marker which impacts on reunification and future plans is that the Irish child welfare system does not share the same tradition of permanency planning that exists in the USA, nor does it have legislative provisions for Residence Orders that exist under the UK Children Act, 1989.

Section Three

The systemic analysis of the networks, combined with the process oriented descriptions at the different junctures can provide a basis for improved case management practice. Enhanced understanding provides an opportunity to implement a practice model aimed at building on the mainly co-operative relationships that exist at the outset of the networks. Specific proposals relevant to the different junctures of decision-making, assessment, support and access are now outlined.

Optimal components of network

A key finding underlying the practice proposals are the optimal components needed to maintain a co-operative network of relationships, as identified through the participants' viewpoints in the study. The optimal aspirations are described as comprising the following features and are presented in Figure 1:

- The family members feel supported and respected by each other, and the agency.

- The agency is satisfied that the child is in receipt of adequate protection, remains in care only as long as necessary, and the care arrangement is built on the principle of normalisation.

- The child is content to live in an environment free from conflict between the adults, where they are loved and cared for.

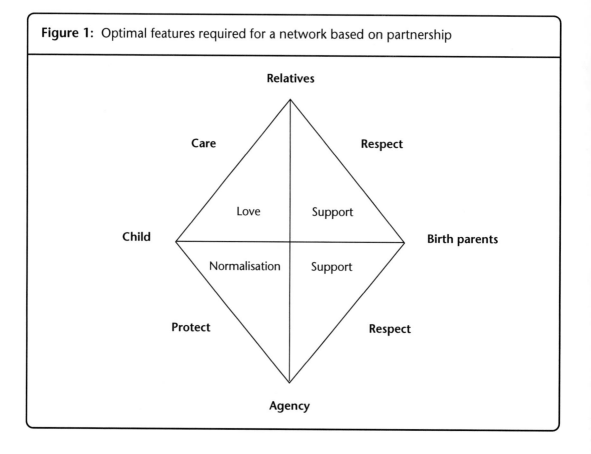

Figure 1: Optimal features required for a network based on partnership

Entering formal relative care: decision-making stage

From a retrospective examination of the impact of case management at the decision- making stage, it is suggested that an opportunity should be provided at this stage for the extended family to meet with professionals, through use of family/professional network meeting. This could provide a platform to:

- Address the issues that led to the need for care.

- Share concerns and to consider the protection agenda.

- Examine options.

- Reach a solution that is based on the care and protection needs of the child.

- Identify the resource availability and requirement needed to support the placement.

- Organise the access arrangements and outlining the mutual expectations of each participants.

It is important that the resources, and stresses of the child and the different family members are considered, and that the available services and the agency expectations are made explicit. The role of a family/professional network meeting is central. In order to maximise the effect of this type of meeting, two principles of the 'family group conference', (Ryburn, 1996; O'Brien, 2000) could be adopted. The first is that the extended family has the ability to make a safe plan for dependent children, unless there are explicit contra-indications, and secondly that the family need time to take into consideration the information brought by the professionals, and to plan in private. Network meetings could provide for inclusive decision-making, where the benefits of a range of views will be applied to the protection issue. The different routes by which the child enters relative care previously outlined will affect the timing of this meeting.

Diversion

The findings at the decision-making stage point to the possibility that some relative care placements, where the agency is satisfied from the outset that the protection needs are safeguarded, could be diverted into a type of family preservation programme. The option of diversion should be considered not only at the initial decision-making stage but also for placements at different stages of development. The applicability of the current case management system for long-term stable networks, especially networks which have low supervision requirements and where support needs fluctuate, emerged as a key issue in the study.

Two alternatives have emerged to address the question of diverting networks to an alternative system. The first is the provision for Residence Orders that exists under the UK Children's Act, 1989, whereby parental responsibility is extended to the relatives, and relatives have access to a means-tested carers' allowance. The second alternative is a 'Designated Relatives Scheme', developed in Chicago, under the 'Home of Relative Reform Plan' aimed at creating a system whereby statutory requirements are kept to a minimum (Gleeson, 1996). In theory, the delegated relative status aims to reduce the level of supervision provided by the agency, and to give the relatives more control over the day-to-day rearing of the children. Gleeson (1996) outlines how this system has not worked as effectively as initially envisaged in the Chicago Scheme. While referencing the lack of research into the failure of the scheme, he postulates that the low uptake reflected relatives' apprehension that, if they agreed to this step, the agency would then expect them to adopt the children. It is of note that this failure occurred in a context in which a permanency philosophy dominates, which is not a feature of the Irish child welfare system.

Systems such as Delegated Relative Status and Residence Orders (Dept. of Health, 1995a) have the potential benefits of:

- Allowing the children to have a 'normal' life.

- Cutting down on the level of intrusion which some relatives and children feel from the agency.

- Saving the agency the expenditure associated with administrative and staff duties in implementing the full regulations of a foster care system.

The delegated relative status has an advantage over the residence order in that there is a greater opportunity to include the birth parents in a dialogue built on the values of respect and partnership, whereas the legal negotiation surrounding a residence order may invoke an adversarial setting in which the theme of incompetent parent is further reinforced. On the other hand, the residence order may provide greater legal safeguards for the children. In discussing an alternative system along the lines of the residence order or the delegated relative status, there is a requirement to ensure that:

- The adversarial nature of the proceedings are minimised.

- A detailed explicit plan is put in place, outlining the purpose of the placement, the duration and the steps to be undertaken if the birth parents are to resume care of the child.

- The children's protection needs are adequately safeguarded in the relative home.

- Relatives providing the child rearing should not be financially disadvantaged by opting out of the foster care system.

- The range of services available to the members of the networks should be made explicit.

- A review mechanism is built in, which is not limited only to an examination of the requirement for continued financial support, as is currently the case under UK legislation, but the review should provide a context in which the viewpoints of all participants are heard. The family group conference may be beneficial for this purpose.

- The birth parents agree that the child will remain with the relative even if their preference is for reunification.

Such provisions, contained in a scheme, could be particularly suitable for co-operative networks. It could also have applicability for some conflictual networks, where reunification is unlikely and where all attempts to reunite the child with the birth parents have failed. As a general point, support services for the birth parents, which aims at helping them come to terms with the reasons for the placement and to be fully involved in making future plans might lessen the conflict in their relationship with the relatives. Such measures require resources, and attention needs to be drawn to the negative effects if diversion is driven principally by budgetary reduction measures, or imposed on relatives (Gleeson, 1996; Link, 1996).

A different assessment approach

The two-stage assessment process, characteristic of relative care, is one of the most damaging features of the current case management system, in terms of re-opening the threat of removing the child, and introducing what is perceived as a long, intrusive and irrelevant process, characterised by lack of openness. In the study, there was little evidence that it contributed significantly to child protection, for the efforts involved.

A different approach, with a short concentrated assessment in the initial decision-making stage, with less voluminous reports and documentation is recommended. The role of the family/ professional network meeting as previously outlined is central. When a decision is made, it should not be second guessed by introducing a new worker who fails to utilise the important information gathered at the decision-making stage through the family network meeting. The study has shown that the practice of allocating a new worker after the emergency placement is made, to conduct the relatives' assessment, risks becoming an unnecessarily long and unfocused process. Two workers, operating as a team would enhance decision-making, by making an assessment of the needs of all the participants and making arrangements for the provision of service, either to be provided by them or to make referrals for specialist services. Co-working would also help to minimise the risk of the participants being marginalised, and scape-goated, which carries potential difficulty for the stability and duration of the placement. The agency resources so released should be re-deployed to specific but separate induction, support and supervision roles with a rigorous system of periodic reviews.

The two-worker case management system[3] needs re-consideration also for more long-term case management of relative care and will be further addressed towards the end of this chapter. The confusion arises principally from a system whereby the workers carry separate responsibility for individuals rather than tasks. It intensifies conflicts when family members are not clear about role demarcation. In the event of difficulties, the separated roles were seen to fuel

---

3. The two worker model used extensively in relative care is a replication of the two worker model used in traditional foster care whereby one worker has responsibility for the child and birth parent and the other worker works exclusively with the foster carer. In relative care this fails to take account of the fundamental differences associated with the family history, how relatives become connected to the agency and the different agency position.

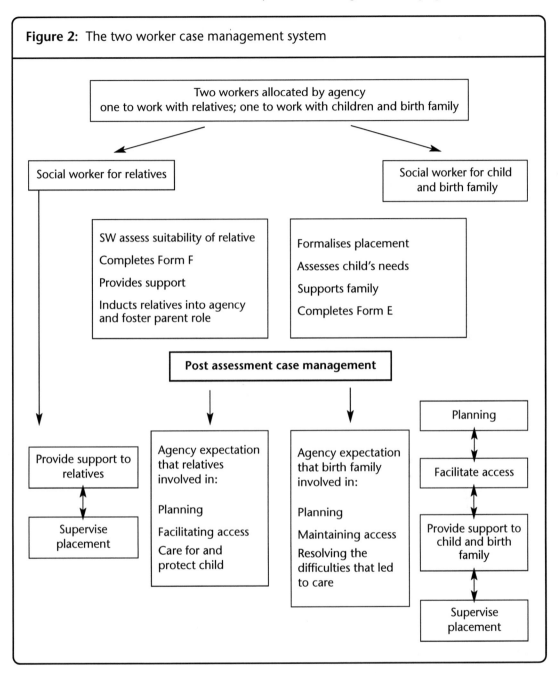

Figure 2: The two worker case management system

Two workers allocated by agency
one to work with relatives; one to work with children and birth family

Social worker for relatives

Social worker for child and birth family

SW assess suitability of relative

Completes Form F

Provides support

Inducts relatives into agency and foster parent role

Formalises placement

Assesses child's needs

Supports family

Completes Form E

Post assessment case management

Provide support to relatives

Supervise placement

Agency expectation that relatives involved in:

Planning

Facilitating access

Care for and protect child

Agency expectation that birth family involved in:

Planning

Maintaining access

Resolving the difficulties that led to care

Planning

Facilitate access

Provide support to child and birth family

Supervise placement

adversarial relationships, with each social worker aligned with their own respective member of the network, rather than engaging in a context in which the differences and difficulties could be discussed.

A number of key features, based firmly on the principle of 'best interests of the child' needs to provide as the foundation for the assessment model:

- The vast majority of relatives are only interested in fostering children from within their own families, and the assessment therefore is in relation to the specific network.

- The vast majority of families will make safe plans for their children. Family involvement is proposed as being in line with a partnership model that values familial ties and obligations as a potentially significant resource in times of crisis. Families, as evidenced in the study, are extremely well-motivated to protect children.

- Asking relatives to identify the factors which they see as qualifying them for the task is closer to the self-selection model, and including a wide range of family, not only the specific relatives in these conversations, should ensure greater security/ stability for the arrangements made and less potential for subsequent intra-familial conflict.

- The agency needs to clarify policy and criteria on which decisions are made and to encourage greater consultation with professionals aimed at ensuring that a flexible approach to working with relatives will develop.

- A flexible approach is necessary in terms of age, accommodation and family composition that reflect the demographic profile of the relative population. The criteria must be geared to ensure the child's needs are met, rather than creating criteria that will exclude many relatives from formal relative care systems.

- Decision-making needs to be localised, and to incorporate two levels (a) family endorsement, in the network meeting, and (b) a rapid system for professional peer review of the facts, leading to decision-making.

Finally, it is important to reiterate that assessment is not an end in itself, and is only one means of ensuring that the children in relative care are adequately cared for and protected. Regular supervision and placement review meetings should be given greater attention in relative care. These should build on the concepts of family consultation, and organised private time for the family, to ensure that dialogue remains fluid, conflict is made explicit if present, and imaginative solutions can be found based on a philosophy of partnership, openness, respect and non-coercive practice.

Support

The blurring of support and supervision activities is associated with many of the more negative experiences in relative care. A framework is needed which distinguishes networks/cases which need high and low support and high and low supervision. It is suggested that such a framework would provide greater clarity about support and supervision requirements, which could enhance the co-operation that exists at the initial decision-making stage of the networks, taken in conjunction with the proposals for re-deploying resources currently used in assessment. This framework can guide policy and practice in formulating the service requirements and protection needs of the individual participants, in the relative networks as these arise over time. This could enhance case management, and help especially to diffuse many of the difficulties associated with the more conflictual networks.

Access

The pain associated with access difficulties was all too evident in the study. It has been suggested that access is a barometer of the state of relationships, as well as being problematic in itself. While the objective of proposals in this chapter has been to avoid evolution to the point where conflict surrounds access arrangements, practice needs to consider the potential for the exclusion of any member of the network. The challenge is for the development of services and practices which facilitate the meeting of different perspectives, and within which the different accounts, aspirations and fears can be shared. To this end, systemic thinking (using the fifth province model) provides a vehicle within which the ambivalent social field can be negotiated and the evolving relationships can be understood.

A way forward—Emerging Networks of Relative Care: 'ENORC'

The above proposals are summarised in a model for working with relative care networks. The model draws on both the family group conference approach and systemic ideas, summarises/incorporates the findings and proposals highlighted in the previous section of this chapter, and provides a framework for case management practices in relative care. This new model is called 'ENORC' Evolving Networks of Relative Care, and is presented in Figure 3. In it the key processes and aspects involved in the new case management model are presented. The different routes giving rise to the relative care placement are illustrated, a rapid assessment model, in conjunction with a family group

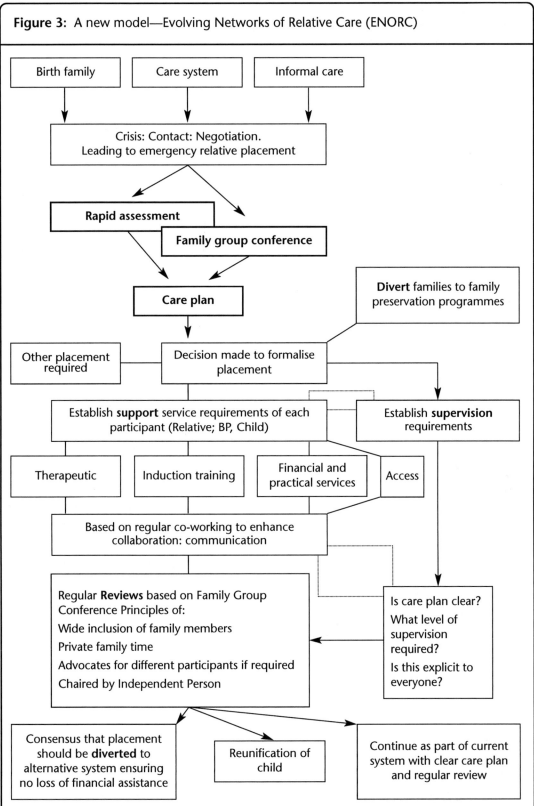

Figure 3: A new model—Evolving Networks of Relative Care (ENORC)

conference in the form of network meetings, is proposed, and the possibility of diverting suitable networks to an alternative programme is depicted.

The proposed model is task rather than role-orientated and particular attention is paid to determining the support and supervision requirements of the various participants. Emphasis is placed on the formal care plan, and regular reviews of the network. As part of the review process, the options of returning the child home, the placement continuing or diverting the network to an alternative programme are considered. The principal differences between 'ENORC' (Figure 3) and the existing case management system are as follows:

- Rapid assessment using a wide definition of family and child protection.
- Family network meeting drawing on principles of family group conferencing is a key structure within which decisions are made.
- An explicit care plan.
- Support and supervision needs assessed separately.
- Focus on assessing individual, dyad and triad needs and designing services to address the multiple needs.
- Work organised according to task rather than role thus having major implications for current two worker model.
- Regular reviews based on principles of family group conference.
- Availability of alternative systems which stable networks can be diverted into, provided relatives do not risk losing required financial support.

The proposals contained in ENORC provide a framework to sustain optimal network configuration, while recognising that the agency will always be peripheral to the family. In this model the role of the agency is to make explicit the protection needs of the child, and to ensure that through open and respectful conversation, the child will be adequately protected in the family. This calls for a new appraisal of risk and child protection criteria, and places relative care and family placement in a central position. Risk-taking is a central feature of practice in child welfare agencies, being a balance of assessed needs and available resources. This practice does not take place in a vacuum. It occurs in a context of heightened public awareness and interest in

child welfare. Likewise the importance of accountability, effectiveness and quality as the cornerstones of public service provision are emphasised.

Concluding comments

The study shows that relative care has emerged as an important care option for children, and that it is embedded in complex relationships at a family/state, and intra-family level. Relative care will not be a solution for all children requiring care. It may be unsuitable due to the unavailability of appropriate resources in the child's network, or the risks associated with the proposed placement may be too high. The diverse needs of children will continue to warrant a range of care options in residential, foster and relative care. Relative care, if operated properly, will not be a cheap care option. If it is used primarily because of perceived budgetary savings, or as a response to the shortage of other alternative care options, and good practice does not develop, then unfortunate results can be predicted.

By considering the benefits for the children and families identified in the study and the analysis of the practical, ideological, economic and social forces that both militate against and support relative care, an effective child-centred care option may be successfully developed for many children. Willingness, commitment and vision is required to embrace 'this age-old tradition and new departure' in a way that is advantageous to all. The framework proposed by this author is being developed in the Mid Western Health Board in Ireland and supported by the Department of Health. Notwithstanding, ongoing research is needed to track the evolving practice of relative care. This should use combined quantitative and qualitative methodologies and be aimed at evaluating its effectiveness.

References

Berrick, J.D., Barth, R.P., and Needell, B. (1994). A Comparison of Kinship Foster Homes and Foster Family Homes: Implications for Kinship Foster-Care as Family Preservation Children. *Youth Services Review*, 16: pp. 33–63.

Berridge, D. (1997). *Foster Care: A Research Review*. London: HMSO.

Byrne, N.O'R. (1995). Diamond Absolutes: A Daughter's Response to her Mother's Abortion. *Journal of Systemic Consultation and Management*, 6: pp. 255–277.

Child Welfare League of America (1994). *Kinship Care: A Natural Bridge.* Washington DC: Child Welfare League of America.

Colgan, F.I. (1983). *Stability, Change and Co-evolution: Implications for Family Therapy.* Masters in Social Science thesis submitted to University College Dublin.

Conway, E. (1993). *Evaluation of Fostering Campaign: October 1991.* Unpublished Internal Document. Dublin: Eastern Health Board.

Department of Health (1990). *Survey of Children in the Care of the Health Boards in 1988: Vol. 1.* Dublin: Stationary Office.

Department of Health (1992). *Survey of Children in the Care of the Health Boards.* Dublin: Stationary Office.

Department of Health (1995). *The Children's Act 1989: Residence Order Study: A Study of the Experiences of Local Authorities of Public Law Residence Orders.* London: Social Service Inspectorate.

Department of Health (1995a). *Child Care Regulations. (Placement of Children with Relatives.)* S.I. No. 130. Dublin: Stationary Office.

Department of Health (1996). *Survey of Children in the Care of the Health Boards.* Dublin: Stationary Office.

Department of Health (1999). *Health Statistics 1999.* Dublin: Information Management Unit, Dept. of Health and Children.

Dubowitz, H., Feigelman, S., and Zuvarim, S. (1993). A Profile of Kinship Care. *Child Welfare*, 72: pp. 153–169.

Dubowitz, H., Tepper, V., Feigelman, S., Sawyer, R. (1990). *The Physical and Mental Health and Education Status of Children Placed with Relatives Final Report.* Baltimore, MD: University of Maryland Medical School, Paediatrics Department, prepared for the Maryland Department of Human Resources and the Baltimore City Department of Social Services.

Gilligan, R. (1991). *Irish Child Care Services. Policy Practice and Provision.* Dublin: I.P.A.

Gleeson, J.P. (1996). Kinship Care as a Child Welfare Service: The Policy Debate in an Era of Welfare Reform. *Child Welfare*, 75: pp. 419–449.

HMSO (1989). *The Children Act.* London: HMSO.

IFCA (2000). *European Foster Care Conference.* August, Cork.

Iglehart, A. (1994). Kinship Foster Care: Placement, Service and Outcome Issues. *Social Service Review*, 16: pp. 107–122.

Ingram, C. (1996). Kinship Care: From Last Resort to First Choice. *Child Welfare*, 75: pp. 550–566.

Kearney, P. Byrne, N., and McCarthy, L. (1989). Just Metaphors: Marginal Illuminations in a Colonial Retreat. *Family Therapy Case Studies*, 4: pp. 17–31.

Kelly, G., and Gilligan, R. (2000). *Issues in Foster Care, Policy, Practice and Research.* London: Jessica Kingsley.

Killackey, E. (1992). Kinship Foster Care. *Family Law Quarterly*, 26: pp. 211–220.

Kusserow, R. (1992). *Using Relatives for Foster Care.* Washington DC: US Dept. of Health and Human Services, Office of the Inspector General, OEI.16-90--2391.

LeProhn, N. (1994). The Role of The Kinship Foster Parent: A Comparison of The Role Conceptions of Relative and Non Relative Foster Parents. *Social Service Review*, 16: pp. 65–84.

Link, M.K. (1996). Permanency Outcomes in Kinship Care: A Study of Children Placed in Kinship Care in Erie County, New York. *Child Welfare*, 75: pp. 509–529.

O'Brien, V. (1996). Relative Foster Care: An Untapped Placement Alternative for Children in the Care System? A Discussion of the Central Issues. *Journal of Child Centred Practice*, 3: pp. 7–21.

O'Brien, V. (1997). *Fostering the Family: A New Systemic Approach to Evolving Networks of Relative Care.* PhD submitted to National University of Ireland.

O'Brien, V. (1997b). Relative Foster Care: A Family / State Discourse. *Feedback: The Magazine of the Family Therapy Association*, 7: pp. 16–23.

O'Brien, V. (1999). Evolving Networks of Relative Care: Some Findings from an Irish Study. In Greeff, R. (Ed.). *Kinship Care.* Ashgate: Arena.

O'Brien, V. (2000). Relative Care: A Different Type of Foster Care, Implications for Practice. In Kelly, G., and Gilligan, R. *Issues in Foster Care, Policy, Practice and Research.* London: Jessica Kingsley.

O'Brien, V. (2000b). *An Evaluation of the Family Group Conference Pilot Project in the Eastern Health Board.* Dublin: ERHA.

O'Brien, V., and O'Farrell, K. (2000). A New Model for Assessing Relative Carers. Unpublished presentation at IFCA (2000). *European Foster Care Conference,* August, Cork.

O'Higgins, K. (1996). *Disruption, Displacement, Discontinuity: Children in Care and their Families in Ireland.* Aldershot: Avebury.

Richardson, V. (1985). *Whose Children? An Analysis of Some Aspects of Child Care Policy in Ireland.* Dublin: Family Studies Unit, U.C.D.

Rowe, J., Cain, H., Hundelby, M., and Keane, A. (1984). *Long Term Foster Care.* London: Batsford.

Ryburn, M. (1996). Family Group Conferences: Partnership in Practice. *Adoption and Fostering*, 20: pp. 16–23.

Task Force on Permanency Planning for Children (1990). *Kinship Care: The Double Edged Dilemma.* New York: Rochester Inc.

Thornton, J. (1987). *An Investigation into the Nature of Kinship Foster Care.* Unpublished doctoral dissertation, New York, Yeshiva University.

Thornton, J.L. (1991). Permanency Planning for Children in Kinship Foster Homes. *Child Welfare*, 70: pp. 593–601.

8 Children Reunited with their Parents: A Review of Research Findings

Elaine Farmer

Introduction

Most books on kinship care make no mention of children who return to their birth parents from substitute care. More extraordinary still, most studies on children looked after all but ignore the most common outcome, which is reunification with parents (for example, see *Social Work Decisions in Child Care*, DHSS, 1985 and, the sequel DoH, 1991). This might suggest that returning children home to their parents is intrinsically unproblematic. Unfortunately, the research that does exist shows precisely the opposite.

The National Children's Bureau report *Caring for Separated Children* (Parker, 1980) was one of the first to provide guidance on the return of children to their parents. The study *Lost in Care* (Millham *et al.*, 1986) which followed 450 children looked after for two years after separation, showed that in fact nearly nine in ten of these children eventually returned home. It also highlighted the fact that if children did not return in the first six weeks after separation their chances of going home reduced, as did their links with their parents and other family members.

In the light of this finding, Vernon and Fruin's evidence from the same research programme (1986) was of concern. They found that many children 'remained in care or in a particular placement, not as the result of an explicit decision that this would be the best course of action, but by default' and Fisher and his colleagues (1986) similarly concluded that 'a good number of discharge processes (according to both families and social workers) occurred without the active involvement of the social workers'. Millham *et al.* (1986) also showed that when social workers expected children to stay in care a long time, or when they felt unable to predict what would happen, children were often destined to lengthy periods in care. The study by Rowe *et al.* (1989) added to this picture. They found that 18% of the children who returned home from care during a two year follow-up returned to care within the study period and 7% did so twice. These figures were similar to those found by Packman *et al.* (1986) and the 22% and

6% found in the research by Millham *et al.* (1986).

Much of this research contributed to the changes in child care policy that were incorporated into the Children Act, 1989. There was a new emphasis on family support and reunion, on the value of contact, on placing children close to their families and schools to achieve continuity and on working in partnership with parents. However post-Children Act 1989 evidence shows that in the UK a tendency for children to move in and out of care has replaced that of children remaining looked after for a single longer period (Packman and Hall, 1998).

A very recent study on foster care again raises the question of whether current practice in returning children from care is adequate. Sinclair *et al.* (2000) found that the number of times children had returned home was a much stronger predictor of the number of foster placements they had experienced than either their disturbance or their age. They therefore conclude that more information is needed about the characteristics of children for whom return will not work, so that either more support can be supplied or more decisive action taken.

It is therefore timely to look at what we do know about returning children to their families, the developments and outcomes for them and which factors differentiate between successful and unsuccessful return. In doing so selective examples of research from both the UK and the United States will be used. Attempting to compare findings from different studies is problematic, due to methodological variations and these difficulties are intensified when findings from completely different child welfare systems in other countries are included. In spite of these limitations some of the research messages about restoring children home are repeated in a number of studies and therefore appear fairly robust.

In the United States reunification has, at least, been a recognised subject of study so there is a body of general research on the topic as well as evaluations of specialist intervention programmes to achieve return. Nonetheless, one prominent American researcher working in the area has commented: 'little research has been conducted on family reunification as such' (Maluccio *et al.*, 1994). The greater research attention paid to reunification in the United States as compared to the UK may, in part, be because whilst in the USA the proponents of permanency planning emphasised that the best chance of permanence for children was with their birth parents, in the UK the permanence movement came to be associated with efforts to arrange for children to be adopted. In the United States, and in theory in the UK, there is a hierarchy of permanence planning options: prevent placement if a child can be safely maintained at home; if care cannot be prevented, return the child home as quickly as possible; or if a child cannot be safely returned, implement another permanent plan (such as adoption, independent living) as quickly as possible (Maluccio *et al.*, 1996). Now we might add that the next plan after return home has been considered would ideally be to place the child with a relative.

What Proportion of Children Return from Care to their Parents?

A number of studies relate to the question of what proportion of children return to their parents from care. Bullock *et al.* (1993) found that 82% of their 450 children in substitute care had returned home to their families within five years. They predicted that almost all children in care would eventually be returned to their families. However, research by Biehal *et al.* (1992 and 1995) found that young people who remained in care until the ages of 16–18 were those for whom a return home has not been possible and very few of these young people were reunited with their families. Although many of these care leavers had some contact with their families in the early months after leaving care, less than a third had reasonably positive, supportive relationships with one or both parents during their transition from care (Biehal and Wade, 1996). The returns of many young people from secure settings (Bullock *et al.*, 1998a) have also revealed particular difficulties. Young people who had long lacked family support, for example, rarely succeeded in creating a new support network after leaving.

In the United States children with multiple disabilities and those from minority ethnic groups (Wattenburg, 1993) were found to be likely to have extended stays in state care. A study by the National Black Child Development Institute (NCBCDI, 1993) found that of a thousand African–American children entering care in six cities in 1986 only half (51%) had been discharged by the end of a 26 month follow-up. Where parental drug abuse was a major cause of separation, the figure fell to just over a quarter (28%), and even those discharged were more likely to return to the extended family than to parents.

Groups such as the National Black Child Development Institute stress the paucity of welfare services, especially housing, that might make a real difference to parents' ability to resume the care of their children (NCBCDI, 1993). Parental drug abuse, particularly involving crack-cocaine, has been a greater barrier to return in North America than in the UK (Curtis and McCullough, 1993). Other authors suggest that the attitudes of foster carers are often a barrier to return, especially when they feel marginalised in the decision-making process. Fein and Staff (1993) suggest that the social work staff of state agencies have caseloads that are too large for the intensive work required for reunification.

What Circumstances Lead to Children Returning to their Families?

The question of how reunification comes about appears to have been investigated in much greater depth in British than in American research. Some children enter care only briefly, say when their mothers are hospitalised, and the return occurs quickly and is relatively unproblematic. Bullock *et al.* (1998) calculate that nearly three fifths of children looked after will be home within six weeks and one in five will go back in the first week. Packman and Hall (1998) found that almost half of the accommodated children in their study had returned home six months after entering care. However, for other children return is much less certain and will depend on conflictual or ambivalent relationships improving, on changes in a child's behaviour or on social services departments believing that the safety of an abused or neglected child is now assured.

Earlier studies suggested that one of the best predictors of reunification was the maintenance of contact between children and their families (Aldgate, 1977; Millham *et al.*, 1986). Since the implementation of the Children Act 1989, levels of contact are considerably higher than previously, so contact levels are unlikely to predict return in the way they did previously. Cleaver (2000) found that the proportion of children now seeing a parent on a weekly basis had increased fourfold on that identified in earlier studies. However, the proportion of fostered children who had no parental visits remained stable. Her findings also showed that contact alone was often insufficient to promote a child's return home. Direct work on existing attachments was often also needed. Similarly, Packman and Hall (1998) found that it was not clear how contact was linked with restoration plans. Other studies have found that little work is undertaken with children's families when children are in substitute care (Farmer and Pollock, 1998; Farmer *et al.*, forthcoming). Assessing the right time for a child to return home, working on relationships between parents and children and dealing with the feelings engendered by separation is highly skilled work and this recent evidence suggests that it is done far too rarely.

Farmer and Parker (1991) in their study of children on care orders returned to their families found that the child's age at removal had an influence on early planning, since by the six months stage it was intended that almost half (47%) of the children who were under two would be returned, as compared with only just over a quarter (28%) of those who were two or over. These early plans turned out to be extremely important since they were significantly associated with the amount of time children spent in substitute care before returning to their families. When an intention to return a child had been recorded on file within six months of the making of the care order, children were reunited soonest and with greatest success. There is evidence to suggest that an active intention to achieve reunification gets children home sooner than a 'wait and see' approach (Gottesfeld, 1970; Vernon and Fruin, 1986; Millham *et al.*, 1986).

A number of other studies have identified length of stay in care as a predictor of reunification. George (1990) found that the probability of return decreased with length of stay in care. Other studies have found that length of stay was associated with child characteristics, the financial hardship of parents, problems affecting the mother–child relationship and with maternal mental illness (Olsen, 1982; Finch *et al.*, 1986; Lawder *et al.*, 1986; Milner, 1987). Interestingly, some studies have suggested that shorter stays in care may be associated with rapid breakdown and return to care (for example

Davis *et al.*, 1993). Similarly, Wulczyn (1991) found that a third of the children discharged within three months re-entered care, compared with 19% of children in care from six months to one year.

Caregivers play a largely unsung role in the return process. Vernon and Fruin (1986) described the part which placement caregivers played in returning children home both when a foster placement broke down and when residential staff pressed for a non-residential placement or demanded a child's removal. Farmer and Parker (1991) noted that sometimes caregivers worked closely with the parents to encourage return and that parents felt more able to trust them when they did so than social workers who held the power to remove their children. Thoburn (1980) found that social workers were sometimes influenced by the views of residential workers or foster carers about whether children should go home.

Barth *et al.* (1985/86), based on a sample of case records of abused children, found that families with the least likelihood of having their children returned to them were those where the child had been abused most severely, where children had school problems and families which had the fewest socio-economic resources, in that order of importance. One study found that children who had been removed from a single parent or from a non-parent were significantly less likely to be reunified than children removed from a two parent family where at least one birth parent was present (Landsverk *et al.*, 1996).

Other research has shown that in reality planned reunifications unaffected by pressure from the child, the parents or the substitute care placement, were very much the exception rather than the rule (Farmer, 1996). Thoburn (1980) concluded that the most influential factor in a child's return was the parents' and child's determination for the family to be together. A distinctive feature of the returns of 'disaffected' adolescents has been shown to be that they often go home because they have arrived at a particular stage in their care careers, for example one in five adolescents in Farmer and Parker's study (1991) 'graduated' home when they left school or when a placement of fixed duration, such as a custodial sentence ended.

Bullock *et al.* (1993) identified three groups of returning children. 'Early returners' are usually children whose families have been temporarily unable to cope. The immediate problems tend to resolve themselves, as parents' return from hospital, depressions lift or an abusive family member leaves. 'Intermediate returners' returned to relatives between six months and two years after separation. The characteristics and problems of this group were similar to those of the early returners but the problems involved took longer to sort out. As a result of their longer separation, change and loss of continuity were far more common for these children than for the first group. As the children remained in care, professionals sought around for other relatives to look after the children or for an unrelated but familiar adult. Another common route home was the collapse of the placement in care.

'Long-term returners' who returned after more than two years in care may have been separated from their families as early as the primary school years as a result of concerns about child protection and child behaviour. Return is frequently informally negotiated between relatives and children, sometimes in defiance of social work decisions and sometimes when adolescents walk out and insist on going home. These children too experience high levels of family change during their absence.

Farmer (1996) also found that fewer than a third of returning children found their families unchanged on their return. Given this evidence, reunification might sometimes more productively be thought of as a new placement, and planned for accordingly, rather than simply the resumption of a former state of affairs (Atherton, 1993). Bullock et al. (1993) have emphasised that the return of children to their families is a process that is at least as complex and stressful as that of separation and intimately connected to it. Reconciliation involves facing up to the failures on either side which led to separation and after a period there is often a major row where all of the hurt feelings are expressed. Overcoming this apparent crisis, when children need reassurance that they will not be sent away again, can lay the foundation for a successful return.

Finally, there are a few children who cannot live at home but who need to return so that their idealised picture of a parent can be tested against the reality. Fein et al. (1983) found that for children 'stuck' in the care system, those for whom reunification was tried, settled more successfully even if they were eventually placed with permanent substitute families.

The Management of the Transition Back to the Child's Family

What do we know about how returns are managed by social workers and what the issues are for children and parents? It is important to understand that a child's return to the family involves a major transition in which the child's relationships and roles at home and school have to be renegotiated. The children themselves will have changed and they bring with them their experience of loss as a result of disruptions in their relationships with their parents and siblings as well as of moves between foster care and residential placements. Not only this, but as we have seen, they were usually returning to changed families. Two things follow from this. One is the need for a positive ritual to mark the child's transition home, such as a celebration meal or a special certificate to be given to the parents and child. In practice, parents in the author's study often said that they felt that the child had been 'dumped' back with them. The other is recognition of the difficulties involved in any major transition. It follows that efforts to ensure as much continuity as possible are likely to ease the transition.

There are three particular areas in which social workers can make a major contribution to the maintenance of continuity for children. First, regular contact between the child in out-of-home care and the family has been shown to be a crucial precursor to a child's return. For example, the study Lost in Care (Millham et al., 1986) showed that intensive efforts are needed at the start of a placement to establish such contact and that the pattern set at the beginning tends to continue. Social workers can do much to facilitate links and remove obstacles such as distance, cost or anxiety. In addition, children need to maintain their contact with their wider network of local friends as well as family (see for example Berridge, 1997; Cleaver, 2000).

A second area in which the child needs continuity is in retaining a sense of belonging in the family. It is important that children see that their bed and their room remains the same and that their possessions are left untouched. Moreover, efforts need to be made to maintain the children's roles in their families in relation to parent figures and siblings, so that the family does not assume a way of functioning which excludes them. The third area of continuity concerns school or day care. Given the changes, which the child has to undergo when going home, it is especially hard if the move also means a change of school, with the associated disruptions to schoolwork, routine and relationships with peers and teachers. Social workers can help enormously by arranging, on entry to care, for children to stay in the same school or day nursery. This will pay dividends when the child returns home.

One important facet of achieving continuity by maintaining children's support networks is the nature of the child's substitute care placement before reunification. Children benefit when 'inclusive' foster families or residential homes are used (Thorpe, 1974; Holman, 1975; Aldgate, 1977; Sinanoglu and Maluccio; 1981) where the skills are in place both to encourage contact between children and their families and to assist parents in working towards the child's return. In the USA some agencies have initiated programmes with the explicit intention of developing the role of foster carers as role models and support figures for parents and it has been shown that foster carers can play a positive role as parent counsellors, parent aides and parent educators (Lee and Park, 1980; Simmons *et al.*, 1981; Davies and Bland, 1981). Some of the parents whom the author interviewed made it clear that good relationships with foster carers had greatly assisted them in maintaining links with their children and restoring their morale.

One interesting finding here, in this volume, from research in the USA is the particular contribution which placement with relatives can make to the maintenance of children's links with other family members (Fein *et al.*,1983; Davis *et al.*, 1996; Berrick *et al.*, 1994), and, perhaps for this reason it has been suggested that return home is particularly successful where children are placed with relatives during the reunification work (Maluccio *et al.*, 1986). There are also strong arguments for black and minority ethnic children to be placed with relatives where cultural views about the shame of a child being placed outside the family might make reunification especially difficult.

However, more recent research from the USA suggests that in fact, reunification with birth parents happens less frequently from placements with relatives or friends than from unrelated carers (Berrick *et al.*, 1994; Dubowitz *et al.*, 1993; Thornton, 1991; Scannapieco and Jackson, 1996; Wulczyn and Goerge, 1992). This finding was also shown in the study by Rowe *et al.* (1989) where only a third of children returned to parents from relative placements as compared

with over half (55%) from other kinds of substitute care. More understanding of this important finding is needed. It may be that placement with relatives is used where the prospects of return are remote or it could be that in some instances the complex intra-family dynamics involved in placements with relatives actually militate against children returning to their parents. Certainly, recent research has shown that placement with relatives raises particular issues about the alignment of birth parents in the four-cornered relationship between agency, carers, child and parents which do not arise in the same way in unrelated placements (O'Brien, 1999, 2000). One American author has suggested that when family reunification leads to a net loss of income for the extended family it may act as a brake on restoration (Courtney, 1996).

In addition, a study by Landsverk and his colleagues (1996) which found that the rate of reunification was not very different for children placed with kin or unrelated carers, showed that different variables predicted reunion in the two groups. Thus, whilst these researchers found that externalising behaviours and behavioural/ emotional problems reduced the chances of children being returned to their parents from placements with unrelated carers, the same effect was not as evident when children were in kin care. Indeed, none of the indicators of psychosocial functioning in this study were significantly related to reunion from kin care. It was also notable that significantly more of the children with unrelated carers as compared to children in kin care had emotional and behavioural problems, developmental and learning difficulties and physical handicap or acute physical problems. It may be that relatives choose not to take an emotionally or behaviourally disturbed child into their care and that the greater numbers of disturbed children with unrelated carers opens up a greater potential for this factor to have an impact on the reunification decision. This study also found that children from kin care who had been removed because of neglect or caretaker absence were much less likely to be reunified than children removed for reasons of sexual abuse, physical or emotional abuse. Removal for reasons of sexual or emotional abuse also predicted return for children placed with unrelated carers.

Social workers can do much to assist children and their families with the major stresses which accompany the reunification itself. Practitioners can play an important part in rebuilding parents' confidence in themselves as parents and in preparing them for what they should realistically expect when children return. The interviews in Farmer and Parker's study (1991) revealed that many parents were taken by surprise by the difficulties that their children had in settling back with them. Regular visits and stays before the return had not revealed what was to come. Once the 'honeymoon' period was over children tested out and showed their distress in a number of ways such as in temper tantrums, defiance, jealousy, nightmares and clinging behaviour. Practical help and advice on how to deal with these behaviours was needed from social workers and other professionals, as well as reassurance that such difficulties were to be expected. Parents said that they would have welcomed the opportunity to talk to others who had had similar experiences, for example in a parents' group. They had also wanted access to a crisis service so that they would know that they could telephone and get help from someone familiar at any time of the day or night (see also Trent, 1989). However, in practice, parents had often concealed these problems from their social workers for fear that the children would be removed again.

How Well Does Reunification Work?

Research before the Children Act by Rowe *et al.* (1989) showed that satisfaction with returns declined as the children's ages increased. Combining their two measures of success, whether the placement lasted as long as expected and met desired aims, nearly half (46%) of returns of children under the age of five met both criteria, compared with only a quarter (23%) of the returns of children over 10. Similarly, Fein *et al.* (1983) found, along with other researchers, that children who were older at the time of discharge from care had less stable reunions. Research has also shown that disrupted returns are associated with longer periods in care (Lahti *et al.*, 1982; Fein *et al.*, 1983; Farmer, 1996).

Another factor associated with successful returns (Farmer and Parker, 1991) is that either there had been no change in the children's families in their absence or only an adult had changed, not the other children in the family. This suggests the crucial importance of the child's relationships with siblings and step-siblings and their critical impact on the child's

relationship with the parents, for example through sibling rivalry and competition for the parents' time and affection. The relevance of the other children in the household to placement success has also been shown in research on fostering (Parker, 1966; George, 1970; Berridge and Cleaver, 1987). Packman and Hall (1998) also showed that the more change during separation, especially changes of placement, the less likely was a successful reunion (see also Block and Libowitz, 1983). Other changes, such as in the composition of the child's birth family in the child's absence, also had a disruptive effect.

The prospects of successful reunification have been shown to increase when children are returned with brothers and sisters (Farmer and Parker, 1991). Presumably children can offer each other support in the processes of readjustment and in re-establishing their rights to territory. Moreover, siblings who return together provide each other with continuity: something these children badly need. Again, this finding replicates those in studies of substitute care (see for example Whitaker *et al.*, 1984; Berridge and Cleaver, 1987).

In the author's study (1991) somewhat different factors were associated with the successful return of adolescents, those termed the 'disaffected', that is adolescents on whom care orders had been made for offending, not attending school or because they were beyond their parents' control. First, reunification with the family was more likely to be a success if the young person had made regular visits home prior to return. Second, there were more unsuccessful returns when the young people had had a previous unsuccessful placement at home. Third, a place to stay and assistance were often offered by the child's wider network of extended family and friends. A quarter of the adolescents moved themselves on from their returns to parents to live with relatives or friends. There is clearly scope for practitioners to endeavour to harness such resources and to offer practical and financial support to assist the child's network to offer care when living at home is no longer the best option (see also Marsh and Peel, 1999). The fourth factor that needs careful attention is that of education. These adolescents had experienced frequent moves, with corresponding changes of school and of friendships, with major consequences for educational progress. It should not therefore be surprising that nearly two-thirds (60%) of the whole group had school attendance problems when they returned. Many of the teenagers had special educational needs and they were more likely to settle with their families when appropriate special education was provided.

Two other predictors of disrupted return, from American research, were first, limited parental skills, as shown by communication problems with the children, insufficient understanding of child development and poor handling and discipline, and second, limited support from extended family, friends and neighbours (Festinger, 1994).

Social and environmental variables have also been shown to prevent successful returns home, including: poverty, receipt of public assistance, exposure to drugs and inadequate housing (Jones, 1998; and Schuerman *et al.*, 1994). Non-white children were more likely than white children to return to care, and Schuerman *et al.* (1994) also found that reunification failure was more frequent with single parent families. Isolation and poverty in these families may increase stress and lower parental effectiveness.

In the UK Packman and Hall (1998) found that breakdown of return was more likely when the initial separation was because of parental mental illness, alcohol or drug misuse (see also Schuerman *et al.*, 1994). Tensions between siblings and concerns about child protection were also associated with further separation. Difficulties during reunification were related to children with a tendency to violence or self-harm, but offending did not increase the risk of breakdown. Difficulties with schooling also affected the success of reunion (see also Lahti *et al.*, 1982). Reunification failure has also been found to be associated with neglect as the presenting problem (Hess *et al.*, 1992; Davis *et al.*, 1993; Courtney, 1995).

Block and Libowitz (1983) found that successful adjustment of children was associated with how well planned the return home was, for example if it was expected and occurred on time. These authors also found that disrupted reunions were not associated with frequency of caseworker contacts or with the response of parents to social work services prior to the child's return. Disruption was related to parental inability to cope with the child. This research suggests that intensity of services alone is insufficient to bring about successful outcomes. The content and mix of services needs to be considered. Similarly, Farmer (1996) highlighted the important contribution that proactive social work, continuous social work involvement, and decisive planning can make to successful reunification.

Outcomes of Reunification

Returning children on care orders to their parents carries risks. Farmer and Parker (1991) found that a quarter of all the 'protected' children in their study (42 children) were neglected or abused during their placement at home. This re-abuse rate is in line with those found in other studies of children in high risk situations (Barth and Berry, 1987; Farmer and Owen, 1995; Gibbons *et al.*, 1995). However, most of the children continued to stay with their families. Only nine were removed as the direct result of their abuse or neglect. A great deal of effort was put into supporting placements with the family and attempts were made to absorb further incidents of concern in preference to removing the child.

The authors judged that for about half of the children the return home was beneficial, for one in five it was detrimental and the rest fell somewhere in between. It was of considerable concern to find that nearly half of the reunifications, which in the researcher's view were detrimental for the child, had lasted for over two years. It became apparent that renewed abuse and neglect might be tolerated if the social worker believed that the family was generally co-operative (see also Dingwall *et al.*, 1983; Farmer and Owen, 1995). At the two year follow-up the researchers found that 38% of the returns of the 'protected' children had broken down. In 40% of these the breakdown was caused by difficulties in the relationships between the parent(s) and child and 21% by abuse or neglect. Another fifth (21%) of endings were because the parent(s) were no longer able to look after the child, for reasons of homelessness, illness or imprisonment. Over a third of the 63 children whose return ended moved directly to another parent, relative or friend.

It was notable that for the adolescents in this study (1991) their stay in care had rarely led to sustained improvement. Of the young people who were on care orders for offending two-thirds re-offended when they were returned home. For the adolescents removed for not attending school things were no better: two-thirds failed to attend school regularly after reunification. But it was the teenage girls who showed an even more worrying trend. Almost half of them became pregnant during the placement at home (44%).

This is an extremely high rate when compared with that for teenage girls in the 'protected' group (14%) and even more so when compared with pregnancy rates for this age group in the population (approximately 3%).

By the end of the two year follow-up period half of the adolescent returns had disrupted. Offending (31%), the breakdown of relationships between the child and parent/s (29%) and the young person's decision to move away (21%) dominated the reasons for the returns ending. A particularly interesting finding was that just under half of them (45%) moved themselves on to live with relatives, friends or occasionally the other separated parent. Not infrequently this new arrangement did not last and the young people moved again, usually to one or both parents, and some moved a third or fourth time. The mobility of these adolescents mostly within the extended family, but also including friends, was probably an attempt to solve or escape problems in the previous household. For some moving on was probably a learned response to difficulty.

It is some cause for optimism that many of these young people were in contact with their extended families, and we know from research on leaving care that some of these adolescents seek some stability by moving in with a partner's parents and establishing their own families very early (Speak, 1995; Biehal *et al.*, 1995). Marsh and Peel (1999) have shown that a range of relatives and non-relatives (especially foster carers) may assist looked after children in the transition to independence, although still more extended family support might be forthcoming if social workers did more to include the wider family and friends in plans at this stage. Instability after leaving care is associated with instability within the care system. A study by Biehal and her colleagues (1995) demonstrated that young people who had experienced many moves in care tended to continue the pattern of instability and frequent moves after leaving care. In addition, research by Garnett (1992) emphasised that the 'long-term stable' care leavers did much better in terms of education and employment than 'teenage entrants' or the 'long-term unsettled'.

In the UK there have been very few innovative reunification programmes, which have also been evaluated (unlike in the USA, for example, Lewis and Callaghan, 1993 and Fraser *et al.*, 1996). In one of those specialist restoration programmes in the UK, Trent (1989) described how 36 children were reunified with their families, even though permanency plans away from the birth parents

had originally been made. At follow-up one to six years later, in over half the cases (52%) the child and family were still together. She notes that 'placing children back home is risky, time-consuming and hard work' (Trent, 1989: p. 54). Maluccio *et al.* (1994), on the basis of a wealth of research data and experience, stress the importance of reunion informing all planning, even prior to separation, early and consistent contact with parents and the important role of the extended family. Awareness of the impact of separation and loss so that it informs all interventions by professionals is also seen as crucial.

Conclusion

This brief review of the literature suggests considerable consensus about some of the key factors in returning children from care to their families. A number of studies emphasise careful decision-making, early planning and intensive work with the child and family both before and after reunification. Other factors that appear robust show that some of the factors that are related to the breakdown of reunification are the same as those that relate to the disruption of placements in care. However, research since the Children Act suggests that children now have more moves into and out of care than previously and that this is connected with more unsuccessful returns home. It appears then that the Children Act has encouraged more returns, but that either decisions have been taken before real change has occurred or insufficient support has been provided. More information is needed about the characteristics of children for whom return will not readily work, so that either more support can be supplied or more decisive action taken to arrange another form of permanent placement.

The role of placements with relatives in relation to restoration is important but uncertain. On the one hand such placements encourage contact with parents. On the other, they make return to parents less likely. Clearly, more information about the interaction between these two types of placement is needed. Nonetheless, placements with relatives and with parents have a number of features in common: they have as yet attracted little research in this country and local authorities show a much greater willingness to provide financial assistance and support when children are placed with unrelated carers than when they are living with their parents or relatives. Nonetheless, the state does in many cases pay considerably more for kinship care than it pays to support poor parents to care for their own children (Courtney, 1996). As interest in placements with relatives and friends increases we must ensure that returning children to their parents does not become even further the 'poor relation' within the child welfare system.

References

Aldate, J. (1977). *The Identification of Factors Influencing Children's Length of Stay in Care*. PhD thesis, University of Edinburgh.

Atherton, C. (1993). Reunification: Parallels Between Placement in New Families and Reunifying Children with their Families. In Marsh, P., and Triseliotis, J. (Eds.). *Prevention and Reunification in Child Care*. London: Batsford.

Barth, R.P., Snowden, L.R., Broeck, E.T., Clancy, T., Jordan, C., and Barusch, A.S. (1985/86). Contributors to Reunification or Permanent Out-of-Home Care for Physically Abused Children. *Journal of Social Service Research*, 9: pp. 31–45.

Barth, R.P. and Berry, M. (1987). Outcomes of Child Welfare Services Since Permanency Planning. *Social Service Review*, 61: pp. 71–90.

Berrick, J.D., Barth, R.P., and Needell, B. (1994). A Comparison of Kinship Foster Homes and Foster Family Homes: Implications for Kinship Foster Care as Family Preservation. *Children and Youth Services Review*, 16(1/2): pp. 33–63.

Berridge, D. (1997). *Foster Care: A Research Review*. London: The Stationery Office.

Berridge, D., and Cleaver, H. (1987). *Foster Home Breakdown*. Oxford: Basil Blackwell.

Biehal, N., Clayden, J., Stein, M., and Wade, J. (1992). *Prepared for Living? A Survey of Young People Leaving the Care of Three Local Authorities*. London: National Children's Bureau.

Biehal, N., Clayden, J., Stein, M., and Wade, J. (1995). *Moving On. Young People and Leaving Care Schemes*. London: HMSO.

Biehal, N., and Wade, J. (1996). Looking Backward, Looking Forward: Care Leavers, Families and Change. *Children and Youth Services Review*, 18(4/5): pp. 425–445.

Block, N.M. and Libowitz, A.S. (1983). *Recidivism in Foster Care*. New York: Child Welfare League of America.

Bullock, R., Little, M., and Millham, S. (1993). *Going Home: The Return of Children Separated from their Families*. Aldershot: Dartmouth.

Bullock, R., Gooch, D., and Little, M. (1998). *Children Going Home: The Re-unification of Families*. Aldershot: Ashgate.

Bullock, R., Little, M., and Millham, S. (1998a). *The Care Careers of Young People in Long-stay Secure Treatment Units*. Aldershot: Ashgate.

Cleaver, H. (2000). *Fostering Family Contact*. Norwich: The Stationery Office.

Courtney, M.E. (1995). Re-entry to Foster Care of Children Returned to their Families. *Social Service Review*, June.

Courtney, M.E. (1996). Kinship Foster Care and Children's Welfare; The California Experience. *Institute for Research on Poverty*, 17(3): pp. 42–48. University of Wisconsin-Madison.

Curtis, P., and McCullough, (1993). The Impact of Alcohol and Other Drugs on the Child Welfare System. *Child Welfare*, LXXII: pp. 533–542.

Davies, L.J. and Bland, D. (1981). The Use of Foster Parents as Role Models for Parents. In Sinanoglu, P.A. and Maluccio, A.N. *Parents of Children in Placement: Perspectives and Programs*. New York: Child Welfare League of America.

Davis, I.P., English, D.J., and Landsverk, J.A. (1993). *Going Home, and Returning to Care: A Study of Foster Care Reunification*. San Diego State University, College of Health and Human Services, School of Social Work and the Child and Family Research Group.

Davis, I.P., Landsverk, J., Newton, R., and Ganger, W. (1996). Parental Visiting and Foster Care Reunification. *Children and Youth Services Review*, 18(4/5): pp. 363–382.

Department of Health (1991). *Patterns and Outcomes in Child Placements*. London: HMSO.

Department of Health and Social Security (1985). *Social Work Decisions in Child Care: Recent Research Findings and their Implications*. London: HMSO.

Dingwall, R., Eekelaar, J., and Murray, T. (1983). *The Protection of Children: State Intervention and Family Life*. Oxford: Blackwell.

Dubowitz, H., Feigelman, S., and Zuravin, S. (1993). A Profile of Kinship Care. *Child Welfare*, 72: pp. 153–169.

Farmer. E. (1996). Family Reunification with High Risk Children: Lessons from Research. *Children and Youth Services Review*, 18(4/5): pp. 403–424.

Farmer, E., and Parker, R. (1991). *Trials and Tribulations: Returning Children from Local Authority Care to their Families*. London: HMSO.

Farmer, E., and Owen, M. (1995). *Child Protection Practice: Private Risks and Public Remedies*. A study of decision-making, intervention and outcome in child protection work. London: HMSO.

Farmer, E., and Pollock, (1998). *Sexually Abused and Abusing Children in Substitute Care*. Chichester: Wiley.

Farmer, E., Moyers, S., and Lipscombe, J. (forthcoming 2000). *The Fostering Task with Adolescents: A Prospective Study*. Research Report for the Department of Health.

Fein, E., Maluccio, A., Hamilton, V., and Ward, D. (1983). After Foster Care: Outcomes of Permanency Planning for Children. *Child Welfare*, LXII: pp. 485–558.

Fein, E., and Staff, I. (1993). Last Best Change: Findings from a Reunification Services Program. *Child Welfare*, LXII: pp. 25–40.

Festinger, T. (1994). *Returning to Care: Discharge and Re-entry into Foster Care*. Washington DC: Child Welfare League of America.

Finch, S., Fanshel, D., and Grundy, J. (1986). Factors

Associated with the Discharge of Children from Foster Care. *Social Work Research and Abstracts*, 22: pp. 10–18.

Fisher, M., Marsh, P., Phillips, D., with Sainsbury, E. (1986). *In and Out of Care: The Experiences of Children, Parents and Social Workers*. London: Batsford.

Fraser, M.W., Walton, E., Lewis, R.E., Pecora, P.J., and Walton, W.K. (1996). An Experiment in Family Reunification: Correlates of Outcomes at One Year Follow-up. *Children and Youth Services Review*, 18(4/5): pp. 335–361.

Garnett, L. (1992). *Leaving Care and After*. London: National Children's Bureau.

George, V. (1970). *Foster Care: Theory and Practice*. London: Routledge and Kegan Paul.

Gibbons, J., Conroy, S., and Bell, C. (1995). *Operating the Child Protection System. A Study of Child Protection Practices in English Local Authorities*. London: HMSO.

Goerge, R. (1990). *The Reunification Process in Substitute Care. Social Services Review*, LXIV: pp. 422–457.

Gottesfeld, H. (1970). *In Loco Parentis: A Study of Perceived Role Values in Foster Home Care*. New York: Jewish Welfare Association.

Hess, P.M., and Folaron, G. (1992). *Disrupted Reunification: 62 Families' Experiences. Supplemental Descriptive Data and Final Report*. Indianapolis, IN: Indiana University School of Social Work.

Holman, R. (1975). The Place of Fostering in Social Work. *British Journal of Social Work*, 5(1): pp. 3–29.

Jones, L. (1998). The Social and Family Correlates of Successful Reunification of Children in Foster Care. *Children and Youth Services Review*, 20(4): pp. 305–323.

Lahti, J. (1982). A Follow-up Study of Foster Children in Permanent Placements. *Social Service Review*, 56: pp. 556–571.

Landsverk, J., Davis, I., Ganger, W., Newton, R., and Johnson, I. (1996). The Impact of Child Psychosocial Functioning in Reunification from Out-of-Home Placement. *Children and Youth Services Review*, 18(4/5): pp. 447–462.

Lawder, E., Poulin, J.E., and Andrews, R. (1986). A Study of 185 Foster Children Five Years After Placement. *Child Welfare*, 65: pp. 241–245.

Lee, J.A.B., and Park, D.N. (1980). *Walk a Mile in My Shoes: A Manual on Biological Parents for Foster Parents*. W. Harford Center for the Study of Child Welfare, University of Connecticut.

Lewis, R., and Callaghan, S. (1993). The Peer Parent Project: Compensating Foster Parents to Facilitate Reunification of Children with their Biological Parents. *Community Alternatives*, V: pp. 43–65.

Maluccio, A.N., Fein, E., and Olmstead, K.A. (1986). *Permanency Planning for Children: Concepts and Methods*. New York: Tavistock.

Maluccio, A.N., Fein, E., and Davis, I.P. (1994). Family Reunification: Research Findings, Issues and Direction. *Child Welfare*, LXXIII(5): pp. 489–504.

Maluccio, A.N., Abramczyk, L.A. and Thomlison, B. (1996). Family Reunification of Children in Out-of-home Care: Research Perspectives. *Children and Youth Services Review*, 18(4/5): pp. 287–305.

Marsh, P., and Peel, M. (1999). *Leaving Care in Partnership: Family Involvement with Care Leavers*. London: The Stationery Office.

Millham, S., Bullock, R., Hosie, K., and Little, M. (1986). *Lost in Care: The Problems of Maintaining Links Between Children in Care and their Families*. Aldershot: Gower.

Milner, J. (1987). An Ecological Perspective on Duration of Foster Care. *Child Welfare*, 66: pp. 113–123.

National Black Child Development Institute (1993). *Parental Drug Abuse and African American Children in Foster Care: Issues and Findings*. Washington DC: NBCDI.

O'Brien, V. (1999). Evolving Networks in Relative Care: Alliance and Exclusion. In Greef, R. (Ed.). *Fostering Kinship: An International Perspective on Kinship Care*. Aldershot: Ashgate.

O'Brien, V. (2000). Relative Care. A Different Type of Foster Care: Implications for Practice. In Kelly, G., and Gilligan, R. *Issues in Foster Care: Policy, Practice and Research*. London: Jessica Kingsley.

Olsen, L. (1982). Services for Minority Children in out-of-home Care. *Social Services Review*, 56: pp. 572–585.

Packman, J., Randall, J., and Jacques, N. (1986). *Who Needs Care?* Oxford: Blackwell.

Packman, J., and Hall, C. (1998). *From Care to Accommodation. Support, Protection and Control in Child Care Services*. London: The Stationery Office.

Parker, R. (1966). *Decision in Child Care*. London: Allen and Unwin.

Parker, R. (1980). *Caring for Separated Children*. London: National Children's Bureau.

Rowe, J., Hundleby, M., and Garnett, L. (1989). *Child Care Now. A Survey of Placement Patterns*. London: British Agencies for Adoption and Fostering.

Scannapieco, M., and Jackson, S. (1996). Kinship Care: The African American Response to Family Preservation. *Social Work*, 41(2): pp. 190–196.

Schuerman, J.R., Rzepnicki, T.L., and Johnson, P.R. (1994). *Outcomes in Evaluation of the 'Family First' Reunification Program of the Department of Children and Family Services*. Final Report. Chicago: Chapin Hall Centre for Children at the University of Chicago.

Simmons, G., Gumpert, J., and Rothman, B. (1981). Natural Parents as Partners in Child Care Placement. In Sinanoglu, P.A. and Maluccio, A.N. *Parents of Children in Placement: Perspectives and Programs*. New York: Child Welfare League of America.

Sinanoglu, P.A., and Maluccio, A.N. (1981). *Parents of Children in Placement: Perspectives and Programs*. New York: Child Welfare League of America.

Sinclair, I., Gibbs, I., and Wilson, K. (2000). *Supporting Foster Placements*. Report to the Department of Health, Social Work Research and Development Unit, University of York.

Speak, S. (1995). *The Difficulties of Setting up Home for Young Single Mothers*. Findings Series, Social Policy Research No.72. York: Joseph Rowntree Foundation.

Thoburn, J. (1980). *Captive Clients: Social Work with Families of Children Home on Trial*. London: Routledge and Kegan Paul.

Thornton, J.L. (1991). Permanency Planning for Children in Kinship Foster Homes. *Child Welfare*, 70: pp. 593–601.

Thorpe, R. (1974). *The Social and Psychological Situation of the Long-term Foster Child with Regard to his Natural Parents*. PhD thesis, University of Nottingham.

Trent, J. (1989). *Homeward Bound: The Rehabilitation of Children to their Birth Parents*. Ilford: Barnardos.

Vernon, J., and Fruin, D. (1986). *In Care: A Study of Social Work Decision Making*. London: National Children's Bureau.

Wattenberg, E. (1993). Children in the Minnesota Child Welfare System. *Community Alternatives*, V: pp. 143–144.

Whitaker, D.S., Cook, J., Dunn, C., and Rocliffe, S. (1984). *The Experience of Residential Care from the Perspectives of Children, Parents and Care-givers*. Final Report to the SSRC, Department of Social Policy and Social Work, University of York.

Wulczyn, F. (1991). Caseload Dynamics and Foster Care Re-entry. *Social Service Review*, 65: pp. 133–156.

Wulczyn, F.H., and Goerge, R.M. (1992). Foster Care in New York and Illinois: The Challenge of Rapid Change. *Social Service Review*, 66: pp. 278–294.

9 Kinship Care: A Family Rights Group Perspective

Robert Tapsfield

The difficulties that many kinship carers experience in obtaining the support and services they need illustrates the confusion and uncertainty that currently exists in social services departments about local authorities' proper role in supporting kinship care. It would be wrong to lay all the blame for this at the door of social services departments as they are probably reflecting a wider uncertainty about the state's role in supporting kinship care. To put it bluntly, does the state or the family have the primary responsibility for providing for children who cannot be cared for by their birth parents? And, what is the state's role in promoting and supporting kinship care for those children who cannot live with their birth parents?

Families have been caring for children who cannot be cared for by their parents for generations, across all cultures. Expectations on which family members are most likely to take on this caring role and expectations about how such decisions will be made vary between cultural groups and between families in those groups. What is universal is some expectation that the wider family has a responsibility to care for children whose parents are unable to look after them. This is not to say that all children who cannot be cared for by their parents can always be cared for by relatives. They cannot, and many factors may intervene to make this impossible, including poverty and a breakdown in family relationships. However, in considering local authorities role in promoting and supporting kinship care, it is important to remember that kinship care is not a local authority service. Kinship care is a feature of the way in which families operate and it can be supported and encouraged by local authorities, or, it can be unsupported and undermined.

The question for social service departments is, what is their role in supporting and promoting kinship care? How best should they do this? The experiences of many families not only illustrates the current confusion that exists but also highlights the need for policies that properly promote and support kinship care for children who cannot live with their birth parents.

The Experiences of Families

The following accounts from relatives who called Family Rights Group advice service illustrate the difficulties that many families experience:

> Mrs H had been caring for her two grandchildren for two months. Social workers and the police had removed both children from their mothers care because of concerns about neglect. The social workers had brought the children to the grandmother 'rather than place them with foster carers'. The grandmother had been told that the children could not return to their mother's care until the condition of the mother's flat had been substantially improved. Social services had offered financial assistance to pay for some of the costs of improving the home conditions. Mrs H was concerned that she had not seen the social workers since they brought the children to her, she was unsure about the long-term plans for the children, and was suffering financially. She received no payment from the local authority for the children and was unsure whether she was entitled to any financial support.

Grandparents are often prepared to help out in an emergency when the immediate needs of the child comes first, without considering longer term questions about financial support, and people like Mrs H who help out in a crisis can find themselves without adequate financial support. Negotiating for this at a later date can be difficult and any payment will be at the discretion of the local authority. The legal status of Mrs H's grandchildren is also uncertain, as is Mrs H's role in any decision making about the children's future:

> Mrs P had been caring for her seven and eight-year-old grandchildren for six months following her daughter's death. The children's father had not seen the children for some while. There had been court hearings over contact when the daughter was alive and the father who did not have parental responsibility had been given supervised contact for one hour a fortnight. The supervision requirement was imposed because of serious child protection concerns. In fact the father's contact had been very irregular and had stopped entirely before the mother's death. Mrs P called Family Rights Group after she had been advised by the father's solicitor that he was intending to seek a residence order for both children. She believed the children would be at risk if they were cared

for by their father and suspected that he was seeking a residence order to assist him in obtaining accommodation for himself.

Mrs P had sought legal advice but had discovered that she would not be eligible for legal aid as she worked part-time. She could not afford to pay for solicitors to act for her. Because of her concerns about the risks to the children should their father obtain a residence order, she had approached social services for assistance. Social services informed her that they were unable to help as the children were being well cared for and were not currently in need. Mrs P was not seeking ongoing financial support, although the financial burden of caring for the two children was considerable, but she wanted assistance with the legal costs of securing the children's placement with her.

Many grandparents who take over the care of their grandchildren without social services involvement face considerable difficulty in obtaining assistance at a later stage. For Mrs P the cost of using a solicitor to obtain a residence order was prohibitive and although it is possible to make an application for a residence order without involving a solicitor, this can be a daunting prospect. Although Mrs P believed the children would be at risk if they were allowed to live with their father, social services declined to help because the children were not at risk currently.

Families' views about whether they need or are entitled to financial help differ and are likely to depend both on their financial resources and on the cultural expectations that influence how the family members view their responsibilities to each other.

Many families take over the care of relatives' children without expecting or seeking ongoing financial help. But many families do require financial assistance and see this as essential if they are to take on the care of an additional child or children.

Mrs L had been caring for her niece and nephew since their mother died ten years ago. She had been asked by social services to look after the children and had agreed on condition that social services offer her financial support. Mrs L had brought up her own children and was now working full-time. She was reluctant to give up full-time work and return to a life on benefits, but was prepared to look after her niece and nephew if she received financial support and help in obtaining suitable accommodation. The local authority agreed to make regular payments to Mrs L for both children. The children were not subject to a residence order as their mother had appointed Mrs L as the children's guardian in her will. The local authority eventually found Mrs L more suitable accommodation and negotiated with the new authority, where Mrs L now lived, for them to

continue making payments for both children. These were to be reviewed annually and the new authority said the payments would cease when the children reached sixteen. This duly happened despite Mrs L's representations that the children, who were in full-time education, were as expensive to care for after their sixteenth birthday as they had been before.

Mrs L was clear that she could not have looked after her niece and nephew if the local authority had not agreed to offer her financial assistance and help with obtaining suitable accommodation. Although she knew that the financial assistance was subject to an annual review, she did not believe it would cease when the children were sixteen, as the cost of looking after them would not change on their sixteenth birthday. However, she could do nothing when the local authority decided to cease financial support, and she could not now decide to stop caring for her niece and nephew who she had looked after for ten years. Mrs L's health had deteriorated and she was unable to work and so became financially totally dependent on income support for herself and the two children.

Mrs N wanted to care for her niece who was in local authority care and applied to become a foster carer. The local authority said they did not approve relatives as foster carers but agreed to pay a residence order allowance and recommended that the court make a residence order. The aunt was concerned that the residence order allowance she would receive would be less than the allowance she would receive if she were a foster carer. There were also no assurances that the residence allowance would be maintained throughout her niece's childhood.

Mrs N was clear that she saw no need for her niece to remain in local authority care and she herself was not looking for the other support that might be available to her as a foster carer. She was concerned about the long-term financial implications for her of becoming a parent at a time of her life when she had not planned for this. She wanted to ensure that she would receive continued financial support from the local authority should she continue to need this.

Many relatives seek to become foster carers because they want long-term financial support even though they do not relish the thought of being assessed as a foster carer and the child does not otherwise need to remain looked after. Local authorities vary in their readiness to approve relatives as foster carers when the primary reason for approval is to secure long-term financial support.

Mr T had offered to care for his 14-year-old grandson who was living with foster carers but was reported to be very unsettled. Mr T had informed social services of his offer and had discussed this with his daughter, his grandson's mother, who was happy for her son to live with his grandfather. Social services had not expressed much interest in the proposal. They had not indicated they had any objections but had done nothing about following up the family's offer.

Many relatives are unsure of how the local authority makes decisions and how they can influence this process. Their information about reviews and child protection conferences may come from the child's parents and they may feel reluctant to push for a greater involvement. This uncertainty about how to become involved can be interpreted by social workers as ambivalence, a lack of interest and concern, or even on occasions an inability to put the child's needs first.

The Difficulties for Kinship Carers

The situations outlined previously are typical of the difficulties described by callers to Family Rights Group advice line. These difficulties reflect the uncertainty that exists in local authorities about their proper role in supporting and promoting kinship care. There are social workers and social service departments who see kinship care as the responsibility of families and think that there is an expectation on relatives to step in and look after children whose own parents are unable to do this. They think families should take on these responsibilities without seeking any help from the state. Other social workers and social service departments see kinship care as the responsibility of the state and as an alternative to residential or stranger foster care. They think relatives should receive adequate financial and other support to care for children who might otherwise be looked after in stranger foster care or residential care. These different views lead to social services departments and social workers offering very different services to families. These can best be seen by considering the very different approaches local authorities have to relatives as foster carers, the varied policies about residence orders and residence order allowances, the absence of information about support for relatives and the lack of policies about how the wider family is involved in decision making.

Relatives as foster carers

In a number of local authorities over twenty per cent of the children who are fostered are fostered by relatives who are approved as foster carers. In other local authorities very few, less than five percent, of children are fostered with relatives. Waterhouse's national study of foster care (1997) found the proportion of relatives who were foster carers ranged from thirty per cent in one authority to none at all. These are striking differences that are unlikely to be accounted for by variation in local need. The implications for relatives is that whether you will be able to become a foster carer is likely to depend more on where you live than on the needs of the child or children you are caring for.

Local authorities also vary in the level of fostering allowances paid to relatives. Some local authorities treat relative and non-relative foster carers identically and some offer different levels of financial support to relatives. Where this occurs relatives will be offered lower levels of financial support. There may be reasons for paying relatives at lower rates and Greeff (1999) suggests that internationally, relatives who are foster carers tend to be paid less than non-relatives. The difficulty for relatives is that there is no consistency in how they are treated and there is often a lack of openness about decisions. Relatives who are foster carers may not be aware of being treated differently from non-relative foster carers. They may not be aware that they are receiving a lower level of service.

Historically, fostering services have been developed as if foster carers were not relatives. The particular needs of relatives who are foster carers have been ignored. It is only recently that the fact that significant numbers of foster carers are relatives has been recognised. The NFCA Handbook *Family and Friends as Carers* (NFCA, 2000) is an important attempt to meet the needs of this group. However, the emphasis of the National Foster Care Standards is on promoting an increasingly professional fostering service. Unfortunately, this may not meet the needs of kinship carers who seek financial and other supports but who are unlikely to see themselves as a part of a professional foster service.

Residence order allowances

Local authorities are able to pay residence order allowances in respect of children who are subject to a residence order. The Children Act 1989, which introduced residence orders and gave local authorities the power to pay a residence order allowance, did not restrict this allowance to children who had been in local authority care. In practice, local authorities may be more likely to agree to a residence order allowance when this leads to children being discharged from care. Not only is such a plan seen as securing a permanent placement for a child, but the plan will also cost the local authority far less than if the child had remained 'in care.' The implication for relatives is that obtaining financial support may be easier when children are in foster care or residential care and the local authority can see a financial saving if relatives care for the children with a residence order and allowance. Relatives who take on the care of children and then seek financial help may find it more difficult to obtain than relatives who make clear that they will need financial support agreed before they take on the caring role.

A survey conducted by the Grandparents' Federation (1996) showed wide discrepancies between local authorities in the payment of residence order allowances. We know that there is not only variation in the readiness to pay a residence order allowance, but also in the rate of any allowance paid, and in the length of time an allowance will be paid for. Again, the implications for relatives are that the availability and amounts of a residence order allowance is likely to depend on where you live, and not on the needs of the child.

The lack of information

The difficulties for relatives are exacerbated by the lack of information that is available on how local authorities support kinship carers. The Grandparents' Federation survey found that only one authority had written information about services that were available to support relatives who were caring for children. Evidence suggests that it is very difficult for families to ascertain whether their local authority is sympathetic to relatives as foster carers, whether they encourage relatives to take out residence orders, or what level of support is available to kinship carers in any circumstances.

Involving the wider family in decision making

The tendency of social services departments is to work with parents and children. Most usually

this will be the mother. Partnership is seen in terms of working with children and parents and not with the wider family. Even when social workers are aware that the wider family is involved, there is often uncertainty and hesitancy about formalising their involvement. Part of the reason for this may be because the individual who is receiving a service may be reluctant to involve their wider family and social workers have felt constrained by the need to respect confidentiality. Family group conferences have shown that many families are happy to involve the wider family and that the reluctance to do so may be more to do with professional resistance than family reluctance.

It is to be hoped that the *Assessment Framework for Children in Need and Their Families* (Department of Health, 2000) and its emphasis on family and environmental factors will encourage social workers to not only ask about the wider family but seek to involve them when appropriate. The development of family group conferences have encouraged some departments to consider how and when to involve the wider family and in those situations when a family group conference is held, the wider family will be involved and should be better placed to negotiate for the services they need.

Legislation and research

The difficulties that relatives experience stand in contrast to the legislative support for kinship care. Research evidence also suggests that children's needs are better served by kinship care than stranger care.

Three key principles that underpin much of the Children Act 1989, partnership, the importance of contact and the emphasis on supporting families, all support kinship care. Section 23 of the Act goes further than this and requires local authorities to place children with relatives unless this is not consistent with the child's welfare:

> ...any local authority looking after a child shall make arrangements to enable them to live with a relative, friend or other person connected with him, unless that would not be reasonably practicable or consistent with his welfare.

The Children Act imposes a duty on local authorities to seek a home for children within their extended family if they cannot be cared for by their parents. It is hard to see how the Children Act could have been more supportive or encouraging of kinship care. In practice, however, there are very real difficulties for relatives getting their views properly considered by courts, because relatives are not automatically entitled to be a party to proceedings. They need to make an application to become a party. Relatives also experience difficulties because they are not automatically entitled to legal aid when making applications for residence orders.

Although there is little research into kinship care, what research studies there are in this country and in the USA all suggest that kinship care is a positive option for children who cannot live with their birth parents. Rowe (1984), for example, found that:

> ...children fostered by relatives seemed to be doing better in virtually all respects than those fostered by others and that children fostered by relatives also saw more of their natural parents.

Rowe concluded that:

> ...there appeared to be considerable advantages to children being fostered within their extended family.

Berridge and Cleaver's study (1987) showed that the placements of children fostered with relatives lasted longer than children placed with non-relatives. Berridge, in his research review of foster care (1997) commented on the surprisingly low profile of kinship foster care given the evidence of positive outcomes for children. Research findings in this country have tended to confirm the findings of research studies in the US where kinship placements have been found to be more stable, and placements last longer.

The reluctance to promote and support kinship care

If the legislation and research evidence support kinship care, why are social services departments so reluctant to embrace it? This is even more surprising considering the difficulties local authorities are finding in recruiting sufficient foster carers and the additional potential benefits of saving the local authority the high cost of residential care. The reasons for social services departments' lack of commitment to kinship care are complex. However, in my view there are three main issues that are especially prominent.

Firstly, the social services may be fearful of being overwhelmed by demand if they were to advertise support services for kinship carers. We do not know how many children are being brought up by relatives in this country.

Information currently exists only about the children who are fostered by relatives but there is likely to be a far greater number of children who are being cared for by relatives and who are completely unknown to social services. The 'fear' of social services departments is that if they were to advertise support services, including financial support to kinship carers, they would be overwhelmed with demand. This 'fear' ignores the deterrent that that intrusion by social workers carries. Most families chose to organise these things between themselves without the 'prying' of social workers, if they have the resources to do this. Such families would be unlikely to choose to involve social services even if more support was available. Families who approach social services for help are likely to do this because they need assistance either to make appropriate decisions about children or because they need support, which may include financial support, to take on what can be a very complicated task.

Secondly, there is the fear of a loss of professional control and the added complications of involving the wider family. Working with the wider family can lead to social workers 'believing' they are in less control. Relatives who are foster carers can be seen as a threat by social workers because they are likely to know more about the children and the family than the social worker and they may not be as compliant as non-relative carers. The allegiances of relatives who are foster carers are more likely to be with the wider family than with social services. In contrast, non-relative foster carers may have allegiances to the social services department that approved them and has supported them. The relationship that the kinship carer has with the child is also likely to be much stronger than the relationship the social worker has with the child and the social worker is consequently likely to have less influence over the placement.

Working with the wider family can certainly add to the complexity of the task for the social worker. There may be disagreements between family members and the social services department, and disagreements between the family members themselves. It may be that the concerns about a child in the family are themselves a cause of family tension. The wider family may legitimately claim some say over the future care arrangements for a child and may therefore try to influence the social services plan. It is perhaps understandable why social workers shy away from working with the wider family where such difficult relationships exist, believing, erroneously, that it may be better for the child to be separated from such family conflicts.

The loss of control and added complexity of involving the wider family can make social workers reluctant to take on this task and if this happens a kinship placement will become much less likely.

Thirdly there are the assumptions about parents who fail. One common assumption is that parents fail because of the poor parenting they themselves received. The inevitable focus on weaknesses in families who fail to care for their children leads to assumptions that these weaknesses exist within the wider family. The wider family are then written off and it is assumed that they cannot be a resource to the children who are in need. If the wider family seek to become involved, this is interpreted as part of the problem—it is not seen as a part of the solution. Social workers who operate from a deficit model of family functioning are more likely to assume and see weaknesses in the wider family and there will be a tendency for the whole family to be labelled and seen as the problem. The focus for social work intervention is the need to rescue the child from the family and place them in a new family that is free from dysfunction.

Those authorities that have introduced family group conferences have had to work to promote a more positive view of the wider family. The evidence from family group conferences is that when families meet together they invariably produce a plan that the professionals feel able to support (Marsh and Crow, 1997). However, despite the research evidence that supports family group conferences, there is still resistance to them, even within departments that have established projects.

The Advantages of Kinship Care

Given the reluctance of local authorities to promote and support kinship care, it is worth emphasising the potential benefits of kinship care over stranger care for children. The benefits listed are in addition to the research evidence already cited that points to increased stability and positive outcomes for children fostered with relatives:

- Kinship placements are better able to reflect a child's cultural background and therefore better able to encourage a sense of identity and self-esteem. Kinship placements enable children to live with people they know and people who know them. The trauma of

separation is likely to be reduced for children who can live with members of their extended family.

- Kinship placements reinforce identity. They do this by providing children with information and knowledge about their family; they preserve significant attachments and they offer membership of a family.

- Kinship placements are likely to facilitate connections and contact with members of the birth family.

- Kinship placements strengthen families, they work with and build on the strengths of families and promote family responsibility.

- Kinship carers have an investment in children in their family that is qualitatively different to the investment of non-related carers.

A Policy for Kinship Care

It is unlikely that services for kinship carers will significantly improve unless policies are developed nationally and locally that promote and support kinship care. In developing policies, local authorities must consult with and involve parents, kinship carers and children. As we have seen, it is the experiences of families that inform us of the failings in current policies and practice. If this same experience is used to develop and shape services in the future, it will be more likely that services meet the needs of families who use them.

Policies to support kinship care need to be seen within the wider context that recognises and values the contribution the wider family and the community make to caring for children. The wider family, which of course may include friends, is often particularly significant for children whose parents are struggling or unable to meet their needs.

Policies that support kinship care must also be placed within the wider context of kinship involvement. It is not sufficient to provide support and financial assistance for kinship carers if relatives are routinely excluded from decision-making about children who are in need of care and protection. Kinship involvement requires that local authority Children Services Plans include statements that recognise and welcome the involvement of relatives when decisions need to be made about children in need of care and protection.

Family group conferences are an effective way of involving the wider family network, which may include friends in decision making about children. They engage the wider family and can mobilise family support to enable children to live with their parents if this is possible. For children who cannot live with their parents, family group conferences can establish if kinship care is possible. Local authorities should be required to offer a family group conference in all situations when children are looked after and there is not a rehabilitation plan.

Article eight of the Human Rights Act 1998 states that 'everyone has the right to respect for his private and family life, his home and his correspondence'. This should be seen as giving children the right to live with their wider family when they cannot live with their parents, and giving the wider family the right to care for children and to be offered necessary support.

In practice kinship care should be the placement of choice for children who cannot live with their birth parents. Active steps should be taken to seek a kinship placement for all children who become looked after and ensure that relatives are provided with sufficient income and access to support services to care for children who cannot be cared for by their birth parents. Financial and other support should be offered whilst requiring the minimum intrusion into family life that is necessary to ensure children's safety. Financial support must be based on need and not on the legal status of the child.

Currently local authorities provide very different services in very different ways. Some variation probably reflects differences in local circumstances, but the extent of the variation means that the services are likely to depend more on where you live than on need. The way forward is a nationally agreed approach to supporting kinship care. This will require a national framework for supporting kinship carers. Such a framework should ensure that relatives can obtain the financial and other support they need without requiring children to become or remain looked after by the local authority. The framework should be accompanied by guidance that covers issues like assessment, assistance with legal costs, and ongoing support services.

A national framework for supporting kinship care and local policies for delivering the service need to be supported by improved access to the courts for relatives who are or may become kinship carers. This could be achieved by giving an automatic right to legal aid for relatives making residence order applications in care proceedings. There should also be a requirement on courts to satisfy themselves that every effort has been made to arrange a kinship placement before a care order or adoption order is considered.

Conclusion

The experiences of the families who phoned Family Rights Group advice line highlights the lack, and varied nature, of services that are currently available to support kinship care. Kinship carers have great difficulties in obtaining services that meet their needs. This lack of services probably reflects the confusion and uncertainty that exists about the role of the state in supporting kinship care. Given the obvious and demonstrated benefits for children, who cannot be cared for by their parents, of growing up within their wider family as opposed to stranger foster care or residential care, there is a need to develop a framework for supporting kinship care. This framework must ensure that relatives receive the support services and financial help they need to care for children who cannot be cared for by their parents and that this help is given whilst requiring the minimum of intrusion into family life that is necessary to ensure children are safe.

References

Berridge, D., and Cleaver, H. (1987). *Foster Home Breakdown*. Oxford: Blackwell.

Berridge, D. (1997). *Foster Care: A Research Review*. London: HMSO.

Department of Health (2000). *Framework for the Assessment of Children in Need and their Families*. London: Department of Health.

Grandparents' Federation (1996). *Residence Order Allowance Survey*. Grandparents' Federation.

Greeff, R. (1999). Kinship, Fostering, Obligation and the State. In Greeff, R. (Ed.). *Fostering Kinship*. Aldershot: Ashgate.

Marsh, P., and Crow, G. (1997). *Family Group Conferences in Child Welfare*. Oxford: Blackwells.

NFCA (2000). *Family and Friends Carers' Handbook*. London: National Foster Care Association.

Rowe, J., Cain, H., Hundleby, M., and Keane, A. (1984). *Long-term Foster Care*. Batsford/BAAF.

Waterhouse, S. (1997). *The Organisation of Fostering Services*. London: NFCA.

10 Making Kinship Partnerships Work: Examining Family Group Conferences

Paul Nixon

…a move away from the traditional paternalistic system of welfare in which the child is rescued by the bureaucracy, to one where the family is seen as the priority carer and protector and is supported to undertake this role.

This quotation from Connolly (1994: p. 90) describes the perceived shifts of thinking necessary for family group conferences to fully develop in the UK. The same could be said of other kinship care difficulties discussed elsewhere in this book (Ed.).

Introduction

This chapter considers the ways in which Family Group Conferences (FGCs) promote family participation and kinship care by making families central to decision making about child placement, contact and services for children. The chapter will also outline the challenge of FGCs to traditional social work systems and what is required for FGCs, and thereby kinship care, to become more embedded and accepted. FGCs can provide a way for kin and communities to be central to those decision-making processes about child welfare. The development of Family Group Conferences is described and consideration given to its impact on child care practice in the UK. Highlighting the differences in both practice and philosophy with more orthodox patterns of social work, this chapter will explore developments in New Zealand and analyse their relevance to practice under the Children Act 1989.

The early discourse on FGCs in the UK focused on how this approach could be delivered in a way that was empowering to families; stressing the importance of partnerships between families and professionals, engaging effectively with family and community resources, promoting culturally sensitive practices and enhancing family responsibility in decision making (Morris, 1995; Morris and Tunnard, 1996). A 'strengths-based family perspective' underpins all these concepts philosophically. While FGCs appear to provide a different way of working with and *thinking* about families, the process can easily and paradoxically be reduced to a methodology or technique for professionals to *use on* families. Therefore the professional, organisational and political context in which FGCs are being introduced is key to understanding the meaning, which is then attached to words like 'partnership', 'responsibility' and 'empowerment'.

Central to the argument in this chapter, are the ideas that partnerships, FGCs and successful kinship care policy and practice are intimately related, and require different ways of thinking and acting, but are not commonly reflected in current orthodox models of social work provision. The wider context in which FGCs are being introduced will also define and possibly determine the nature of the work. Political denial of the links between poverty, social inequality and parenting problems has made strengths-based and inclusive practices difficult to realise. Most of the families who come into contact with social workers live in poverty and poverty is the biggest risk factor in children's lives (Gulbenkian Foundation, 1995; Oppenheim and Harper, 1996). Inequality in the UK has grown significantly in the last 30 years, the number of people with less than 40% of average income, who are the very poorest, is rising (Howarth, 1999: p. 12). Poverty continues to damage children's health and well-being well into adulthood (Gregg *et al.*, 1999). For example Cleaver and Freeman (1995) found that two-thirds of families caught up in the child protection process lived 'on the margins of society' and faced problems more extreme than the serious allegations with which they were confronted. It can be argued that the use of public funds to support relatives caring for their family members is inconsistent with the more conservative political desirability of self-sufficiency and by implication lower taxation (Iglehart, 1994), but if kinship care is to get the best for children and partnerships are to be meaningful, families may well need and should receive, as a right, significant resources provided by the state.

Families, Social Work and the Children Act 1989

The history of child care services in the UK (and elsewhere) has been built upon changing assumptions about the rights of children, the responsibilities of the families and the role of the state in relation to children. The Children Act 1989 sought to 'construct a new consensus' (Parton, 1991) on these rights and responsibilities and finding the right balance lies at the heart of the Act. The intention to achieve a better 'balance' of power between families and professionals is evident throughout the legislation and a more collaborative social work style is implicitly encouraged, although agencies retained distinct powers through the courts.

It is this author's contention that the growing interest in FGCs reflects the underlying and continued frustrations over the inability of practitioners and their agencies to work collaboratively or manage the practice tensions between the role of families and the state in relation to children. Research evidence shows that partnership approaches are still conspicuously 'thin on the ground' (DoH, 1991; Thoburn *et al.*, 1995; DoH, 1995a; Bell, 1996). Interest in FGCs grew with the realisation that this novel approach appeared to provide a practical format for partnership, in ways which the Children Act 1989 failed to deliver. The Children Act 1989 sought to achieve not only changes in policy and practice but also in *attitudes* about children and families. It was hoped that the new law would produce 'very fundamental changes in thinking...partnership, participation, choice, openness, parental responsibility and every child's need for both security and family links' (DoH, 1989: p. 1).

Despite these good intentions the evidence suggest that families still have limited influence on choosing their preferred outcomes to interventions or on the type, quality or quantity of services delivered (Thoburn *et al.*, 1995; Bell, 1999; Freeman and Hunt, 1999). 'Partnership' with families has been described as 'an idea in search of practice' (Ryburn and Atherton, 1996). Practitioners find themselves operating within organisational structures and a culture in which service users voices are routinely marginalised. Thus the terms and conditions of 'partnerships' between families and professionals might be better described as 'limited participation' pre-set by the professional/organisational agenda (Braye and Preston-Shoot, 1995). Allied to these difficulties is the growing concern that the roles and values of social work are being pushed increasingly towards coercion, 'gatekeeping' and social control (Cooper, 1995; Parton, 1997a; Jack, 1997). After the Children Act 1989, services were

reconceptualised so that children would be 'accommodated' (s. 20) rather than received 'into care' and this was intended to help support rather than supplant families in their role. The aim was to provide respite that would prevent permanent family breakdown.

Given the importance of families to children, there is a surprising dearth of information about the way families function, for example there is scant empirical research on the role fathers play in families (Burghes *et al.*, 1997). Utting noted a 'shortage of data relating to the part grandparents, brothers, sisters, uncles, aunts and cousins play in children's lives' (1995: p. 28). Family composition has changed significantly over recent years although families have remained of primary importance in most people's lives (McGlone *et al.*, 1996; ONS, 1997).

The current administration has reasserted its intention to strengthen the role of extended families in the upbringing of their children and has acknowledged that grandparents and other relatives are often the most important sources of day care, support and contact for many children (Home Office, 1998). Yet the Children Act 1989 did not integrate the fundamental principles or assumptions about FGCs that were introduced in New Zealand. It is of direct relevance for United Kingdom kinship care developments to reflect on the emergence of FGCs there.

Family Group Conferences in New Zealand

In 1989 the *Children, Young Persons and Their Families Act* in New Zealand was inaugurated. The legislation was similar in philosophy to the Children Act 1989 (England and Wales) and both pieces of legislation were influenced by similar shortcomings in existing child care services that had tended to reduce the role of families as carers and as decision-makers for children (Marsh and Allen, 1993).

Yet it was different. The New Zealand legislation was novel in that it took a 'family group perspective' (Tapp, 1990) while being founded on ancient notions of family and community decision making (Wilcox *et al.*, 1991; Hassall, 1996). The inclusion of the word 'family' in the title of the Act underlines the intention to strengthen and maintain family groups (Connolly, 1994), a fundamental assumption being that the welfare of children is generally bound up with the well-being of their families.

An interplay of factors precipitated change in New Zealand. The growing concern over the perceived disintegration of traditional family structures produced a series of pro-family policies that occurred in tandem with a programme of decentralising government, promoting 'local solutions of local problems' (Barbour, 1991). In social work there was pressure to de-institutionalise children and a growing dissatisfaction with foster care that corresponded with a criticism over social works' failure to involve the extended family in the placement and protection of the children (von Dadelzen, 1987). Moreover there were some fundamental shifts towards the greater openness and participation to a more 'consumer' orientated model of social work (Wilcox *et al.*, 1991).

The children of the Maori community in particular, were grossly over-represented in public care and often placed with white European carers. There were very few Maori social workers and interventions were based on white European (*Pakeha*) values and assumptions that were imposed on the indigenous population. Little was being done to support the *whanau* (extended family), *hapu* (clans) and *iwi* (tribe), and in practice these structures were being undermined. A Ministerial Inquiry was commissioned and produced a report on the Maori Perspective for the Department of Social Welfare called *Puao-te-ata-tu* (day break). This pivotal report envisaged a greater community and family involvement in the care of, and decision making for children.

> *The Maori child is not to be viewed in isolation, or even as part of the nuclear family, but as a member of a wider kin group or hapu community that has traditionally exercised responsibility for the child's care and placement. The technique, in the committee's opinion, must be to reaffirm the hapu bonds and capitalise on the traditional strengths of the wider group.*
>
> (Puao-te-ata-tu Department of Social Welfare, 1988: p. 29)

In this context an approach called the Family Group Conference (FGC) became central to the new laws for children in New Zealand. The FGC is predicated on principles of inclusion, partnership and culturally sensitive practice. The FGC approach seeks to engage the knowledge, skills and resources of both formal (professional/agency) and informal (family/community) systems within the child's ecological network. Through the work of an independent co-ordinator these two communities are brought together; and families in their widest sense, are

encouraged to take up decision-making responsibilities. The role of the state and other service providers to facilitate and resource plans and decisions. The key practice stages of FGCs have been described in detail elsewhere (Nixon, 1992; Morris, 1995; Marsh and Crow, 1998) and need not be repeated here.

The FGC provides a single and unified model to involve families in the decision-making and goes much further than the Children Act 1989 (England and Wales) in *requiring* a significant change in social work practice in relation to family participation. However, some concern has been expressed in New Zealand over the balance of responsibility being tipped too heavily in favour of the family group (Tapp, 1990; Geddis, 1993) and in attempting to empower families, the interests of the child may sit in the shadow of the needs of the family.

The overall evidence from New Zealand appears to be positive about the legislation and the practice of FGCs (Maxwell, 1991; Thornton, 1993). Fundamentally this new approach made practitioners re-conceptualise the way they thought about families and services. This then raises the questions about practice in the UK and if and how such ideas about FGCs have been received and acted on.

Family Group Conferences in the UK

Family Group Conferences are still relatively new to the UK and how they will best operate under our legislation is still unclear. FGCs have been transplanted and practised in a variety of contexts, adapted to suit local, regional and political needs.

In both New Zealand and the UK, local differences have led to variations in practice (Thornton, 1993; Lupton and Stevens, 1997) so for different political groups the concepts of 'responsibility' or 'empowerment' may have both liberating and regulatory potential (Baistow, 1994/5; Lupton, 1998; Lupton and Nixon, 1999). Within a context where resources and services are being cut, FGCs can quickly be reduced to a procedure or mechanism that is concerned with 'gatekeeping', resource rationing or social control, rather than community building and family decision-making. The implementation of FGCs in the UK has been based upon introducing the model as a *good practice* construct rather than a radical legal construct. Consequently it has focused on winning over the 'hearts and minds' of practitioners and stemmed from the desire to improve practice under our existing laws which have congruent principles. This has meant that the prevailing professional, procedural and organisational cultures and structures have remained intact with negative implications for its implementation. This then raises the questions about where the decisions really lie?

Family or professional decision-making?

In the past professionals have made a decision and you didn't feel it was the right one. The family make a better decision 'cos they have a larger picture. Social workers only have a small picture.

(family member quoted in Lupton *et al.*, 1995)

Arguably most of the orthodox models of child welfare decision making are built on a culture of professional expertise and control, in which (through the acquisition and application of specialist knowledge), professionals are believed to 'know best' (Ryburn, 1991a). This key assumption, by itself, reduces the importance of family participation. This is no more evident in the working relationships between practitioners and families that are operationalised through systems that are designed by the professionals and physically and conceptually dominated by them. By contrast the FGC approach aims to see each family as unique and an expert on itself, so that the plans made by families reflect their culture, needs and aspirations, rather than those of the professional. The FGC therefore conceptually turns the orthodox models on their head, becoming a family meeting to which professionals are invited to attend.

Implementing FGCs in the UK has highlighted the difficulties in operating two different approaches based on quite different assumptions and practices. FGCs consequently appear to conflict with, rather than compliment usual decision-making processes. These difficulties are compounded by the increasing use of legal, managerial and procedural mechanisms to deal with children's placement needs, which have the effect of marginalising families. This legal 'colonisation' and managerial annexation of planning for children's permanency has had the net effect of moving children and their families even further away from the locus of decision making process. Unlike the placement of children with professionally selected, sanctioned and trained strangers that requires legal and procedural definition of roles and responsibilities, kin placements are characterised by the fact that carers' have a pre-existing relationship with the child. This relationship has its own importance, validity and meaning that is independent of any court order.

As one grandparent expressed:

This child is my grandchild now and forever. He calls me 'grandma', I call him 'my baby'. I don't need a court to tell me what to do. I'll be here for him as long as he needs me. If some social worker tells me to adopt my own grandchild I'll tell her she's crazy. I'm his grandparent, not his parent. It would just confuse everything to pretend I'm his parent. We couldn't be anymore permanent than we are now.

(Grandmother quoted in McFadden, 1998: p. 10)

Developing a collaborative approach through a FGC has the potential to give families a greater say over the lives of their children. The process does not in itself however, mean that professionals relinquish their power as this still operates through courts; knowledge of procedures and the control of resources, but it does provide a format for better partnerships to develop. Despite some of these limitations the introduction of FGCs in the UK seems to have provided a greater opportunity for families to participate much more in decision-making and share responsibilities more evenly with practitioners. (Lupton *et al.*, 1995; Marsh and Crow, 1998).

The original idea that decision-making should be driven by families came from the community. Yet it is professionals who have designed the FGC service, constructed the standards and in doing so may have, to some extent at least, colonised and diluted the original spirit behind FGCs.

The need to value kin more

Implicit in the FGC approach is the intention to build on family strengths. Child care social work still however has a tendency towards a 'deficit-model' of families 'in need' focusing mostly on problems and weaknesses, with practice often built on assumptions of child or parental pathology, that is still underpinned by an inadequate knowledge and evidence base (Ahmed, 1990; Parton *et al.*, 1997b). The FGC approach by contrast adopts an ecological approach to social work, attending to the wider context and seeking to engage the strengths in the child's family. Stereotypes of a 'typical family', a nuclear family, with married parents and 2.4 children are far from the reality for many of us, yet public and media images continue to promote this hegemony. Families that do not reflect this image can be disadvantaged by negative expectations of both public and professional groups alike (Fry and Addington, 1984) while research shows us that it is not the composition of family but the quality of relationships that are the key to children's' well-being (Schaffer, 1990). However, the invidious effect of misplaced beliefs about *ideal* family types can affect who gets a service or the way it is provided. So for example in adoption work the most recent evidence from BAAF is that 95% of adopters were married couples, 55% being from social class 1 to 3 (McCurry, 2000).

Current orthodox social work has tended to reduce the concept of 'family' to parents or more particularly turn the focus on mothers and are likely to 'blame the mother' (Farmer and Owen, 1995). By contrast, children and parents often perceive their family in broader terms seeing relations and friends as natural networks and sources of support (McGlone *et al.*, 1998; Morrow 1998). However, if wider families are ignored or overlooked in decision-making processes affecting children, a lack of engagement and commitment to the plans made by professionals is likely. This can form a cycle of mistrust and misunderstanding, which has a corrosive effect on relationships between families and professionals.

The value of kinship ties for children appears to have been frequently overlooked or ignored by professionals (DoH, 1991; Home Office, 1998). In a review for the Department of Health, Berridge (1997) found that placement with kin for example, was still greatly under-used *despite* evidence on its value. Fostering with relatives was seldom found in his review and he concluded that; '…this is particularly curious given that research has consistently found very positive outcomes for children fostered with relatives' (Berridge, 1997: p. 17).

A number of reasons could be proposed for this 'curious' reluctance to involve kinship networks in the care of children. It may be that professionals see involving the kinship group as time consuming, complicated, unpredictable or even unsafe. Perhaps it could relate to some of the following factors:

- Professionals have less control over kin placements.

- More control over agency foster carers or residential placement.

- Lack of time or will to work collaboratively.

- Uncertainty over the legal mandates and implications.

- Assumptions of inter-generational family 'deficits' or 'bad blood'.

- A lack of understanding of kin networks.

The term kinship care may refer to the informal arrangements which take place outside the child welfare system and the jurisdiction of the courts, or the formal arrangements which are arranged or approved by the child welfare agencies or through the courts. There remain a number of definitional problems over what is meant by kinship care. For example, does it refer specifically to extended family or a wider group of non-relative friends of family, which has also been known as *fictive kin* (McFadden, 1998).

Research into kinship care is encouraging, showing that placements tend to be more stable and generally last longer with less changes of placement than with traditional foster carers (Berridge and Cleaver, 1987; Berrick *et al.*, 1994; Dubowitz, 1990; Gabel, 1992). Kinship care has also been considered particularly to meet the needs of children from black and ethnic minorities (Berrick *et al.*, 1994). Rowe *et al.* (1984) found kin care held qualitative advantages over 'stranger care'; particularly the role grandparents would play. In relation to fostering with relatives, Rowe found placements with kin to be more stable (1984: p. 75). The most obvious reason for this may be that a placement within the extended family involves a special commitment to the child from carers and being placed with wider family reduces the trauma to the child of the effects of separation from the parents (Dubowitz *et al.*, 1993).

In adoption work in the UK, kin is often overlooked. Trent (1989) showed that even those children where adoption was initially considered the only viable plan, could be restored to parents and other relatives. Indeed Ryburn (1995) showed that in half of 74 contested adoptions no prior consideration was given to the placement of children within their wider kin networks. Walton *et al.* (1993) illustrated how focused efforts could restore children to kin networks, when placement with strangers was initially seen as the only alternative. It seems clear that the option of placements with extended family provide the child and parents greater choice in the decisions about which placement would be best for them and this fits with the governments *Quality Protects* agenda.

Critics, however, argue that permanency planning is overlooked in kinship placements and therefore children are left in a harmful situation of 'legal limbo' (Sheindlin, 1994). Indeed the use of FGCs in the UK have been hampered by professional concern about the potential lack of meaningful family commitment within kin networks to children. Interestingly research into FGC practice highlighted that FGC co-ordinators had more difficulty getting professionals to FGCs than family members (Lupton *et al.*, 1995).

While conservative social work appears to frequently overlook the importance of kinship ties, the practice of FGCs has started to reassert the value of kin. The FGC enables the family group to act with collective responsibility for the child. One national study on FGCs showed that those children in the UK offered an FGC were more likely to be placed with extended family (than with orthodox methods) and that placement was more likely to be stable (Crow and Marsh, 1997: p. 18).

FGCs can also provide a supportive function, strengthening family connections. In New Zealand the involvement of extended family has served to increase the support around the original care givers (Hassall and Maxwell, 1991). In the UK extended family members were also far more likely to be involved in offering support to their kin than with traditional approaches. Marsh and Crow examined 80 FGCs in UK, and in 94% of these families offered some level of support and in 31% of cases offered to look after the children for at least some period of time (Marsh and Crow, 1998).

Research in New Zealand, where FGCs have been running longest, indicates a significant reduction of children in the public care (Maxwell and Robertson, 1991) although there have been problems with official record keeping, so comparisons have been problematic. On the basis of the existing research from New Zealand, Thornton concluded that 'Families are more involved than ever in making decisions and taking responsibility for their children. Fewer children are being separated from their family or *whanau* than for many years' (1993: p. 29).

The Importance of Contact, Continuity and Identity

There is a growing recognition of the importance of identity and continuity in children's lives. Families provide the most enduring relationships for children and young people and the importance of the maintenance and promotion of links with families, even for those children who cannot live with their parents, is well documented. (Rowe *at al.*, 1989; Millham *et al.*, 1986; DoH, 1991; Bullock, 1993).

The FGC allows the family to make decisions that reflect their traditions and culture, thereby offering a culturally sensitive model respectfully reinforcing the importance of identity and contact within families. Indeed for many families from Black and ethnic minorities this may be their usual way of decision making and it is important not to present this back to them as a professional idea.

If, as seems the case, FGCs are able to provide a wider range of kin carers for children this will ensure children can live with carers they know and trust, potentially reducing any trauma they can experience when they are placed with strangers. Research shows a greater chance of contact between parents and child if the child is placed with the extended family (Berrick *et al.*, 1994; Rowe *et al.*, 1984). Moreover, it maintains children's sense of identity and self-esteem which flows from knowing their family history and culture. Kinship care also promotes children's connections with siblings which we know is important (Wedge and Mantle, 1991) and strengthens the abilities of families to give children the support they need (Child Welfare League of America, 1994).

A growing body of knowledge is demonstrating children's needs for emotional ties which endure over time, and the integration of all the child's experiences of family (Fahlberg, 1994). This links to the notion of continuity and contact so that children connected to extended family and community networks experience a continuing of caring relationships (McFadden and Downs, 1995). Furthermore, where children who are adopted retain links with their families of origin, research has shown that placements are less likely to disrupt and that children benefit from improved self-esteem and clearer self-concept (Ryburn, 1995). However, in order for any of these partnerships between children, kith and kin, and social services even to be considered, prior to any partial realisation, and benefits assessed, there needs to be agreed ways of making decisions.

Collaborative assessments

The way social problems are understood and defined will vary greatly according to class, culture, religion, ethnicity and geography. Family structures, values, beliefs, attitudes and behaviours are mostly socially constructed and generate different patterns of parenting behaviour (Giovannoni and Becerra, 1979) that may be apparent to each family, but less so to outside professionals. The latter are likely to see the problems of 'others' through the filters of their own values, beliefs, training and agency role but these perceptions are given a greater legitimacy through the formalised process of 'assessment'. Ryburn (1991b) argues that claims to assessment providing rigorous objectivity should be treated with caution:

> Every statement made in an assessment report by a social worker is at least as much of a statement about that particular social worker, in the wider context of her role and agency, as it is a statement about those who are being assessed.

> (Ryburn, 1991b: p. 21)

Most assessment processes are based upon 'expert questioning' or 'procedural' models of assessment (Smale and Tuson, 1993; Smale et al., 2000). These mainly focus on family pathologies and deficits, or agency criteria of 'eligibility' and rely on professionals or agency determining 'need' and what questions should be asked of 'others'. Far less attention is paid in these models to understanding or harnessing family strengths or their own definitions of their needs or difficulties. (See Pitcher's chapter in this volume regarding a collaborative assessment framework —Ed.) The ecological perspectives underpinning the FGC approach take into account all aspects of the family and their environment. Focusing less on parental pathology, ecological approaches recognise the unique cultural characteristics and interconnectedness of kin and the resources in their family system (Minuchin, 1974; Garbarino and Kostelny, 1993). For example, Scannapieco and Hegar (1996) argue that kinship care assessments are different from orthodox models and should give an opportunity for the strengths of the family to emerge.

In collaborative assessments practitioners need to take account of all members of the family systems and strengths. The assessment approach that needs development in this context and with FGCs in particular has been described as the *'exchange'* model (Smale and Tuson, 1993; Smale et al., 2000). The exchange model aims for greater user participation and attempts to give clients a greater say over their needs. Exchange is more complex, takes longer and involves more people.

> ...the process involves working with people to understand their differing perceptions and interests and to arrive at a compromise...Instead of the worker making 'an assessment' and organising care and support for people, which carries the implicit assumption of control, the worker negotiates to get agreement about who should do what for whom.

> (Smale and Tuson, 1993: p. 16)

Professionals can still dominate the FGC by predetermining agendas and setting extensive 'bottom-lines' so changes in practice are needed to help professionals 'let-go'. In one study (Lupton et al., 1995) professionals had been trained not to direct families about their preferred plans and yet 40% of professionals still instructed the family about what they thought should be the outcome of the FGC! Developing an open, honest and clear dialogue and exchange with families is necessary to develop the partnerships within the FGC process and ongoing work with potential kin carers.

Conflicts, agreements and resources

A central concern of critics of the FGC approach is that families in crisis cannot make good or safe decisions about their children, either because they are too 'dysfunctional' or fear that powerful individuals will manipulate the conference for their own ends. However, the weight of numbers at FGCs means that influence is more diffuse or evenly shared. Furthermore, the sharing of information and 'secrets' (from both family and professionals) challenges and confronts the secrecy on which much abuse is sustained. It is likely that the inclusion of a wider family network, not directly facing the problem, will offer greater care and protection for the child than the professionals could on their own (Nixon, 1992). There is a risk, however, that FGCs could reinforce power imbalances in families and the process needs to take account of this concern. By widening the circle a wider group can act with collective responsibility for the child within the family, beyond its weakest link. Furthermore, the co-ordinators can actively exclude certain family members, like a perpetrator of abuse or violence, from the conference itself in the child's interests. The identification of supporters and advocates for vulnerable children or adults at the conference preparation phase, can do much to ensure vulnerable individuals have a voice in the process (Pennell and Burford, 2000).

The FGC sets out to ensure that the decisions made for children are safe and to strengthen the network of help and concern around the child. Families often report that the FGCs are stressful and often difficult (Marsh and Crow, 1998) but also that they prefer this approach to leaving matters in the hands of professionals. It represents the family taking ownership of the problem solving process. FGCs plans are often more detailed and imaginative than those put forward by professionals. This may be because they are drawing on a wider base of information about *their* family. In practice, review of FGCs decisions are important so that plans can be followed through, ensuring resources are put in place. This has been highlighted in the research (Lupton *et al.*, 1995; Lupton and Stevens, 1997; Smith and Hennesey, 1998) and is becoming translated more thoroughly into practice.

Attention needs to be paid to resourcing issues as families may be placed in an invidious position of having decision-making responsibilities without being able to access resources that may ultimately make those decisions effective. There is a significant risk that the rhetoric of family responsibility is easily translated into a reduction of resources from the state. A key task then is to get senior management and political support for this approach, ideally with flexible budgets dedicated to the implementation of FGC plans. An assessment of financial costs of FGCs has been difficult but overall the research noted that there might be little difference in cost between traditional meetings and FGCs. (Lupton and Stevens, 1997; Marsh and Crow, 1998). It is unlikely therefore that FGCs can cut service costs. Research shows that kinship carers typically have fewer of their own financial resources than do state paid foster parents (Berrick *et al.*, 1993) so properly resourcing plans and kinship carers is key to achieving the best outcomes for children. For example, after one FGC where grandparents secured a residence order, they found it hard to manage on income support and child benefit (see also Laws and Broad (2000) on kinship carers views on this point—Ed.).

Conclusion

The central argument in this chapter has been that good kinship care policy practice and partnership approaches are closely related concepts. It appears that both, however, have not been a priority in day-to-day social work in the UK, nor are they present in any substantive way in many

of the departmental policies, resources and structures that shape practice. Family Group Conferences are one practical way of recognising and responding to the importance of kinship ties for children and partnership issues for families and practitioners. But this is not without its health warning. It's easy to see how FGCs can easily be transmuted or reinterpreted as a way of reducing resources provided by the state to families or becoming hijacked by the organisational agenda. The value of kinship ties and fictive social networks is not just about providing placements, but the whole continuum of the child's experience from improving contact to reinforcing positive identity, through to improving the quality of decision making for children.

For practitioners working in hierarchical and disabling structures it will not be easy to practice principles that require trust, flexibility and 'respect for people' skills, if they are not themselves treated in that way. There needs to be a move away from procedural and managerial responses to ones that 'open up' possibilities rather than restrict and close down creative practice. Social workers will not be able to work in an enabling way with families unless they themselves are enabled within the systems and structures with which they operate. To date state agencies have mostly led the development of FGC work but this must change. Much more must be done to involve the community and service users in shaping FGC praxis. The ideas originally came from the community in New Zealand, but to a great extent the interpretation of the principles has almost exclusively become the domain of professionals. There is much work to be done on improving the implementation of this approach, developing good practice knowledge and more has still to be learnt from research about long-term outcomes. All of this will only be successful if families, communities and kin are actively involved, participating in decision making at all levels, from policy planning to practice.

References

Ahmed, S., (1990). *Black Perspectives in Social Work.* Birmingham: Venture Press.

Atkin, W.R. (1991). New Zealand: Let the Family Decide: The New Approach to Family Problems. *Journal of Family Law*, 29(2): pp. 387–392.

Baistow, K. (1994/5). Liberation or Regulation? Some Paradoxes of Empowerment. *Critical Social Policy*, 42: 14(3); pp. 34–46.

Barbour, A. (1991). Family Group Conferences: Context and

Consequences. *Social Work Review.* New Zealand Association of Social Workers.

Bell, M. (1996). An Account of the Experience of 51 Families Involved in an Initial Child Protection Conference. *Child and Family Social Work,* 1(1): pp. 43–56.

Bell, M. (1999). *Child Protection: Families and the Conference Process: Evaluative Research in Social Work.* Aldershot: Ashgate.

Berrick, J.D., Barth, R., and Needell, B. (1994). A Comparison of Kinship Foster Homes and Foster Family Homes: Implications for Kinship Homes as Family Preservation. *Child Welfare Research Review,* 16.

Berridge, D. (1997). *Foster Care: A Research Review.* London: HMSO.

Berridge, D., and Cleaver, H. (1987). *Foster Home Breakdown.* Oxford: Blackwell.

Braye, S., and Preston-Shoot, M. (1995). *Empowering Practice in Social Care.* Buckingham: Open University Press.

Bullock, R., Little, M., and Millham, S. (1993). *Going Home: The Return of Children Separated from their Families.* Dartmouth: Aldershot.

Burghes, L., Clarke, L., and Cronin, N. (1997). *Fathers and Fatherhood in Britain.* London: Family Policy Study Centre.

Child Welfare League of America (1994). *Kinship Care: A Natural Bridge.* Washington DC: Child Welfare League of America.

Cleaver, H., and Freeman, P. (1995). *Parental Perspectives in Cases of Suspected Child Abuse.* London: HMSO.

Cleaver, N. (1995). Another Arm of the Bureaucracy? (NZ) *Social Work Now,* July.

Connolly, M. (1994). An Act of Empowerment? The Children, Young Persons and Their Families Act 1989. *British Journal of Social Work,* 24: pp. 87–100.

Cooper, A. (1995). Scare in the Community: Britain in a Moral Panic-Child Abuse (part 4). *Community Care,* 3rd–9th August.

Crow, G., and Marsh, P. (1997). *Family Group Conferences, Partnership and Child Welfare: A Research Report on Four Pilot Projects in England and Wales.* Sheffield: University of Sheffield.

Department of Health (1989). *The Care of Children: Principles and Practice in Regulations and Guidance.* London: HMSO.

Department of Health (1991). *Patterns and Outcomes on Child Placement.* London: HMSO.

Department of Health (1995a). *Child Protection: Messages from Research.* London: HMSO.

Department of Health (1995b). *The Challenge of Partnership in Child Protection.* London: HMSO.

Dubowitz, H. (1990). *The Physical and Mental Health and Educational Status of Children Placed with Relatives: Final Report.* Baltimore, MD: University of Maryland Medical School.

Dubowitz, H., Feigelman, S., and Zuravin, S. (1993). A Profile of Kinship Care. *Child Welfare,* 72: pp. 153–169.

Fahlberg, V. (1994). *A Child's Journey Through Placement.* London: BAAF.

Farmer, E., and Owen, M. (1995). *Child Protection: Private Risks and Public Remedies.* London: HMSO.

Fisher, M., Marsh, P., Phillips, D., and Sainsbury, E. (1986). *In and Out of Care: The Experiences of Children, Parents and Social Workers.* London: Batsford.

Freeman, P., and Hunt, J. (1999). *Parental Perspectives on Care Proceedings.* London: The Stationery Office.

Fry, P., and Addington, J. (1984). Professionals' Negative Expectations of Boys from Father-headed Single Parent Families: Implications for the Training of Child Care Professionals. *British Journal of Developmental Psychology,* 2: pp. 337–346.

Gabel, G. (1992). *Preliminary Report on Kinship Foster Family Profile.* New York: Human Resources Administration, Child Welfare Administration.

Garbarino, J., and Kostelny, K. (1993). Neighbourhood and Community Influences on Parenting. In Luster, T., and Okagaki, L. (Eds.). *Parenting: An Ecological Perspective,* pp. 203–225.

Geddis, D. (1993). A Critical Analysis of the Family Group Conference. *Family Law Bulletin,* 3(11): pp. 141–144.

Giovannoni, J., and Becerra, R. (1979). *Defining Child Abuse.* New York: Free Press.

Gregg, P., Harkness, S., and Machin, S. (1999). *Child Development and Family Income.* York: Joseph Rowntree Foundation.

Gulbenkian Foundation (1995). *Children and Violence, Report of the Commission on Children and Violence convened by the Gulbenkian Foundation.* London: Gulbenkian Foundation.

Hassall, I. (1996). Origin and Development of Family Group Conferences. In Hudson, J., Galaway, Morriss, A., and Maxwell, G. (1996). *Family Group Conferences: Perspectives on Policy and Practice,* pp. 17–36. Annadale, NSW: The Federation Press/Criminal Justice Press.

Home Office (1998). *Supporting Families: A Consultation Document.* London: Stationary Office.

Howarth, C., Kenway, P., Palmer, G., and Miorelli, R. (1999). *Monitoring Poverty and Social Exclusion.* York: Joseph Rowntree Foundation.

Iglehart, A. (1994). Kinship Foster Care: Placement, Service and Outcome Issues. *Children and Youth Services Review,* 16: pp. 107–122.

Jack, G. (1997). An Ecological Approach to Social Work with Children and Families. *Child and Family Social Work,* 2: pp. 109–120.

Lawes, S., and Broad, B. (2000). *Looking After Children in Extended Families: Carers Views.* Leicester: Centre for Social Action, De Montfort University.

Lupton, C., Barnard, S., and Swall-Yarrington, M. (1995). *Family Planning? An Evaluation of the FGC Model.* SSRIU Report No. 31. Portsmouth: University of Portsmouth.

Lupton, C.. and Stevens, M. (1997). *Family Outcomes: Following Through on Family Group Conferences.* SSRIU Report No. 34. Portsmouth: University of Portsmouth.

Lupton, C. (1998). User Empowerment or Family Self-reliance? The Family Group Conference Model. *British Journal of Social Work,* 28(1): pp. 107–128.

Lupton, C., and Nixon, P. (1999). *Empowering Practice? A*

Critical Appraisal of the Family Group Conference Approach. Bristol: Policy Press.

Marsh, P., and Allen, G. (1993). The Law, Prevention and Revolution: The New Zealand Development of the Family Group Conferences. In Marsh, P., and Triseliotis (Eds.). *Prevention and Reunification in Child Care*. London: Batsford.

Marsh, P., and Crow, G. (1998). *Family Group Conferences in Child Welfare*. Oxford: Blackwells.

Maxwell, G. (Ed.) (1991). *An Appraisal of the First Year of the Children, Young Persons and Their Families Act 1989*. Officer for the Commissioner of Children.

McCurry, P. (2000). Adoption Campaign Wins Boost from New Research Data. *Community Care*, 12th–18th October: pp. 10–11.

McFadden, E.J. (1998). Kinship Care in the United States. *Adoption and Fostering*, 22(3): pp. 7–15.

McFadden, E.J., and Downs, S.W. (1995). Family Continuity: The New Paradigm in Permanence Planning. *Community Alternatives*, 7(1): pp. 39–60.

McGlone, F., Park, A., and Roberts, C. (1996). Relative Values: Kinship and Friendship. In Jowell, R., Curtise, J., Park, A., Brook, L., and Thomson, K. (Eds.). *British Social Attitudes: the 13th Report*. Aldershot: Dartmouth.

McGlone, F., Park, A., and Smith, K. (1998). *Families and Kinship: Family and Parenthood Policy and Practice*. London: Family Policy Studies Centre.

Ministerial Advisory Committee (1986). *Puao-te-Ata-tu: The Report of the Ministerial Advisory Committee on a Maori Perspective for the Department of Social Welfare*. Wellington: DSW.

Minuchin, S. (1974). *Families and Family Therapy*. London: Tavistock Publications.

Millham, S., Bullock, R., Hoise, K., and Hack, M. (1986). *Lost in Care*. Aldershot: Gower.

Morris, K. (1995). *Family Group Conferences: An Introductory Pack*. London: Family Rights Group.

Morris, K., and Tunnard, J. (Eds.) (1996). *Family Group Conferences: Messages from UK Practice and Research*. London: Family Rights Group.

Morrow, V. (1998). *Understanding Families: Children's Perspectives*. London: National Children's Bureau.

Nixon, P. (1992). *Family Group Conferences: A Radical Approach to Planning the Care and Protection of Children*. Unpublished paper. Winchester: Hampshire CC Social Services Department.

Office for National Statistics (1997). *Social Focus on Families*. Pulling, J., and Summerfield, C. London: The Stationery Office.

Oppenheim, C., and Harper, L. (1996). *Poverty: The Facts*. London: Child Poverty Action Group.

Parton, N. (1991). *Governing the Family: Child Care, Child Protection and the State*. London: Macmillan.

Parton, N. (Ed.) (1997a). *Child Protection and Family Support: Tensions, Contradictions and Possibilities*. London: Routledge.

Parton, N., Thorpe, D., and Watham, C. (1997b). *Child Protection: Risk and the Moral Order*. Basingstoke: Macmillan.

Pennell, J., and Burford. G. (2000). Family Group Decision-making and Family Violence. In Burford, G., and Hudson, J. (Eds.). *Family Group Conferences: New Directions in Community Centred Child and Family Practice*. New York: Aldine de Gruyter.

Rowe, J., Hundleby, M., and Garnett, L. (1989). *Child Care Now: A Survey of Child Care Patterns*. Research series 6. London: BAAF.

Rowe, J., Cain, H., Hundleby, M., and Keane, A. (1984). *Long Term Foster Care*. London: Batsford.

Ryburn, M. (1991a). The Children Act: Power and Empowerment. *Adoption and Fostering*, 15(3): pp. 10–15.

Ryburn, M. (1991b). The Myth of Assessment. *Adoption and Fostering*, 15(1): pp. 20–27.

Ryburn, M. (1995). Adopted Children's Identity and Information Needs. *Children and Society*, 9(3): pp. 41–64.

Ryburn, M., and Atherton, C. (1996). Family Group Conferences: Partnership in Practice. *Adoption and Fostering*, 20(1): pp. 16–23.

Scannapieco, M., and Hegar, R.L. (1996). A Non-traditional Assessment Framework for Formal Kinship Homes. *Child Welfare*, 75(6): pp. 567–582.

Schaffer, H. (1990). *Making Decisions about Children: Psychological Questions and Answers*. Oxford: Blackwells.

Sheindlin, J.B. (1994). Paying Grandparents to Keep Kids in Limbo (Op-Ed.). The New York Times, August 29th: p. 415. Cited in McLean, B., and Thomas, T.C. (1996). *Informal and Formal Kinship Care Populations: A Study in Contrasts*, pp. 489–505. Child Welfare League of America.

Smale, G., and Tuson, G. (1993). *Empowerment, Assessment, Care Management and the Skilled Worker*. London: HMSO.

Smale, G., Tuson, G., and Statham, D. (2000). *Social Work and Social Problems: Working Towards Social Inclusion and Social Change*. Basingstoke: Macmillan Press.

Smith, L., and Hennessy, J. (1998). *Making a Difference: Essex Family Group Conference Project; Research Findings and Practice Issues*. Chelmsford: Essex County Council Social Services Department.

Tapp, P. (1990). Family Group Conferences and the Children, Young Persons and Their Families Act 1989: An Ineffective Statute? *New Zealand Recent Law Review*, pp. 82–88.

Thoburn, J., Lewis, A., and Shemmings, D. (1995). *Paternalism or Partnership? Family Involvement in the Child Protection Process*. London: HMSO.

Thornton, C. (1993). *Family Group Conferences: A Literature Review*. Lower Hutt, New Zealand: Practitioner's Publishing.

Trent, J. (1989). *Homeward Bound: The Rehabilitation of Children to their Birth Parents*. Ilford: Barnardos.

Utting, D. (1995). *Family and Parenthood, Supporting Family Breakdown: A Guide to the Debate*. Joseph Rowntree Foundation.

von Dadelzen, J. (1987). *Sexual Abuse Study. An Examination of the Histories of Sexual Abuse Among Girls Currently in the Care of the Department of Social Welfare*. Wellington, New Zealand: Department of Social Welfare.

Walton, E., Fraser, M., Lewis. R., Pecora, P., and Walton, W. (1993). In-home Focussed Reunification: An Experimental Study. *Child Welfare*, 72(5): pp. 473–487.

Wedge, P., and Mantle. G. (1991). *Sibling Groups and Social Work: A Study of Children Released for Permanent Family Placement*. Avebury: Aldershot.

Wilcox, R., Smith, D., Moore, J., Hewitt, A., Allen, G., Walker, H., Ropata, M., Monu, L., and Featherstone, T. (1991). *Family Decision-making: Family Group Conference Practitioner Views*. Lower Hutt, New Zealand: Practitioner's Publishing.

11 Assessing Grandparent Carers: A Framework

David Pitcher

When a child cannot be looked after by their own parents, somebody else must take on this task. The responsibility for assessing such alternative carers is one of the most important the local authority has. This is especially the case because a child in need of substitute care may well have been affected by abuse, neglect or traumatic experiences, and will need carers who are not just competent, but who are able to understand difficult or perplexing behaviour, and who can help repair some of the damage that has been done. For those professionals working with vulnerable children, there can surely be few skills more needed than those in assessing those who will care for them.

The contribution this chapter makes is to describe the framework that I, together with my colleagues, have devised for assessing grandparent carers for Plymouth City Council. In undertaking an assessment of prospective carers, we bring the findings of research, and the principles of best practice, to bear on the complex, day-to-day circumstances of individual people.

'When Grandparents Care'

The essential starting point for our framework was to understand the experiences of grandparents who had been assessed. In 1999, I interviewed all the grandparents in Plymouth whom we knew were caring for their grandchildren where they would otherwise be in local authority foster care due to abuse or neglect. This amounted to thirty-three families. We interviewed a number of the grandchildren, and their parents separately. We also consulted with the social workers involved in making, assessing and supporting the placements. We asked questions about the circumstances of the placements, the feelings of those involved, and how the assessments were experienced.

Our five key findings:

1. For most grandparents who care, it is clear that there is real delight in their grandchild.

2. Taking on a grandchild is unlikely to improve any family relationship, except with that grandchild.

3. Grandparents and grandchildren feel isolated. They feel different from their peers, and are unlikely to know anyone else in their situation.

4. Grandparents feel unsure about their rights and entitlements, but also do not like to ask for help.

5. There are big variations in levels of practical, financial and other support from Social Services. This often depends more on the history of the case than the current need.

Our five key recommendations to the Social Services Department:

1. That grandparents who wish to should be given the opportunity to meet and to support each other.

2. That there should be clear information about entitlements at the beginning of a placement. Financial help and help with transport should be available quickly.

3. That it would help if the local authority had a clearly stated policy on grandparents, especially on financial allowances.

4. That social workers carrying out assessments should do so with confidence, but should make sure that they properly explain how and why it is being done.

5. That right at the beginning of a placement, grandparents should decide a plan for what would happen if things did not work out, and to ensure they have proper, agreed support in place from Social Services and/or family. They may well need help in doing this.

As regards assessment, 'When Grandparents Care' revealed that:

- The vast majority of grandparents expect to be assessed, and feel reassured that everything is being 'checked out'.

- During an assessment, grandparents are likely to be overawed by the perceived power of Social Services, and terrified that the child will not be placed with them. Unless dealt with, this leads to a distorted assessment, and the social worker feeling the grandparents are not being honest.

- Social workers often begin their assessment in the 'normal' way, by looking at history of childhood, but without explaining why this is necessary. This leads to misinterpretation by grandparents.

- Social workers are seen as most helpful when they are friendly and informal, and acknowledge differences in age and experience; and when they acknowledge other pressures the grandparents face.

- It is possible to undertake an assessment in a hopeful, positive and supportive way without sacrificing rigour.

The Study has led to a number of developments, including the formation of a monthly support group, 'Parents Again', for grandparent carers, the introduction of a welcome pack for grandparents who are considering taking on the care of a grandchild, and a clear statement in Plymouth's Children's Services Plan addressing the council's position in respect of all grandparents and other relatives.

When a child's grandparents come forward, or are proposed as carers for their grandchild, this evokes many 'gut level' reactions in workers. In reality, the issues are almost always quite complex. Each situation contains surprises, and demands a systematic appraisal. This is illustrated in Figure 1, which demonstrates the potential risks and benefits to a child of placement with grandparents.

Identifying Potential Carers

In many, if not most, cases, the child's grandparents are already part of the scene. They may be the ones expressing concern to the department, or they may be supporting the grandchildren in a difficult situation, perhaps visiting daily or having them at weekends. There are, however, a number of reasons why potential carers may not be immediately identified. Sometimes, abusing families may keep grandparents out, thus preventing what is happening in the family becoming known. Grandchildren, too, may be encouraged by their parents to conceal what is going on, out of loyalty.

It is a good start to ask the child's parents who there may be in the family who might be able to care for their children. However, just because they do not know of anyone does not mean there may not be.

Drawing up a family tree with the family will help identify forgotten potential carers, or potential carers whom the family may not wish to be considered. This is especially the case where families have separated, and perhaps the paternal side may be ignored.

Paternal, as well as maternal, grandparents should be considered as potential carers. Great grandparents may also be possible carers.

How can an assessment be both rigorous and supportive?

There are cases when assessments alienate the grandparents because of a thorough but clinical approach; or, where the emphasis is on 'support' (sic) and difficult questions are not addressed. Perhaps the workers feel that the placement is already decided, especially if the child is already with the grandparent?

This has led to a perception that approved standards are lower for grandparents than for foster parents, and in the United States an officially sanctioned two tiered system does operate.

It is our belief that an assessment can be both a positive experience for the carer *and* cover all the difficult issues in depth.

The following indicators show how this can be achieved:

1. By ensuring that the grandparents understand that it is their ability to meet their grandchild's needs that is being assessed, not their worth as human beings. This needs to be emphasised throughout, and by beginning with a shared and, if possible, agreed statement of the child's needs.

2. By discounting manifestly unsuitable carers in the first or second interview, so that for those who continue to be assessed the worker genuinely believes in their potential. Again, 'unsuitable' always means unsuited to meet the child's needs at the moment, not 'unfit' people.

3. By establishing a high level of honesty right at the beginning, and sharing ideas with the grandparents throughout, rather than coming up with pronouncements at the end.

Figure 1:

Potential benefits	Issues for assessment	Potential risks
1. Family is likely to see the child as less problematic than would a non-relative carer	**1.** Child's need for care ⇓	1. There may be concerns about age, health, housing etc.
2. A less drastic change for the child, especially if there is already a strong bond	**2.** Child's need for stability and continuity ⇓	2. It cannot be assumed that the child knows, or likes the relative
3. It is usually what the child wants		
4. Greater likelihood of lifelong contact with all family members	**3.** Child's need for identity ⇓	3. Other values may be more important. **Best** interests…?
5. Child can see that some members of their family have succeeded		4. The child may remain in a dysfunctional family system
6. If a parent feels less threatened good quality contact is more likely	**4.** Family's relationship towards birth parent ⇓	5. The carer may be very negative towards the birth parent, or conversely be collusive
7. The child is less likely to worry about their parent		
8. Placement less likely to break down, or need professional support	**5.** Family's need for professional support	6. The family is less likely to receive money, training and ongoing personal support
		7. Social services' involvement or control may seem intrusive or unnatural

A formal mid-assessment review is suggested in our model.

4. By incorporating future support into the assessment, rather than seeing it as 'getting them through Panel'. The purpose of an assessment is not just to check potential carers out, but to identify the support the carers need, and to ensure this is properly set up.

5. By observing the grandparents develop as a response to the assessment, rather than seeing them as a static unit to be described. 'Difficulties' become opportunities for change.

6. By ensuring the grandparents understand why the assessment is needed, and why each area needs to be covered.

7. By being friendly and not too formal; by being reliable and consistent.

8. By the worker acknowledging differences in experience, age, race and possibly beliefs.

9. By the worker acknowledging the grandparents' fears, and also the other things that are going on in their lives at the moment.

Approval standards for grandparents may be different, but are never lower, than for unrelated carers. A shortage of resources is not a good reason to place a child with someone who cannot meet his or her needs.

An assessment does not need to continue if the worker does not believe the potential carer can meet the child's needs. The worker should explain fully in writing, why s/he is not proceeding, with the emphasis on why the child's needs would be unmet. The report must suggest other enhanced roles the carer may place in the child's life, if possible, and areas for change. The worker's manager should countersign this report, with a written comment from the manager. The report should be available to the grandparents.

Where possible, an assessment should not be undertaken by the social worker responsible for the child, but by a separate, independent person who can continue to offer support and advice post approval.

An assessment should not be skimped or rushed simply because a child is already placed with the carer.

Planning the assessment

Preparation for the assessment is important, and in this action we suggest ideas which may help.

We all bring our own self to the assessment. Before beginning, the worker might take a little time to consider:

● What is my response to the word 'grandparent'? How much of my feeling is shaped by my own grandparents, whether good or bad, or by my role as a grandparent or parent? Try word association!

● Is my age an issue? This may sound silly, but research suggests that social workers relate most sympathetically to a person of around their age: whether a grandparent or a parent. This is also the case for race and class.

● To what extent are you feeling pressure to approve due to there being no other placements? This pressure could come from you, or from your manager.

● How do I feel about a grandparent asking for help? Studies have shown that many social workers, just like many grandparents, feel they have less right to do so than other foster carers.

● What is the grandparent's view of my power? How does this make me feel?

The worker's assessment is only opinion, not fact, and somebody else's would be quite different. But it is likely to be accurate if:

● It is based on a variety of sources, not just what the grandparents themselves say. The worker should brainstorm all the people who could give information!

● It is based on what the worker observes, not just what he or she is told. For this reason, it is best to carry out the assessment over time. A period of a few months will reveal how the potential carers respond to various events as they unfold, and also to what extent they change.

● How will the worker share what he or she observes? How will it be recorded? Remember that, in assessments, 'everything is information!'

● It is well recorded, with verbatim comments as much as possible. Keep original recordings. The worker should decide how they are going to record, e.g. during/after the sessions, or if two workers, the one not leading the discussion.

● The worker listens to, and values, what they are made to feel by the grandparents, especially if they have begun by looking at their own attitudes. It can help to write down feelings immediately after each visit.

- Somebody else is involved in the assessment. This could be a colleague, or careful supervision; or a 'second opinion' during the assessment, especially where there are hard questions. Supervision will help in examining intuitive feelings.

- The potential carer contributes to the assessment. They may write about their childhood, or keep a written or audio diary of certain situations or over a period of time. This increases their sense of power and motivation, and gives the Panel an unmediated sense of what they are like. However, this should never be a substitute for face-to-face work, but rather as a tool for discussion and for comment.

- The worker forms 'hypotheses', which are constantly adapted and revised in the light of new information, rather than opinions which, research tells us, are often formed very early and very quickly on meeting a new person, and we then organise information around them! Remember that opinion plus power can be a heady combination.

- The worker understands the significance of the differences between him/her and the grandparent. It is important to realise that a person can experience discrimination even where the worker has the best intentions.

If it is done well, an assessment is helpful to the person being assessed, gives confidence, and helps the family discover its strengths and resources. Badly done, an assessment can be intrusive, alienating to the potential carer, and give the department a false sense that the child's needs are being met.

A Format for Assessment

Having set out the principles, we are now able to look at the detail of the assessment process.

Session one: to place or not to place?

People come forward to care for their grandchildren for many reasons, and it is important to screen out grandparents who may not be suitable as early as possible. Sometimes there may be a single, objective reason such as a conviction for an offence against a child. Or there may be more intangible reasons, which the worker will pick up and will need to identify.

There are times when it is right for the child to be placed with grandparents straight away. The difficulty with this is that it may be almost impossible to move them on if it is decided that it is not in the child's best interests to remain with them.

'Unsuitable' grandparents may continue to be important people for the child, and may even be able to become successful carers at a later date.

Grandparents should not be encouraged to take on the care of their grandchild unless they have a clear, realistic understanding of alternatives and the issues they may face. They should undertake the role willingly, and not be pressured due to a shortage of other placements. The social worker should be careful not to play on guilt. The grandparent should agree with the child's needs to be placed away from home.

Never forget: It's OK for a grandparent to say 'No!'

In this session, the worker will need to explore, among other things:

- Does the grandparent agree with the local authority's concerns and description of their grandchild's needs?

- In talking about their grandchild is the grandparent's emphasis on the actual child, or on ideas of duty or loyalty?

- Does the grandparent believe that it is 'right' for a grandparent to parent a grandchild?

It may be that, at this stage, the worker will feel that the placement is not going to be viable. One lesson we have learned is that if grandparents do not acknowledge the seriousness of the alleged abuse, do not write them off without considering whether they may be going through a period of shock if they have only just heard about the abuse—especially sexual abuse. They may need time and help to come to terms with it.

If a grandparent is not suitable, it is best if he or she can see that this is so, and so make their own decision not to continue. It should not feel like a personal rejection.

Session two: beginning the assessment

Once the worker has decided to proceed, they need to establish a clear understanding about the assessment. The assessment is similar to that for all foster parents, with the big difference that the grandparent already knows (or at least has knowledge of the child) and this will be the only child they are approved to care for. This simple difference makes the experience of caring at once more difficult (stigma, isolation, family pressures) and easier (a known child, who is already loved and bears family traits.)

At the beginning of an assessment it is good practice to give the grandparent written information about the format of the assessment, with an indication of time scales. This might also include advice on rights to ask for a service, legal issues (such as who also may care for the child overnight), etc.

An agreement on other issues can be developed. Ensure you will have a quiet room, without interruptions.

At some point during the assessment, both grandparents must be seen individually: where there are other members of the household, whether children or adult, these too must be interviewed individually and their views set out.

Among the issues the worker will want to explore in this session are:

- To explain why the assessment is needed and what will be covered, and why; explain the form it will take; give written assessment schedule; confidentiality; how you will take notes; establish honesty; discuss their fears; get a general picture of what else is going on; acknowledge differences in age, sex, culture, race, etc. Look at the social worker's statement of child's needs.

- To look at practical issues: housing, school, neighbourhood, car/transport.

- To get a brief picture of the carers' personality. If a couple, ask each to describe the other's good and annoying points! How would they describe their marital relationship. If single, who else is around? Who else is part of, or visits the home.

- To ask about the grandparent's view of the type/length of placement, and compare it with the department's.

Session three: 'Tell me about Katie'

'When Grandparents Care' identified that appreciation of the child as an interesting, endearing and individual person, is the key factor in successful grandparent/grandchild placements. It is this delight that engenders resilience in the placement. And it is here that the assessing worker has the advantage over assessments of foster carers, where they can only guess at how the carer will respond, using videos and case studies.

A child placed with relatives is likely to be no less confused and traumatised than a child placed in any other form of care, and the child needs just as much skilled and sensitive handling.

Talking about the child, and the carer's relationship with the child, is a good, logical place to begin from their point of view, and gives some good clues as to their suitability to care.

During this session, the worker should allow the grandparent to talk freely, with as little guidance as possible.

Does the grandparent seem to like the grandchild as he or she is? Is there evidence of shared humour, pleasure in his or her company, and a sense of the child as belonging with them? If siblings or multiple placements are being considered, it is especially important to examine the extra pressures this brings. Our research showed that sibling placements lead to considerably greater stress.

Session four: gathering support

The purpose of an assessment is not just to check potential carers out, or to 'get them through Panel', but to identify the support they need, both as carers for the child and in their own right. The ability to identify and ask for help is to be seen as a positive sign, not a sign of weakness or failure. Not all support needs to be provided by Social Services: there needs to be a mix of support from a variety of sources.

Several research studies have shown that family carers are offered less help, ask for help less, and that social workers believe less help is needed.

This session, positioned quite early on in the assessment to allow ongoing discussion, gives the grandparent 'permission' to think about support, and the chance to look at needs in detail. Being clear that support may be needed can be an important way of letting a grandparent know that we are committed to working with them in a sympathetic and understanding way.

In exploring the need for support, it is important to be as detailed and realistic as possible, and to include the grandparent's feelings about asking for, and receiving, help, including help for themselves in their own right.

The worker and the grandparent are now beginning to draw up a support plan, which will be a separate document identifying all the support, from whatever source, that will be available.

Session five: values, priorities, behaviour

By this stage, the worker will be beginning to develop a feel for the family. There are a number of models for describing family interaction, and these describe such factors as communication styles, family roles, alliances and boundaries, closeness and distance, levels of expressed emotion, the balance between flexibility and organisation, and many others.

The conversation might include:

- What was it like parenting your children? What would you like to have done that you didn't? Mistakes? What did you do right? What is/will be different this time? (This depends not only on you, but also on society and the child's needs!)

- How did you/will you discipline? Does this show understanding of the child's needs as expressed in behaviour? Does the grandparent demonstrate flexibility and intelligence? Beliefs about corporal punishment. Give actual examples, with detail, of actual and hypothetical situations.

- Beliefs. Not only religious practice, but philosophy (e.g. vegetarianism) standards, what is acceptable on TV, ear piercing, swearing. How does this compare with what the parents believe? With what the child is used to? This is especially important for short or medium term placements. How are values/beliefs betrayed by language, e.g. 'druggie', 'bible basher', etc.? Are your values the same as what the child's parents would have wanted?

- Beliefs about the importance of education and school.

- How does/will the grandparent cope with adolescent issues, e.g. sexuality, smoking, staying out late, drugs, alcohol, etc.

- How great is the grandparent's need for rewarding behaviour from the grandchild, whether overt (e.g. expectations of gratitude) or less obvious (e.g. achievement at school?)

- How will the grandparent get involved in the grandchild's life: friendships, interests, organised activities…?

It may be helpful to build in a mid-term review at about this stage. It gives an opportunity to ensure that all parties are happy, and to express your views about the assessment. This could be a formal Review, with a manager, or a more informal point at which the worker says, 'this is what I feel so far.' It is important to avoid 'big surprises' at the end of the assessment.

Session six: readjusting family relationships

When a grandparent takes on the care of his or her grandchild, every relationship changes. This needs to be anticipated and understood and, like all change, it has the potential to cause conflict.

The Grandparent Survey showed that no relationship consistently benefited from taking on a grandchild, except that with the grandchild. Mother–daughter, and relationships with partner, and with other children, and friends, are all at risk.

Grandparents have told us about the costs of taking on a grandchild: exhaustion, loss of friends and social life, guilt, anger and disappointment. They have also described the benefits: a new sense of purpose, new interests, being valued, keeping young, and having the opportunity to rework past mistakes.

What were the grandparent's plans for the future? How did you imagine it? How do you feel about what might have been?

This session looks in greater detail at family life as it is now. Care should be taken not to imply there is a right way of ordering family life that should be conformed to. The worker must convey respect and interest. Many lifestyles can be safe and meet children's needs, even though the worker may not follow them. Many views and opinions are compatible with meeting a child's needs, even though the worker may not share them. Where personal questions are asked, their purpose should be clear to the grandparent. When views are expressed that the social worker does not share, these will be listened to with respect.

How are decisions made in the family. Who and how? Who has the power, in what area? What causes arguments, and how are they resolved. How is affection shown?

Session seven: involving the child in the assessment

We know that a child being cared for by grandparents is likely to have many worries: feeling different from his or her friends, worry about their parents, confusion about their grandparents' changed role, and anxiety about the future. Grandparents, anxious for reassurance that all is well, do not always feel able to address these worries. The child's perceptions, and hence their feelings and experience, will be shaped by their level of thinking and age, and this deserves careful thought.

It is important to hear what the child is saying, and this is no less important just because they are with family or because there appears to be 'no choice' about where they can be.

All assessments will involve at least one individual consultation with the child involved, and this should be separately recorded in the assessment. If a child is too young, specific periods of observation must be substituted. The social worker must demonstrate that they have thought about the best ways to engage the child in a way they understand.

Flexibility and sensitivity are called for if a child seems very shy, or there are lots of professionals who have already spoken to them. In this case, there may be a way of obtaining the child's view through a professional or other person the child already knows and trusts.

Session eight: lessons from the past

The feedback we have received from the grandparents who had been assessed suggests that this vital dimension be explored at this later stage in the assessment, when trust has been developed and the purpose and value of the assessment is clear, rather than at the beginning of the assessment. The worker will by now already know much of the family background, so they are revisiting and exploring what has already been said. Grandparents need to be reassured that this is not gratuitously intrusive or fault finding. It could well be that they will find it a worthwhile opportunity to make sense of their life events for themselves. This may develop into several sessions.

The grandparent's capacity to reflect on past behaviour and life patterns is as important as the actual facts, though these must be presented. This reflects a person's life as at once a dynamic process tending towards health, and the fact that a person's behaviour does develop patterns or 'scripts'.

People may prefer to write (or tape record) something about themselves. This can be very helpful, but it should not be used as a substitute for the social worker's interview. The social worker should use the material in the interview.

Session nine: working with the agency

Grandparents' experiences, opinions and expectations will be varied, some based more on fantasy or imagination than reality. Some may expect the impossible, while others may be alienated and cynical. In fact, the only thing that can be said with certainty is that whatever the expectation, it will be different from the social worker's. And this too will probably be quite different to how things will eventually work out! Especially for grandparents whose grandchildren are subject to Care Orders, a good working relationship is absolutely essential and research shows that if grandparents do not go with this, their grandchildren will be worse off. The ability to accept a partnership with Social Services, and to make positive use of this, is a key factor to be assessed.

The worker may want to consider:

- What has been the grandparent's previous experience of social workers/Social Services?

- How does the grandparent feel about social workers coming round regularly, regular reviews, the need to ask for approval for major decisions, etc.? (Some will feel embarrassment or indignation, others will expect more than we can give).

- Is the grandparent looking at things realistically? Social workers go sick, are unavailable, cases are unallocated, or unwelcome decisions are made. It is important to consider Social Services as it really is. Ask: 'What do you expect?'

- What is the level of understanding of Social Services' plans? Active participation, passive co-operation, confusion?

- How does the grandparent talk about Social Services to/in front of the child?

- Does the grandparent understand the need for, and the limitations of therapy for the child?

As well as sessions with the grandparent and child, the worker will need to speak to two referees, neither of whom should be related to the applicants. Their contribution is a legal requirement, and, unlike the rest of the report, is not seen by the person being assessed.

In addition, the worker may want to speak with:

- Parents. Even though they may be unsuitable as carers, they can contribute a valuable perspective, and their views should be sought.
- Grown up children. What was it like being brought up?
- The school (if the child is already placed).
- Ex-partners, in some circumstances (but never when there has been violence).

Conclusion

The assessment framework I have set out has already resulted in grandparents being assessed in a way that they better understand, and is contributing to the requirements of *Quality Protects*. To sum up good practice in assessment, we suggest 'Plymouth's Twenty Principles' in Assessing Grandparent Carers, see Footnote 1 at end of Chapter. Individual social workers in Plymouth are using this grandparents assessment framework and the local authority is in the process of adopting it. Questions about where the national *Framework for the Assessment of Children in Need and their Families* (Department of Health, 2000) will fit in, and/or work alongside this local framework remains to be seen. At every time, in every local situation, and every individual, there will be differences of emphasis and content. There never can—and never should—be a definitive assessment guide.

Our experience in Plymouth, however, points to three things above all:

- **Be confident:** virtually all the grandparents we have spoken to say they expect to be assessed, and find it reassuring that their grandchild's welfare is being taken seriously. Social workers sometimes feel intrusive or awkward about assessing people who may already have such a strong relationship with the child, but so long as the purpose and nature of the assessment is properly understood, this is likely to be accepted and even welcomed.
- **Be aware of your power:** many grandparents have told us about the fear, even terror, they have at the perceived absolute power of Social Services. In these circumstances, an honest assessment is impossible. Sometimes, hostile or evasive

responses are a result of this. Use your authority, but be aware of just how the grandparents may really be feeling.

- **Be creative:** both in the content and in method, use your imagination and what the family brings, and find a way to share your ideas with colleagues!

Once this is complete, the worker is ready to set out the assessment in writing. Doing this is not 'paperwork' but a creative task! The report should include a separately set out Support Plan and Record of the Child's Views, or description of observation of the child.

Plymouth's twenty principles in assessing grandparent carers

1. Paternal, as well as maternal, grandparents should be considered as potential carers. Great grandparents may also be possible carers.

2. The purpose of an assessment is not just to check potential carers out, but to identify the support those carers may need, and to ensure this is set up.

3. Approval standards for grandparents may be different than for unrelated carers, but they are never lower. In any placement, a child's identified needs must be shown to be met.

4. The social worker undertaking an assessment of a grandparent carer should FIRST have a written statement of the grandchild's needs, provided by the child's social worker. It is the grandparent's ability to meet these needs that is being assessed.

5. An assessment does not need to continue if the worker does not believe the potential carer can meet the child's needs. The worker should explain fully, in writing, why he or she cannot proceed, with the emphasis on why the child's needs would not be met. The letter or report must suggest other roles the grandparent may play in the child's life, if possible.

6. Where possible, an assessment should not be undertaken by the social worker responsible for the child, but by a separate, independent person who can continue to offer support and advice post approval.

7. An assessment should never be skimped or rushed simply because a child is already placed with the carer.

8. In complex cases, two workers should carry out an assessment. Where difficult questions

arise, a second opinion visit by an experienced Family Placement Worker is best practice.

9. Grandparents should not be encouraged to take on the care of their grandchild unless they have a clear, realistic understanding of the alternatives, and of the issues they may face.

10. If grandparents do not seem to acknowledge the seriousness of any alleged abuse, the local authority should consider whether they may be going through a period of shock. They should not 'write them off' without considering this.

11. At the beginning of an assessment, it is good practice to give the grandparent written information about the format of the assessment, with an indication of time scales and the kind of checks and references required. This might also include written advice on rights, legal issues, etc.

12. At some point during the assessment, both grandparents must be seen individually. Where there are other members of the household, whether children or adults, they too must be interviewed individually and their views set out.

13. A child placed with relatives is likely to be no less confused and traumatised than a child placed in any other form of care, and the child needs just as much skilled and sensitive handling.

14. Where a placement involves a sibling combination, it is important to examine the extra pressures this relationship brings.

15. A grandparent carer should be supported in his or her own right. This support can take a variety of forms. Support from other grandparents may be valuable, and for those who need it, Social Services will look favourably on requests for help with transport and babysitting.

16. All assessments submitted to Fostering Approval Panel should include a clearly identified Support Plan.

17. Where personal questions are asked as part of an assessment, their purpose should be clear to the grandparent. When views are expressed that the social worker does not share, these will be listened to with respect.

18. A grandparent's capacity to reflect on past behaviour and life patterns is as important as the actual facts or his or her life.

19. All assessments will involve at least one individual consultation with the child involved, and this should be recorded separately in the assessment. If a child is too young, specific periods of observation may be substituted. The social worker must demonstrate that he or she has thought about the best ways to engage the child.

20. Parents, even though they may be unsuitable as carers, can contribute a valuable perspective, and their views will be sought.

References

Department of Health (2000). *Assessment of Children in Need and their Families.* London: Department of Health.

12 Looking after Children Within the Extended Family: Carers' Views

Sophie Laws

Introduction

Increasingly, childcare policy in the UK encourages the idea that children's welfare is best served when families are supported in looking after their own children, avoiding institutional care wherever possible. Where children cannot continue to live with their birth parents, a placement within the extended family or friendship network brings many potential benefits. Such a placement would generally be seen in social work as a desirable outcome. However this does not mean that local authorities necessarily have a clear view as to how best to support such families.

This chapter summarises the key issues from a research study, undertaken by the author, which examined the experiences and views of carers who have taken on the care of children from someone in their extended family or friendship network.[1] What is it like for them? What do they think about kinship care? What kinds of support have they received from social services, and what have they thought about it?

In 1997 a local study of kinship care work in Wandsworth was undertaken by Bob Broad and that study, the *Child Placements with Relatives and Friends Research Project* recorded policy and practice developments in extended family placements in that borough.[2] Essentially that study set out to identify the number, type, and legal situation of all such placements where the local authority had played some part in arranging an extended family placement. It recorded that between January 1992 and December 1996 there were 116 such placements,

and studied 70 of these in more depth. This article draws on that study where it can give information on a larger group of families.

In 1999 Wandsworth social services department decided to fund a focused piece of research on the views of users (here kinship carers), through its local Management Action Plans in response to the Department of Health's Quality Protects Programme. This study, then, sought to look in more depth at the issues identified in the 1998 study, from a kinship carers perspective.[3]

Sample and methods

From the original (1992–1996) sample of 70 children, 35 children were identified as still living with the relative or friend. These children were cared for by 22 carers. Ten carers agreed to be interviewed. Eight refused or were known to have gone away, and four could not be contacted.

The placements examined here, through these ten carers' interviews, are a sample of placements which have continued for at least two years, and can be described as 'mature' kinship care placements.[4]

This study collected the views of ten women who are carers for children from within their extended families or friendship networks. Respondents were interviewed in their own homes, using a semi-structured questionnaire. The interviews were conducted in a conversational style. The intention was for carers themselves to determine the issues which were most important to them.[5]

---

1. The full report of this research project, entitled *Looking After Children Within the Extended Family: Carers' Views* (2000) by Sophie Laws and Bob Broad, and produced in partnership with the London Borough of Wandsworth Social Services Department is published by and available from the Centre for Social Action, De Montfort University, Scraptoft, Leicester LE7 9SU.
2. Bob Broad, *Child Placements with Relatives and Friends Research Project: Final Report*, 1998.
3. The project was managed by Dr. Bob Broad and undertaken by Dr. Sophie Laws, the researcher on the project.
4. This study concentrated on collecting the views of carers. The experience of the children and young people themselves is the focus of a further research project in Wandsworth, conducted by De Montfort University and funded by the Joseph Rowntree Foundation.
5. The questionnaire was drafted in consultation with members of the kinship care advisory group, and then discussed and piloted with three kinship carers who had agreed to help in designing the research.

Who were the carers?

All the carers in this sample were women. Women formed the great majority of kinship carers in the larger sample of the original study as well, though there were a small number of male carers. The following tables describe the sample in outline.

Table 1: Relationship of carer to child	
Maternal grandmother	4
Sister/half-sister	2
Aunt	2
Friend/not blood relative/'aunt'	2
Total families	10

In the 1998 Wandsworth research study, grandparents accounted for 39% of the cases (the same proportion as in this study), followed by aunts at 26%. Friends cared for 11% of the children.

In eight families there was one child, in one three and in another four. Altogether there were at least five families where these children had siblings who were placed elsewhere, including some in foster care with non-family members. In the sample for the 1998 study, 59% of the children were noted to have siblings. The question of to what extent and with what consequences children may be separated from their siblings in these placements could usefully be investigated further in future research.

Table 2: Ages of children cared for	
Years old	**Number**
5	1
7	3
12	2
13	1
17	3
18–25	5
Total children	15

The 1998 study found that 30% of the children were under 5, and this group are missing from this research, though of course some children had been with the same carer since they were younger.

The children had been with these carers for anything from 2^1/$_2$ to 8 years, with an average of nearly 5 years' stay. These are strikingly long-term placements, compared to the instability of many 'care' placements. One grandmother had altogether cared for four of her daughter's children over the last 14 years, and the youngest is now 12, so she has some more years of caring ahead of her.

Five of the carers were Black and five white. In two families there was a white carer looking after Black children, and in both cases other members of the family were also Black.

Carers' Experiences of Kinship Care

How the children came to be with this carer

The situations which lead to a kinship care placement are diverse. The reasons why the birth parents were unable to care for the child were not pursued in depth, but it was clear that alcohol and/or drug problems were a factor for six mothers. Mental health problems were an issue for several of them. One mother was dead. Three had spent time in prison. In no case was active abuse of children by their mother mentioned, but neglect was a frequent reason for concerns for the children. One young child had been sexually abused by her grandfather.

This generally reflects the picture as described by social workers for the '98 study, though child abuse or neglect was a more commonly given reason in that study. Reasons behind the problems were not directly probed for in these interviews.

For example these summaries come from the carers' accounts:

- Carer is half sister to child. Child was one of a number of children from her father's second marriage. This child was particularly neglected, and was put in a home: it was near to the sister's house, and the parents used to visit her with the child when they visited at the home. One day a social worker asked her if she would have him to live with her.

- Mother of children very depressed. Children went back and forth between the two households over years. Grandmother eventually took over care of children one by one, after child protection concerns.

- Child approached the woman, who was a friend. Child was already living with her aunt: her mother had been murdered.

- Carer's daughter went to prison for a drug-related offence for five years when the child was two years of age. Was going to be fostered, but the grandmother would not part with her granddaughter. When she came out of jail, the child went back to her mother for about 18 months, but there were concerns for her safety. She came back to the grandmother as a fostering arrangement at the age of seven up to the present (age 12).

For the purposes of this research, we tried to clarify typical routes to this type of placement—whether social services approached the carer or vice versa etc. In five cases, the carer had offered to care because the children were at risk of becoming 'looked after'. But for many families the situation was much more complicated than this, with children coming and going between different family homes before any social services intervention, for example. In another example it was technically the carer who approached social services, but this was because the child herself had asked her if she could come and live with her. In three cases at least, the child had already been 'looked after' in a children's home or foster care when they came to the carer.

Fathers were rarely mentioned in accounts of why the children were facing problems.[6] Their role could be looked at further in future research. In one case the carer said that relationship difficulties added to her daughter's problems, and several accounts referred to 'bad company' as endangering the child. One father had sought to care for his children, after they became 'looked after', but his drug use was felt to weaken his case, and the grandmother fought him for custody of the children.

Two carers mentioned difficulty in persuading social services to take action, when they were concerned about the safety of the children when they were with their mothers. One mother became very depressed, and was not feeding or caring for herself or her children:

> *It was very difficult to get social services to listen that the children were not OK with their mother: one of the social workers told me that I was the problem of my daughter, which annoyed me very much. My daughter had no help from social services…It was the MP who got help for them in the end.* (2)*

Impact on carers' lives

Asked about the impact of taking on caring for this child, carers' responses varied from:

> *…not [much] really. I had to deal with jealousy from my son.* (4)

To another who said it had changed her life:

> *…absolutely. He's so demanding.* (1)

Both these carers already had young children at home, but in the latter case the child she took on has learning disabilities. One grandmother said, after 14 years of caring for her daughters' children:

> *My life has been put on hold…It's a full time job.* (9)

In seven out of the ten cases there were other children at home, usually only one but sometimes up to five others. But for three carers, they had no other children at home when they took on up to four children as a kinship carer.

Five carers reported some jealousy or quarrelling between the cared-for child and their own children:

> *My little boy got upset sometimes.* (13)

Several talked about the importance of being fair, for example when buying things for the children, and one said that she had to educate her other children about the need for 'lap time' for this one. (7)

One carer mentioned the satisfaction she has taken from being a kinship carer:

> *It made me feel very worthwhile, that I was doing a good job. People admired me for it. She was a credit to me…People like me are recognised by neighbours, not by anyone official.* (13)

---

6. Cf John M. O'Donnell's account of the invisibility of fathers to social workers in kinship care cases in the USA, 'Involvement of African American Fathers in Kinship Foster Care Services'. *Social Work*, Vol. 44: No. 5, September 1999; pp. 428–441.

* Numbers in brackets are code numbers assigned to the different respondents. Where you see…in the text, there is matter omitted.

Outcomes for the children

Several carers felt that great progress had been made since the children came to them:

> She was tearful at first: it was a very difficult first year. She had been in foster care for a year. Improvements were because she has cousins to play with, more contact with her mother and her brother, who lives with the grandmother. She is now more confident, more talkative, she has stopped wetting the bed, she has settled in at school: a delight. (7)

> …when he came, he was aggressive to us. It was what he used to see go on in his own house. He's never been ill. He used to always be ill when he was in foster care. He's come through a lot, considering what he's been through. [He] was a problem child when he came to me. Now he comes in, says, 'where's Nanny?', follows me around. He's very close to us. He's an ordinary, happy little boy. (10)

One carer emphasised that the child had never been seen as a 'problem':

> Is no problem, never was, just found himself in this situation. He is OK. He stays out of things, e.g. dramas with his mum. He tries to keep things OK with his mum, and to keep the law away from his mum. As long as he is fed and sheltered, he is OK. (3)

A teenager with a disability is going to independence training sessions at college, and hopes to move out and live independently in the next couple of years.

When asked about the children's welfare, a number of the carers made some reference to contact with their birth parents. For example:

> She knows she's got a mother. But if asked where's her mum, she points to me. It's 18 months since [birth mother] has been to see X. She's still drinking. (6)

Others had more positive contact to report:

> She's a nice kid. Highly strung, wants her own way. She's idolised by everybody. Good relationship with her dad and her half sisters and brothers. (9)

In the interviews we asked a direct question about how the carer thought it was for the child having social services involved. None said it was worse, and six felt that it was better for them. The question was not always clear to people, and some responded in relation to social workers' current involvement. One response was interesting:

> It saved his life, but he absolutely hates it. He's nice to [the social worker] when she comes, but after she goes he says, 'why's she coming to check on me now?' (1)

The alternative to kinship care?

We also asked what the carers thought would have happened to the children if they had not come to them. Most said the child would have gone into care. Most thought fostering the most likely outcome, though for some younger children adoption might have been possible. One said 'fostering, but there would have been a lot of anger from the family.' A grandmother said:

> He would have gone from foster care to foster care. He wouldn't have survived: he was on his way out. He was really ill when he came to us. Fleas in his head. Boots too small, sores on his feet…He's never been ill here: he was always ill when he was in foster care. (10)

Another said:

> X is an extremely hard to place child. If I hadn't taken him he would have been in a home, not fostered. I know what happens in homes; I was brought up in a home. I haven't even got to say it…In a home, he would have been got hold of: he's a prime target. He'd have been their little rent boy. (1)

One woman said that if the child had not come to her, he would have gone to someone else in the family. But he chose to stay with her, near where he was living:

> I know lots of people who've been in care, and I don't know one that's come good. Breadline, deadline, dead end street. (3)

The fear of the care system, including fostering, was a strong and unexpected theme in many of the interviews. Their concern about the quality of alternative forms of care is an important motivating factor for many of the carers in this study.

Ongoing contact with birth parents

Another theme which emerged from the interviews was the impact of continuing contact with the children's birth parents. In some cases there was no contact at all, and at the other end of the scale the child's mother was constantly dropping in to her own mother's house. In one family, the care of the child is now shared equally between the carer and the birth mother, who is recovering from alcoholism. The plan is for the child to return to her mother when this is possible.

In relation to mothers, several carers referred to children being affected by their mother's behaviour, especially if she was inconsistent about visits etc. One grandmother noticed how much her grandchildren were affected by their mother's situation. She has mental health problems and has recently had much better support, after a long struggle: and this has affected the children positively.

Carers could find it difficult to deal with when birth parents still took a role in caring for the children. This woman is caring for her young half-brother:

> It's changed the relationship between my dad and me. He drinks. Dad says I'm like a social worker now: too big for my boots. Dad won't back me up on discipline issues, e.g. making him go to college... (1)

Different views on issues like discipline can undermine the carer's authority with the child. One carer felt this happened when the child had contact with her father. Another said:

> My daughter comes every day and interferes in the upbringing of the children...[Child's behaviour is] worse when her mother's around. She sticks up for her. If I stop her doing things, if I think she might mix with unsavoury children, her mother says, 'let her go'. (9)

While some fathers did keep contact with their children, most did not, and this was a source of anger to some carers:

> Their father never bothered. Fathers should see their kids. There should be something to make fathers look after their children. (2)

Perhaps the message is that no assumptions should be made about what will happen in terms of contact with birth parents in kinship care placements. These families have been seriously disrupted and changed, and ongoing contact cannot be assumed. On the other hand for most children their birth parents remained an important part of their lives.

Ethnicity and culture

The 1998 study in Wandsworth found that a greater proportion of kinship carers were African, Afro-Caribbean or of mixed parentage or 'other' ethnic background than would be found in the general population, or indeed in the 'looked after' child population. This is reflected in this study, where half of the carers and 7 out of 10 of the children are Black. Black African, Afro-Caribbean and 'other' people together

constituted only 10.7% of the Borough's population as assessed by the 1991 Census,[7] but accounted for 64% of kinship care placements. The absence of other minority groups should also be noted—where are the Asian families, for example (7% of the local authority's population in the 1991 Census; no kinship care placements)?

A question was asked of all respondents in this study as to how important it was to her for the child to be placed with somebody who was familiar with their family's culture and background. Most of those who commented felt that cultural background was important.

Some comments on why these issues are important:

> I wouldn't have liked to know that X had gone to a white family. If she was a mixed-race child, she could have been integrated into a white family, but she is full Black: mother Jamaican, father Ghanaian. Even if she wasn't with us, her blood family, I think she would have needed to have been with a Black family. (4)

> Music, dancing, speech, culture handed down, reggae culture, slang etc. (7)

> So long as they know about their roots. If they went to a white family, might not know about black kids. It might not, depends if they are living in a multi-cultural area. They at least should go to school with Black kids. But if they were in a white area, growing up in a white family. Then they go to school and someone calls them 'Black', it would be a shock to them. As long as there are other cultures there: at least they'll have an identity. (6)

The question of culture was related for some respondents to other aspects of the family situation:

> You don't know what will happen if a child is taken out of her family. She knows where she's coming from, she's grown up with her nieces and nephews [who are close to her age or older]. Would be hard for her to get into it: easier to understand, having grown up with it all...

> If any rehabilitation is going to take place, it's easier for them to know, than to be out of synch with their culture...That goes for any culture: if you're a Jew, you should be placed with someone who at least knows something of that culture, so if you go back it's not strange to you. (Afro-Caribbean woman) (4)

However another cautions that culture is not the only important issue:

> He knows his culture, knows his granddad is Black. X would never settle down with anybody. It was a

---

7. The question in the 1991 Census asked people to identify their own ethnic group, chosen from pre-set categories. This data may of course be out of date.

coloured woman who had him [foster care], but she didn't look after him well. They struck her off the list [after our complaints].   (10)

Views of social services' help

In this section I will briefly summarise the help respondents wanted and received from social services and from other agencies. Then we will look a little more deeply into the issues they expressed about financial help and about social work help. Questions were asked in an open way, to enable the carers to identify their own priorities.

So what help did the carers receive? All of them were currently receiving financial support: eight an allowance as kinship carers, and two a foster care allowance at a higher rate. For some this financial help had started as soon as they took on the child, but others had cared for children for some time before they got any help. Some people had received financial help at one rate for a short period and then this had changed.

The questionnaire did not ask for detailed financial information, because this had been gathered earlier, but a number of carers volunteered it. Payments mentioned, for those who were not foster carers, ranged from £46 per week to £84 per week. Payments mentioned averaged £65 (six carers gave this information, none of them foster carers). A standard foster care allowance is £108 per week, with increased payments where a child has particular problems, e.g. disabilities.

Some carers additionally received material help for specific costs relating to the child. The cost of a bed or fares was often mentioned.

In terms of advice and support, most of the carers had been visited regularly when the child was first placed with them. In three cases (two of them fostering placements), the child was now regularly seen by her or himself, but in a number of cases the child had never been seen alone by social services.

Help wanted by carers from social services

After asking about the help carers had actually received, they were asked whether there was help they wanted which they did not get. Nine out of the ten carers said that there was help they had wanted which they did not get. They mentioned a wide range of types of help. To summarise:

- financial help:
  - should be paid at fostering rate

  - for wear and tear
  - for school uniforms
  - shoes
  - school dinners
  - fares to school
  - for holidays
- more visits to children
- more visiting of carers
- support group for children
- information (checklists) for carers
- a course for carers
- help to the birth parents after children removed
- more ready response to requests for help

The key question of financial help will be discussed in more detail in a separate section, below, as will the comments about social work support. A typical comment was this:

Why don't we get the same amount as foster carers? I got £40 for school uniform, but it costs far more than that…We have had help with clothes every two years: but this year, they said there would be no help for school uniform. Not offered free lunches. I would like help to take the child on holiday. You need a bit more before holidays, birthdays.   (2)

A strong theme from many of the carers was that they, and other carers, should be checked on more often and more rigorously, partly for support, but primarily as a matter of child protection:

I would like to have been checked on from time to time. I could have been a paedophile. [Social worker] never came to visit her. I was sexually abused myself [in care]. They should have asked her if she was happy: she might have just said yes to me to keep me happy…   (13)

One carer suggested support groups for the children:

Need support groups for children in care: to socialise, get to meet other people. Including younger children. Make them feel they are not the only child in this situation: there are a lot of Black children in care, their hair's not cared for, their skin etc. There should be schemes to help children in care look after themselves, personal hygiene etc. Including kids like X.   (3)

Another wanted to see a structured course for carers where they could talk about difficult issues like how to teach the children about sex; how to help them to think about their future in terms of financial security, etc.

Information was another theme, especially important at an early stage:

> *Checklist of help you can get: I missed out on things through not knowing they were possible.*   (4)

> *When you are a grandparent, you are not told what you can get, where to go, who to see.*   (12)

Help from other services

Carers also mentioned help they needed but did not get from other services. Two mentioned the difficulty they had in getting help with housing issues. In both cases, taking in the child meant that their family was overcrowded.

Two children in this sample have learning difficulties, and both carers had at times struggled to meet their needs. One goes to a mainstream school, but the carer had difficulty finding a suitable school nearby. The child therefore goes some way away, and has to travel by taxi to get there safely. This eats up most of the allowance she receives for her.

The other service mentioned with an important impact on these families was the mental health services, in terms of help to the birth mother of the children. We might also note the high prevalence of alcohol and drug problems amongst the birth parents of the children in this sample, as in the larger 1998 study. This should alert services to the need for cross-boundary working between services which address addictions in adults, and those which concern themselves with child welfare.

Most helpful?

Finance and social work support were the most commonly mentioned assistance that was appreciated:

> *We had two very nice social workers. Helpful. Used to visit the children regularly. Could see the children were looked after properly. If I've phoned in an emergency, they have tried to help.*   (9)

> *Help when my daughter was in prison, and I got X. Somebody to talk to about how I felt having X and that.*   (10)

One carer had issues about handling the child's behaviour, and about contact with the birth father:

> *…the social worker provides good ideas about how to sort things out.*   (7)

One woman specified 'Good advice about becoming a foster parent' (12) as particularly helpful.

Family group meetings were appreciated:

> *Had family conferences and found them really good, really helpful, even though dominated by the mother of the children.*   (4)

Also mentioned was feeling supported by their 'own' social worker, but that assistance was blocked by those 'higher up'.

By contrast to those who had drawn support from social workers, one carer thought 'the cheque' (13) the most helpful thing.

Not helpful?

The next question asked whether there were things respondents had not found helpful in their contact with social services. The most commonly mentioned issue was financial support—the level of it, difficulties accessing it, and the question for some of not being allowed to be foster carers. Some had struggled with very little help when they first took on the children, others still find making ends meet extremely difficult.

Two carers mentioned problems arising from having taken on a Residence Order for the child:

> *It's very hard at times, and now I feel that I've got the Residence Order I'm pushed out of the way. I miss having a key worker.*   (9)

> *There was an issue about the maintenance. We had to get our own solicitors about the Residence Order. It was the solicitor who said unless it was written into the order, we might get no money. Nobody mentioned the maintenance. Social services did advise us to get our own solicitors.*   (4)

Another shared theme, already mentioned, expressed a sense of stigma or blame felt from social services staff:

> *Feeling blamed for my daughter's problems by a social worker.*   (2)

> *When we had to go to this meeting: it's the way we were looked at, it was ridiculous. I do see that they have to protect children. I know you have to be careful, with children. I've never had social services around me, I'm not used to it. We've been through hell and back again…Had to have checks with police, doctors etc. Makes you feel low, we felt degraded…*   (10)

> *There was an incident where my son said that X had touched him in a sexual way. It was like children playing doctors and nurses, but the social worker brought in the Child Protection people, and it was dreadful. The social*

worker said they would have to remove him, get an emergency placement. A policewoman came to interview my son: she did it very sensitively, and was satisfied that there is no problem. I was made to feel dirty, dirty family…   (1)

Another response relating to attitudes was as follows:

It's so legal, it's all bookwork, more than human contact. Be more realistic. The welfare of the child should be more important.   (13)

This theme about feeling things are done 'by the book' is echoed by another carer:

Don't use the text book: 'if that happens, go to number 3 on the page.' Go to people, do it around them, what they're like.   (1)

One carer said that she found unhelpful 'Them not knowing the law' (4), as she only got help with a housing issue when she herself looked up the relevant law about re-housing and 'the welfare of the child', and quoted it to them.

Finally, a theme, which is developed further below: that social services, should visit the children more:

Should visit foster children, talk to them about life, encourage them. Tell them about the future. Some children think they will get lots of help, e.g. get an apartment. They need teaching about reality.   (2)

Financial help

When I had X it was a right ding-dong for social services to pay for anything. It was a hassle to get them to pay for a bed for her. Because we're family, we're treated differently from foster carers. We're not doing it for the money, but we didn't take it up by choice. I feel on the whole, [the local authority] social services are a bit stingy. Things increase every year. Since we got the Residence Order, it was 2 to 3 years ago, each year, even income support increases, it might only be 50 pence, but they do increase it. This has not increased at all. I feel it's lip service. If she had gone into foster care, they could have been paying out £100 per week for each child…We get paid every quarter and now it's on a computer. Before, it would get forgotten, and I've had to ring up and ask them.   (6)

This comment sums up some themes shared by many of the carers interviewed. Many carers talked about the financial help as 'essential'. (1)

I am not in a financial position to help X on my own.   (3)

…couldn't have done it otherwise.   (4)

This last point refers specifically to payments for childcare while the carer works: this was the only carer with a job outside the home.

Most of the carers receiving allowances felt that the rate was too low. Many resented not getting the same level as foster carers. Some pointed out that they do not receive child benefit for these children, reducing their income still more. This removes the government's 'safety net' payment which is made to ensure children's welfare.

A number of specific issues were mentioned by the carers:

- Wear and tear: several carers talked about the damage done to their furniture and fittings by having children around. One grandmother had raised four of her grandchildren as well as her own children, and had used up all her savings doing so. Now that the youngest is a teenager she would like to refurbish the house, but has no resources to pay for it.

- School uniforms, shoes: these items were causing difficulty to many families. Some had had some help with these costs, but amounts paid were small compared to the actual cost.

- Travel to school: fares were an issue for several carers.

- School meals: one carer had been refused help towards school meals by social services. Others, on pensions or student grants, were not able to get free school meals for the children they cared for.

- Holidays: several carers said that the child does not get a holiday every year.

One carer took a different view from the majority on the issue of finance. She thinks that kinship carers should not get more money:

I honestly mean that. If I want to take this child, I should want her anyway, not for the money. Does that mean if the cheques stopped, they'd get chucked out on the street?

She links this to her concern about the quality of foster care: she thinks some people become foster carers for the money:

…they should vet people better. Adults can manipulate children. The social worker should come in as a friend. Should arrive unannounced sometimes. The social worker should say 'I would like to visit when I want'.   (13)

Social work support

A number of carers mentioned greatly valuing emotional support and practical advice they had received from social workers, as we have seen above. While one carer said:

> Social services done nothing.   (13)

most said that they had had good help, at least at the start. Several carers had particularly appreciated prompt help in an emergency.

Many commented on changes in the help they got:

> The first social worker was good, she came every week. Latest one, I don't see her much: she has never been here, we meet at the childminders. Have meetings every so often. There seems to be a steady stream of social workers.   (4)

There was also one negative comment about social workers' attitudes:

> I can speak very well, people can't easily undermine me, but…I feel I have to stand up to social workers. I have been horrified by how I hear social workers talking to people in the office. Because they are in a position of authority: it's as if they think you're stupid if you have to go to social services.   (3)

In only three cases were children still being visited by social workers. Many carers felt that there should be more visiting of children in all types of placement, for their protection. An unanticipated finding of this research was the great concern many carers expressed about the quality of institutional care, and in particular foster care. No question was asked which was expected to prompt this sort of comment, but six carers talked at some length about their concerns:

> When you place children into care, you've got to visit the home. [My grand]children were only allowed into the sitting room when they were asked. X said she was hungry, ate a packet of biscuits, and the foster carer put the child face to the wall. The foster children slept on the floor when there were visitors.   (2)

> …I've seen some children who are in foster care and there's not that close love and affection. There might be when the social worker is around. Children should have their own meeting with a social worker. You could get families where one parent is interfering with the children.   (9)

Three carers made this point about the danger of social workers being deceived about how children are treated:

> In front of social services, everything is fine, they are nice to the children. Behind their backs, the child is lucky to get fed, get washed. I am very family-oriented, child-oriented, and I hate to see children that are not cared for.   (3)

So what is the basis of these views? Recent public concern about abuse in institutional care is a factor. But for several of the carers their experience is very direct. One of the children in the study was badly treated in foster care: the family went to court after they became concerned about the situation at the foster home. This foster carer was later struck off the list.

> X had counselling after leaving foster care. He had lots of foster carers: about four, for 3 months, or 6 months. Back to mum and away again. We got him out before anything had happened to him.   (10)

Two of the respondents also said that they had themselves been in care as children and had been sexually abused. They both regarded abuse as an inherent danger of public care, and were very committed to protecting children from it. The carers felt that people like them should be visited more, and in particular that children should be seen on their own, to protect those children who are unhappy in their placement.

Views on the legal framework of placements

The issues here are perhaps of two kinds. Carers have their own ideas about what their relationship is and should be to the child and to the State, in the form of social services. They also have practical experience of raising children, and of getting support in different ways. This project was primarily focused on carers' views of the help they had received, so much of the material tends to be at the more practical level. However some carers did reflect more broadly on how they saw the situation—in very different ways:

> For the first 3 to 4 months we did not get any help. We don't class it as fostering: we are his own flesh and blood. I couldn't see my grandchild go into fostering.   (10)

And by contrast:

> I am doing them a favour stopping the child becoming a junkie by helping them. Social services are benefiting.   (7)

In terms of what we might imagine to be expected social obligations, different carers, as grandmothers, aunts, sisters or friends, stood in different relationships to the children. But neither their views nor the level and type of support they received appeared to necessarily reflect this. For example both of those who were foster carers were blood relatives to the child.

So what were the legal arrangements surrounding these placements?

Table 3: Legal status of placement

Residence orders	6
Fostering: 'care order'	2
No order	2

Those who were counted as foster carers were in general happy with their situation, though the fact that the birth parents still have parental responsibility was an issue for one of them:

> *His mum and dad have to sign for things, e.g. for a passport: they have parental responsibility. They leave things to me anyway. He has to have an operation: she had to sign for that. Gives me the hump really...I've been looking after him.* (1)

The other carer who was fostering said that her new social worker wants her to change to a Residence Order, but she had not heard any convincing arguments for doing this.

The majority (60%) of this sample has Residence Orders, in contrast to the situation of the larger sample studied in 1998, when only 29% of the placements were of this type. 'No legal order' was more common in that study. This difference may be the result of the present study looking only at long-standing placements, or perhaps the local authority's recent policy[8] of encouraging the use of Residence Orders is a factor.

Several carers said that they had been strongly encouraged by social services to go for the Residence Order. One said

> *Social services paid for the lawyers. They kept mentioning it. I felt if I didn't take it out, [the local authority] social services could take her away any time. Up till that time the children were with us three years. So now I do not need permission to take decisions: but I was doing anything I wanted anyway.* (6)

One carer appreciated the security of the Residence Order.

> *I was encouraged by social services to go for the Residence Order as opposed to them having parental responsibility and her being placed with me. At least this way they can't be taken away. If I have ups and downs, I can be sure the child will stay with me, and keep contact with the rest of the family.* (4)

However, more were uneasy about the situation. One said that since she took out the Residence Order, she gets less money (2). Two carers would have preferred to be classed as foster carers: one grandmother is particularly angry:

> *They were going to let me foster X, but I had some rent arrears and they said that made it impossible. Social services decided I had to take a Residence Order, or they would find foster carers for X.*

She says she cannot afford an annual holiday for X, which fostered children get, and that she and her husband have used up all their savings looking after children, which is why there were rent arrears.

> *When I got this Residence Order, they wrote it out that I'd have a social worker, which I haven't got. If I need to get in touch, it's with the team leader. He's saying, since you got a Residence Order, she's nothing to do with us really...I feel very let down by [the local authority]: they tell you one thing and then afterwards...I think it's disgusting and something should be done about it.* (9)

Several people mentioned the involvement of a solicitor in the process of getting a Residence Order, and that social services had paid for this. The solicitors had advised that the agreement should state what help the carer would get from social services. However some carers found that this did not guarantee that such help would be forthcoming:

> *I am on income support, but I can't claim anything for X. I pay £7 a week for her school dinners. When we did the residence order, the solicitor wrote in that if I lose money caring for X, they will reimburse me. But I am paying for school dinners, fares to school, holidays, shoes, uniforms...* (6)

Advice to social services

Carers were asked what would be their advice to social services, so that they can give better support to people like them in the future. This

---

8. As stated in Wandsworth's *Children and Families Manual*, 1996.

question enabled them to summarise and prioritise their views. These comments were typical:

> Value we carers a lot more. Checking what you need from time to time.I got the feeling it was like an assembly line 'Got this one in under budget, next one along please!' More regular visits and help, rather than waiting till a problem comes up. There should be more written information: what to do if...(especially at the beginning). (7)

> To give more consideration to the carers, and treat them as foster carers. People that are saving social services masses of money. Costs them a lot to keep them in children's homes. And yet they pay grandparents, relatives, a minimum. (9)

> Even though we may be family, we should be treated a lot better financial-wise. Because we are family, we've got the kids and we love the kids: it's not for the money, we took them to save the kids from being fostered, adopted and not seeing them again. (6)

Consultation with carers

One of the motivations of this study was to work towards a generally more responsive service, with greater ongoing consultation of service users. All the carers interviewed were interested to take part in further consultation, and made some comments about how this should be done. For some respondents, they would also value meeting other carers for their own benefit:

> I would like [the local authority] to bring people together at a forum. Where people could network, feed back the pros and cons of it. I felt a bit isolated. Except for [other family member] I didn't know of anybody else that had done it. (4)

Others were more concerned about effective influence on others than about mutual support:

> Bring the head of social services, the top dogs who sit on chairs and pass out judgement, that keep doing the cuts. (9)

> Yes, people should listen to the likes of me that have been there, been abused.

A number of practical issues were raised about the logistics of getting a group together. These are extremely busy people and few had cars.

> I'm a carer plus I have three of my own children. It needs to be during school hours, or better, in the evening, if they would pay for a babysitter. Just let people talk: is better, for adults, the relief of not having to worry about them. If you pay someone, you can focus, if not, have to worry about getting back. (3)

Conclusion

The special contribution of this study is that the carers were asked directly about their own situations, and to identify what was important to them about the help they had received. Carers placed emphasis on financial and emotional/social support. Indeed many said that this help had been essential—they could not have taken on the child without it. And without it, the children would have gone into residential or foster care.

These were long-term placements, from two to eight years, and this stability is valuable for children. Substantial unmet need was identified, however. Nine out of the ten respondents said that they had wanted help that had not been forthcoming. The main themes were the need for more financial assistance, and a variety of needs around social support and checks on carers and children. Carers wanted more, and more accessible, ongoing support. Information was also identified as lacking, and carers recommended the production of a checklist which would assist new kinship carers in knowing what help may be available to them. Some carers were keen to meet other carers to discuss issues of importance to them. Some form of mutual support may be important, perhaps in addition to social work visits.

The typical picture in terms of social work support to carers was that they had had regular, helpful contact with social workers in the early days of the placement, but that this had tailed off to very little over the years.

An unanticipated finding of the study was that many of the carers expressed great concern about the quality of foster care generally. They urged social services to be more rigorous in checking up on foster care placements, and felt that social workers should make a practice of visiting unannounced to both foster carers and kinship carers. As a matter of child protection, it was felt also that children in both types of placement should be seen separately from carers. Some of the children in this sample were reported to have never been seen on their own, though a minority were currently seen three or four times a year.

Some carers said that they had felt 'judged' by social workers during the process of assessment before the placement was made, and urged social services to rethink its attitudes to relatives in these situations. However all appreciated the need for checks on carers, and were willing to accept such checks. It may be that a different sample would feel differently about this.

Another feature of carers' situations that was not entirely expected was that for some families, relationships between the carer, the child and the birth parents remain complicated and problematic. For many of the children, their relationship with their birth parents was seen as a source of some pain.

The situations described challenge an excessively cosy view of kinship care placements. They grow from extended family links, and these links remain an important feature of life for the child, for good or bad. Most of the birth parents were still living, and some were very much a presence in the children's lives, while still having many of the problems which caused the removal of the child. In other families much change has taken place, but there could still be some difficult family dynamics to contend with. Thus, assumptions should not be made about what level or quality of contact children in kinship care placements will have with their birth parents, or about what this may mean for the carer and their relationship with the child.

So, while carers gave a generally positive view of the children's current welfare, the children were not without problems. They had been through some very difficult experiences, and the carers emphasised their needs in terms of building up a sense of security. Two in the sample had learning difficulties, and the carers had found problems in meeting their educational needs. One 17-year-old girl had just run away with an older man, causing her carer great concern, although their relationship had been good to that point. Adolescence clearly presents its own challenges, as to all parents, and one grandmother referred to feeling there were issues her grandchild might not want to discuss with her.

The London Borough of Wandsworth has had a policy of encouraging kinship carers to take out Residence Orders. There was real concern, by carers, that social services will see children of this legal status as 'nothing to do with us', and withdraw support, which would be disastrous for families on very low incomes. This sense of insecurity was exacerbated when social workers sometimes did not respond to phone calls from carers.

Some carers had wanted to be counted as foster carers, and had been refused, and many resented the much higher levels of financial and other support attracted by foster carers. The thinking behind the pressure on carers to take Residence Orders is presumably that these situations should be seen as akin to ordinary families, and this will benefit the children. However these families are more impoverished than others, because they are typically taking on a child or children at a point in their life-cycle when they cannot increase their income at all. The grandparents are pensioners, and most of the others are on income support. Many already have other dependent children. They have not planned to raise more children at this point in their lives, and there can be no expectation that they have resources available to enable them to do this.

It is worth pointing out the gender dimension of the carers' situation, which is generally taken for granted by all concerned. As women, there is a strong social expectation that they will be willing and able to sacrifice their own ambitions and financial future in order to care for others. The hardship women suffer in fulfilling these expectations is less visible, because it is seen as 'natural'. Kinship carers' special situation is hidden by assumptions about the role of women in the family. Women's work in the home is greatly undervalued, financially and otherwise.

The overwhelming message of this research is that the carers feel that being placed with them has been beneficial for the child. For a number of children, ill-health or behavioural problems which they had when they came to the carer have been overcome, and the general picture was very positive. In reaching this end, carers valued social services' help and support. They encouraged social services to promote this type of placement:

> *If children are in foster care and they're not happy and they've got grandparents who can take them, then let them have them. Better than going to foster care with strangers.*   (10)

13 Training Materials for Kinship Foster Care

Ronny Flynn

Introduction

This chapter describes the development of the National Foster Care Association's (NFCA) open learning training materials for family and friends foster care, for carers and for social workers (NFCA, 2000a, 2000b). Although the training material was produced for kinship carers of children who are in public care, the material is directly relevant to all kinship carers whether family and friends foster carers, relative carers or kinship foster carers, all of which terms are used interchangeably in this chapter, reflecting the field as it stands. The chapter ends with some reflections on this training material and gives pointers as to why kinship care may not be perceived as being a priority issue, at least at this point in time.

Background to the training materials

For a number of years the NFCA had been aware of the gap in training and support for family members or friends caring for a child known to them (NFCA, 1993). Regular calls to its Help Line found that these carers had frequent difficulties with finance, their status and their relationship with the local authority. The Children Act 1989 guidance for England and Wales, Children (Scotland) Act 1995 and the Children (Northern Ireland) Order 1995 all state that agencies should explore placement with a child's relatives or friends *before* looking to a placement with non-related carers, but evidence from England showed that this was not common practice. Research by Waterhouse reported the proportion of children placed with kin in local authorities to range from nought to over 30 per cent (Waterhouse, 1997). She noted the lack of information available on these types of placements, and also that these carers were less likely to be allocated a family placement worker than other foster carers. In a follow-up study, Waterhouse and Brocklesby examined the policies and practices of five English local authorities in relation to this type of care, and found that policy and practice was unco-ordinated and varied both within an authority and between authorities (Waterhouse and Brocklesby, 1999). So the needs of this group of children and their carers were not being fully met under the requirements of the Children Act 1989.

In a study funded by the Department of Health and carried out in England for NFCA, Wheal and Waldman (1997, 1999) searched existing training materials, and undertook a survey of training needs of kinship foster carers and social workers. They found no published training materials in England and Wales, although some local authorities were adapting NFCA's *Choosing to Foster* course (NFCA, 1994). Several US training packages were found, but all relied on group-focused training and would have been difficult to use in the UK context where kinship foster carers are relatively invisible and may be geographically spread out. Anecdotal evidence from social workers had suggested that this was the case, and that considerable development work would be needed to engage them in a group training process. The Department of Health agreed to fund NFCA to develop and produce the two substantial training packages described in this chapter, and to distribute a copy to each local authority in England and Wales (NFCA, 2000a and 2000b).

Developing the Training Materials

Open learning provides opportunities for self-study at the learner's own pace and written open learning material was the chosen format for the family and friends, and social worker training materials eventually produced. Practical activities in the form of checklists, sentence completion exercises, charts to fill in, and space to reflect on and record views, thoughts and feelings are an important part of reflective practice and were used throughout the carers' handbook.

The social worker materials were aimed more at encouraging family placement workers and field social workers to train together, so concentrated on methods suited to work in groups. A decision was taken early on to concentrate on carers of children who were in public care and therefore covered by the foster placement regulations, rather than those supported under Section 17 of the Children Act 1989 in England and Wales. This was mainly driven by NFCA's policy of seeking to give kinship carers equal status and recognition with other foster carers, although there is still a policy debate to be had as to whether this is an appropriate system for this group of carers. Some local authorities (see Broad, 1999) support all children with kin using Section 17 money, and a number of authors have advocated for seeing these placements as a completely separate type of care.

NFCA managed the overall project, which included editing, designing and producing the open learning training materials. This contributor was hired on a part-time freelance basis to write the two packages. The research, writing and testing for the published materials was completed in ten months, which necessitated using every contact that would help the process move swiftly along. The amount, structure, content, design and presentation of the materials had not been decided upon, and so had to be developed from scratch. This contributor has specialised in open learning materials that had been developed from a strong and diverse user base, and believed that kinship foster carers, as a group of service users, were a main source of expertise on their training needs, just like social workers were for theirs. However, each would also have ideas for the others' training needs and all would be consulted. The earlier work carried out by Wheal and Waldman (1997) had directly reflected the views of 24 carers and 25 social workers in three local authorities in England, and provided an excellent starting point for the materials development project. Quite early on it was agreed that the social worker package would follow a design and format similar to NFCA's *Choosing to Foster* training materials, whilst it was important that the handbook was as 'user-friendly' and engaging as possible for carers.

The broad aims of the training materials were:

- To raise the status of family and friends foster care.

- To improve the care and support of this group of children.

- To assist carers and social workers to develop skills.

- To challenge discrimination and promote equality.

The development of the materials would draw

on the direct experiences of kinship foster carers and social workers, by including their own case material and quotations throughout. The views of some children and young people in kinship care, and a few children of kinship carers were also included. Carers and social workers would be involved in testing these early drafts that would then be modified as a result of their feedback.

The final draft was critically read by a diverse group that included carers, a young person who had been in kinship care, a disability consultant, social workers, policy makers, academics and other practitioners, as well as a range of NFCA staff and volunteers.

Consulting and selecting materials

Wheal and Waldman's study was supplemented by a number of others. Firstly, a postal survey was carried out of all 245 family and friends carers on NFCA's member database. Information was sought about how long they had been caring, details about the children they cared for, and examples of positive and challenging situations for the children and for them as carers. These family and friends carers were also asked to make additional comments, and if they would like to be put in touch with other kinship caregivers. Finally, they were asked if they would be willing to provide further help in the development of the materials. The process produced 47 separate accounts of experiences, almost all from white English or Welsh women, caring as maternal aunts or grandmothers in 26 different local authorities. The responses in particular richly highlighted the emotional and practical aspects of caring. The strengths and tensions of working within known relationships was what seemed to distinguish these carers' experiences from those of other foster carers. These carers also offered to help further with the project. Interestingly, there were no offers to organise a group of carers to discuss the materials, and only a handful of carers asked to be put in touch with carers in a similar position to themselves. One can only speculate as to the meaning of this lack of response to group activity, which is traditionally the way in which non-related foster carers are trained. Wheal and Waldman's study highlighted the lack of awareness of the need for training felt by some of the carers. Their reluctance to identify themselves as foster carers could help to explain this response. Yet the carers who took part in this survey did so with enthusiasm and commitment, and half of them went on to test the actual materials. It is this enthusiasm that needs to be brought out and developed by local authorities.

All NFCA groups and foster care associations were asked to pass on a request for help to any kinship carers in their membership. This produced a few extra volunteers.

This initial consultation did not bring forward many Black carers or disabled carers, although a number of Black carers had been included in Wheal and Waldman's study. While these may have been underrepresented in NFCA's membership, it was decided to actively recruit as many as possible in the time allowed. So these groups of carers were written to separately, and then followed up by telephone. In addition, local authorities were asked to recruit Black carers as testers as part of their consultation (see below), and this improved the numbers volunteering a little. They were still not satisfactory as the drop out rate was high. This highlights the need for additional time and resources to be built in to the planning stage of a project in order to engage with and recruit less powerful groups of adults. The need to network, and do outreach work to gain people's confidence is also clear. We also do not have a national profile of kinship foster carers in any of the UK countries, and at the time of the research, ethnic record keeping by local authorities was patchy. We do not know, therefore, who uses kinship foster care, although a study of carers supported under Section 17 of the Children Act 1989 in one London borough showed a high proportion of African-Caribbean carers (Broad, 1999). The message about 'representation' was also true for identifying lesbian and gay carers, obtaining the views of children, and including these in the training materials, as well as monitoring the ethnicity of carer and child of those calling the NFCA telephone Helpline.[1]

Wheal and Waldman's study produced a wealth of ideas for content from both carer and social worker perspectives. To add to this, a number of visits and telephone consultations were carried out with local authority workers to help with decisions on priorities for and approaches to the materials. Early research had highlighted great variety in social work policy and practice with this group of carers, which needed checking out. Therefore in addition to the visits, a postal survey of all fostering personnel in English and Welsh local authorities was undertaken. An initial letter was sent to NFCA's contacts in fostering teams, asking for their co-operation with a survey of current practice. Waterhouse (1997) in her survey of local authorities in England had established that 83 local authorities said they placed children with relatives or friends. In a follow-up study with five local authorities, she noted an absence of written policy and procedures on kinship foster care, and ongoing debates about where responsibility for this part of children's services lay (Waterhouse and Brocklesby, 1999). This may have accounted in part for the low response to the training materials survey, which resulted in detailed information from only 10 authorities. Some of this information was collected by telephone; some sent in by social workers. Nevertheless, the information provided by these authorities was most useful in helping to gain a picture of training issues, and highlighted the real need for training in this area! In relation to prioritising the content of the training material to be included, the postal consultation had gleaned a long list of topics that could be included. A review of US and UK literature and training materials was also undertaken. This added as a check on the contents already assembled, but also provided a theoretical and practice overview of the state of kinship care in these countries and nation states, in which to locate the materials. The task was then to organise and select from the list. It was possible to group the contents into a number of broad section headings, for example, 'Divided loyalties?' and 'What is family and friends foster care' that then fitted into broader themes. Each section heading was organised into learning objectives, teaching points and resources that needed collecting, ensuring that all information from research and consultation was included.

---

1. In view of the move to make children and young people more visible as participants in social work and training, this was a sad omission. Parents' views are also not directly represented. Male carers were also very poorly represented, although women with male partners who wrote to us, often included them as joint carers. Lesbian and gay carers were not identified. There is thus plenty of scope for further research and consultation with these under-represented groups although the critical readers helped with these shortcomings, as they provided some of the missing perspectives and expertise. In relation to the analysis of calls made to the NFCA Helpline it seemed that the majority of callers were maternal grandparents and aunts, and enquiries were mostly about financial support clarity and about the relationship between them and the local authority.

What Training? For Whom?: Issues and Practicalities

NFCA's policy for these materials was to treat family and friends carers equally with other foster carers, and find common ground between the two groups that enabled them to work within *existing* local authority systems rather than change them. Contact with the Department of Health reinforced the view that the existing children's legislation and guidance provided all the scope necessary to provide for this group of carers and children. Yet appropriate procedures and information about them was not well organised, and not reaching kinship carers. The training materials thus concentrated more on procedures, legal aspects of caring, and relationships with the local authority and less, the identification of resources and supports, and clarification of the relationship between the kinship carer and social services. These omissions were a disappointment because since kinship foster carers are widely spread out, and unlikely to meet together for any small group training, accessing information on rights, responsibilities and local authority procedures, through this distance learning material, would have enabled them to do their job even better.

Another key theme, which emerged alongside 'information', was that of the changing nature of the carer's role in relation to the children and how written training materials might or might not support carers' needs. The carers who were consulted wanted to help children deal with painful feelings, to communicate more effectively with children and to support them through their life changes. They wanted to understand and manage challenging behaviour and to help them maintain their different identities. They wanted to support them in education and promote healthy living; and they wanted to help them to move on at the appropriate time. The consultation revealed a group of carers who were deeply committed to the best interests of the child. But their responses, as relative foster carers pointed out different needs from other foster carers. Their shared history and existing relationship with the child meant they tended to have relevant information (although some felt useful information was kept from them, for example, if their daughter or son was substance dependent). But they needed to

deal with changes in relationships linked to their role as kinship cared-for children. Some critical readers wondered why the 'carer's role and needs' was not the lead section of the book, given how emotionally charged the task of caring for known children was for many carers. In particular, some with experience of grandparents as carers felt their perspective was not well represented, and wanted to see specific materials targeted at them. There is certainly scope for more targeted materials, although grandparents (usually mediated through the maternal grandmother) were the largest group represented in all the surveys carried out in relation to this project, and contributed freely of their experiences. These carers were not explicitly covered in the materials, though many of the processes, and therefore the sections of the handbook, are relevant to them. Carers wanted time to express and deal with their feelings about having a child they know and care about live with them, when they often didn't expect it. They wanted to work through the fact, that in putting the child's best interests first, they may have to deny their own children support. They wanted to keep the child's relationships with parents alive, but also protect the child from abusive situations. And they needed time to look after themselves and develop their skills.[2]

The social worker training materials aimed to put this group of children and their carers on the local authority agenda so that legal obligations could be honoured and clear and consistent policy in this area discussed. It was, however, very difficult to get local authority managers and workers to free the time to focus on these carers. Nevertheless, we were able to develop a training curriculum that looked at the current service provided by the local authority, examined how decisions were made and how assessment and planning was carried out, and finally how carers were prepared, trained, supervised and supported. The feedback received was that *whatever was produced would be welcomed*, as there was nothing currently available specifically targeted at kinship care.

Our task was then to go through all the processes involved in writing drafts, and test out the materials. Case material and examples collected from carer questionnaires and accounts, and material collected from local authority visits

---

2. These carers had come to us via the social work route, and many were approved as foster carers. We know there are numerous grandparents providing care under private arrangements, or where the child lives with them under a Residence Order, so the child is no longer in public care (Grandparents' Federation, 1996).

made the material come alive. We had asked carers to, for example, send us in an account of their 'day in the life'. We had also asked them to write freely. This material was invaluable, and testers were asked to supplement this with their own accounts.

Black carers, male carers, social workers, fostered children, disabled carers and local authorities were involved in testing the materials. The carers were sent a list of book sections, from which they had to choose any they wanted to test. They were told that each section needed to be tested by five carers, and they would be allocated five of their choosing. 30 carers from 23 different local authorities had volunteered and it was possible to get enough testers to volunteer for each different section. The materials contained some activities for carers to do with children. For example, completing a chart of people important to the child or filling in a 'worry jigsaw'. 20 workers in three local authorities, who set up and ran a group especially for this purpose, tested the social worker materials. A number of other authorities had agreed to run testing groups, but as a result of other priorities had had to withdraw their offers. There was a very comprehensive stage. Some people were asked to pay particular attention to key aspects of the materials. For example, representation of and messages about Black people, disabled people and lesbian and gay people, and to ensure that these groups seemed included as target audiences. The accuracy of references to legislation and local authority policy and procedures was also important.

This approach paid off, and we were able to go ahead with revisions of the materials with a host of suggestions for improvement. For example, some readers pointed out that we had not made it clear how a child might become looked after rather than supported under Section 17 of the Children Act 1989; others that parents' voices were markedly absent (we were not able to do much about the latter at that stage). Many of the carer testers said how much the materials validated their experiences and helped them to realise they were not alone. The empowering nature of training, and open learning methods was thus reinforced. The NFCA finally produced the materials (NFCA, 2000a, 2000b).

Using the Training Materials

Open learning materials enable the learner to be in charge of what they learn, where they learn it and how they learn. They can ask for assistance and

support as they need to, and the 'answers' are located in the materials and in the carer's own experiences rather than in other people. In designing the carer handbook it was envisaged that family placement and social workers would give a copy to each kinship carer they visited. Depending on how much time was available for the first visit, the social worker could either go through the relevant section of the book with the carer, or suggest which sections to focus on first. Carers were encouraged to read the sections that concerned them first, work through the activities with children, family members and friends, and note any issues for discussion with the social worker on the next visit. Telephone or e-mail discussion were also appropriate and carers might be put in touch with each other to discuss the sections of the book. Some local authorities or individual carers might want to initiate a discussion group, and the materials provide a good opportunity for this as they do not need a tutor, just someone who could keep the group going and try and draw out and summarise any points learned.

The Social Worker's Training Guide

This guide (NFCA, 2000b) was prepared in a different way to the carer's handbook. It aims to provide a freestanding resource to enable family placement and social workers, and their managers, to train together. Six modules were developed, which can be run as a logical course from beginning to end over three days. Alternatively, selections could be made and modules combined in different ways to suit different needs and circumstances. Testers had found it difficult to set aside as much time as they felt was necessary for training in this area, so it is also possible to identify small sections that could be discussed, for example, in team meetings. The carer handbook is also seen as a resource for social workers, who may be able to use it to raise issues in a concrete way at policy level, or in supervision. NFCA is planning to run a course for local authority workers and carers who want to use the materials with groups at some stage.

Throughout the development of both these substantial sets of training materials the ambiguous position of kinship foster care became very apparent and work with extended families seemed to receive a low priority in local authorities. Prior to the training epilogue, this following section provides some examination of this proposition.

Why kinship care is a low priority

Although a little more attention is being paid to kinship care, in the form of funded research and a few more publications (Hunt and Macleod, 1999; Laws and Broad, 2000; NCB, 2000; Greeff, 1999), the current situation remains quite static. This is remarkable, given the potential of kinship care to meet the principles of the Children Act 1989, the national objectives for children's social services and the *Quality Protects/Children First* objectives. Messages from the little research that has been carried out in the UK have shown positive outcomes for children. So what is behind the apparent resistance to focus on this children's service? A brief examination of recently published work about families, social work theories, service planning and professional power and autonomy, and making passing reference to the training materials (NFCA, 2000a, 2000b) should help to unravel this critical issue.

Tan (2000) draws our attention to how theories of family dysfunction have influenced how kinship care is perceived by social workers. The social workers' training guide emphasises the research messages on the benefits of kinship care and has training exercises that help social workers make explicit any anxieties about kinship care and challenge myths and stereotypes about them. The evidence from the carers who assisted with the handbook was of a highly committed group who were clear that their first loyalty was to the child, difficult though this was to manage at times. We are now seeing an emphasis on using a family strengths approach to work with these kinship families, which has been published since the NFCA materials were finalised and should also be included in social worker training (Portengen and van der Neut, 1999). Next, to issues about kinship care and social worker power. Ryburn (1998) locates some of social work's reluctance to embrace kinship care as indicative of the challenges it poses to social worker power. Carers who are strangers to the child may be able to align themselves more with social workers, than families can, and this is more comfortable and straightforward for the worker than dealing with complex family relationships. Given the above it is not surprising that these children and carers have been neglected in statistics, research and policy development. Government statistics on children looked-after have not routinely separated out children placed with relatives and friends, but seem to have just begun to do so

(under the heading 'Fostered with Relatives'— Ed.). Foster care in itself has been under researched compared with residential care, in relation to the proportion of children within each setting, and very few studies have looked at kinship care as a specific form of care in itself, rather than embedded in the foster care system. We do not have a national profile of children in kinship care, or their carers as in the US. We do not know which families use the service. In discussions with local authorities when preparing the materials, it was clear that record keeping was inadequate and that there were authorities working outside the legislation and guidance. The regular audit of children in need expected by the government from 2000 may prove invaluable in providing this kind of information. The NFCA training materials encourage social workers to carry out an audit of kinship care placements in the local authority.

Unless local authorities debate the place of kinship care within the range of children's services they provide, it is hard to see how things will change. The local authority survey carried out for the social worker materials showed only one local authority with a clear policy on kinship care: and this was to treat them equally with other foster carers and integrate them into existing training and foster carer groups where possible. Others were genuinely trying to review their existing practice and to develop a policy, but there were tensions in doing this. Historically, field social workers had been responsible for these placements in many local authorities as they were the link with the child's family. In England and Wales, these carers are normally approved under Regulation 11 of the Foster Placement (Children) Regulations 1991, which is meant to be used for emergency and immediate action. However, frequently these placements would then be left with no further assessment, review and little support. Suggestions that family placement workers might take on responsibility for these carers, and that kinship carers might be treated as foster carers met with mixed feelings. Family placement workers often resented the additional demands on their time, and also there was a feeling in some local authorities that kinship carers were not 'worth as much' because investment in them would not benefit a large number of children as in the case of non-related carers. Unless these tensions are debated and a way forward agreed within each local authority, children's services will continue to fudge the issue. O'Brien (2000) and Ryburn (1998) both argue for treating kinship care as a different service from foster care, which would still be able to work within the appropriate legislative frameworks. The NFCA materials advocate for tailoring assessment and support to fit the particular requirements of kin placements, but to try and bring the two groups of carers under the same management and support structure. However, as more information and research is done on kinship care, new ways of working are likely to suggest themselves.

Epilogue

Both sets of training materials, *Family and Friends Carers' Handbook* and *Family and Friends Carers: Social Workers' Training Guide*, were published early in 2000 (NFCA, 2000a, 2000b). It was hoped that the Department of Health would emphasise their usefulness to local authorities in England and Wales by specifying kinship care as part of the Training Support Programme, but this had not happened at the time this chapter was produced in early 2001. To date, take-up of this training material has been slow, and anecdotal evidence suggests that, although they see the value of the materials, local authorities are still not able to make this group of children and their carers enough of a priority to attend to their specific training needs. Given the evidence about its strengths, particularly in relation to meeting anti-oppressive practice objectives and opportunities to work in partnership with families, this is worrying. In May 1998 this contributor wrote that family and friends foster care was the forgotten face of foster care (Flynn, 1998). A recent publication by Laws and Broad (2000) of a small group of kinship carers' views raises many of the issues covered in the NFCA training materials. Further work by these researchers is continuing, with a larger sample, and should provide valuable information for the field. With the increased Department of Health interest, perhaps the situation will change for the children and families involved in kinship foster care.

References

Broad, B. (1999). Kinship Care: Children Placed with Extended Families or Friends. *Childright*, 155: pp. 16–17.

Flynn, R. (1998). *Family and Friends as Foster Carers: The Forgotten Face of Foster Care*. Unpublished paper prepared for the UK Joint Working Party on Foster Care.

Grandparents' Federation (1996). *Residence Order Allowance Survey*. Essex: Grandparents' Federation.

Greeff, R (Ed.) (1999). *Fostering Kinship*. Aldershot: Ashgate Arena.

Hunt, J., and Macleod, A. (1999). *The Best-laid Plans: Outcomes of Judicial Decisions in Child Protection Proceedings*. London: The Stationery Office.

Laws, S., and Broad, B. (2000). *Looking After Children Within the Extended Family: Carers' Views*. Leicester: De Montfort University.

National Children's Bureau (2000). *Kinship Foster Care*. NCB Highlight, No. 179.

National Foster Care Association (1993). *Friends and Relatives as Carers*. London: NFCA.

National Foster Care Association (1994). *Choosing to Foster: The Challenge to Care*. London: NFCA.

National Foster Care Association (2000a). *Family and Friends Carers' Handbook*. London: NFCA.

National Foster Care Association (2000b). *Family and Friends Carers: Social Workers' Training Guide*. London: NFCA.

O'Brien, V. (2000). Relative Care. In: Kelly, G., and Gilligan, R. *Issues in Foster Care: Policy, Practice and Research*. London: Jessica Kingsley.

Portengen, R., and van der Neut, B. (1999). Assessing Family Strengths: A Family Systems Approach. In Greeff, R. (Ed.). Op. cit.

Ryburn, M (1998). A New Model of Welfare: Re-asserting the Value of Kinship for Children in State Care. *Social Policy and Administration*, 32(1): pp. 28–45.

Tan, S. (2000). *Friends and Relative Care: The Neglected Carers*. Unpublished PQ in Social Work Dissertation, Brunel University.

Waldman, J., and Wheal, A. (1999). Training Needs of Friends and Families who are Foster Carers. In Greeff, R. (Ed.). Op. cit.

Waterhouse, S. (1997). *The Organisation of Fostering Services: A Study of the Arrangements for Delivery of Fostering Services in England*. London: NFCA.

Waterhouse, S., and Brocklesby, E. (1999). Placement Choices for Children: Giving More Priority to Kinship Placements? In Greeff, R. (Ed.) (1999). *Fostering Kinship*. Aldershot: Ashgate.

Wheal, A., and Waldman, J. (1997). *Friends and Family as Carers: Identifying the Training Needs of Carers and Social Workers*. Unpublished. NFCA.

14 Promoting Kinship Foster Care: Preserving Family Networks for Black Children of African Origins

Lynda Ince

Introduction

The purpose of this chapter is to focus on the nature of kinship foster care and to explore the underlying reasons for why such an old concept practised within the black family has not had any impact within the British child care system. To what extent can local authorities continue to apply an ethnocentric approach to child care practice when there is a growing need to make a critical appraisal of outcomes for black children and young people who are looked after and being prepared for leaving the care system? This chapter will examine the literature, which suggest that kinship foster care has developed in the United States of America as the first and preferred option for African–American children who must live away from home. Its development in some states is recognised to be a fast growing and deliberate attempt to keep children within their own communities and family settings. However, in Britain the picture has been very different, and is one that has been characterised by a lack of policy initiative and development. In recent years the changing policy context of child care policy, has largely dictated the way in which professionals provide services to children and their families. Such major changes are couched with the legislation, (Children Act 1989) the Children Safeguards Review, (Utting, 1997) the government's response to the Children's Safeguards Review (1998) and the government interventions resulting in *Quality Protects* (1999). In all of these major policy changes there has been a lack of recognition regarding the needs of black children or the place of kinship networks within social policy development. The lack of black theoretical models to assist and guide professional practice in regard to the structure, strengths and versatility of the black family can be cited as one of the main reasons for exclusion at a policy and practice level. Graham (1999) argues that at the very heart of social welfare there is over-reliance on an ethnocentric approach within the provision of services. The understandings which professionals may adopt towards black families and indeed the black community are diametrically opposed to an African-centred world view, particularly in relation to child-rearing practices. It is important to define the term 'black' as used in this chapter. The term 'black' refers to children from African and African Caribbean families. It also used to refer to children of mixed heritage backgrounds with one parent who originates from Africa or the Caribbean. This definition does not in any way devalue other cultural groups, but it helps the writer to stay within defined boundaries and to apply this concept to children who are most likely to be over-represented in the looked after population.

Research evidence has shown that black children of African Caribbean heritage and particularly those of dual heritage are more likely to be looked after and to remain in the care system longer than white children Rowe *et al.* (1984), Bebbington and Miles (1989), Barn (1993, 1997) and Biehal *et al.* (1995). Historically the Department of Health annual statistics have failed to separate out the numbers of black and minority ethnic children who are admitted to or who leave local authority care. The most recent statistic from the Department of Health shows that of the 36,200 children in foster care, approximately 6,400 are living with a relative or friend either within the local authority area or outside the local authority. While the statistical data for 1998/99 clearly outlines the numbers of children who were looked after in foster care and then proceed to break these down by age and gender, no such extrapolation is made by race. It is only recently that the DoH required local authorities to provide ethnic records. There is a lack of knowledge regarding the quality of care black and minority ethnic children receive and how local authorities work with black families and the black community to safeguard their rights to cultural heritage, family and thus to the preservation of kinship networks.

Historical roots of informal kinship networks

In the United States of America informal kinship care is widespread both on an informal and

refers to the
without
rvices. It is
of children who
th their relatives.
indicated that
tes of America has
y by people of
ivoccia, 1996).
O... ...tions of kinship care
came from u... ...ack (1974) who referred
to it as: 'any relative blood or marriage, or any
person with close family ties to another' and by
Billingsley (1972) as a relationship of
appropriation and meanings and one where
blood ties by marriage is not a necessity. People
can automatically become part of a family unit or
indeed form a family unit simply by deciding to
live or to act towards each other as a family
(Takas, 1993). The Child Welfare League of
America also officially defines informal kinship
care as:

> *The full-time nurturing and protection of children by*
> *their parents, relatives, members of their tribes or clan,*
> *god-parents, step-parents or other adults who have a*
> *Kinship bond with the child.*

(CWLA, 1994: p. 387)

It is important to make a distinction between
kinship care and kinship foster care. The concept
of kinship care is not in itself a new one, but has
been established as common practice in Africa,
the West Indies, New Zealand, in other minority
ethnic cultures and particularly amongst the
Maori communities where kinship care has
always been prevalent. In such communities the
concept of family does not necessarily rest with
parents alone. (Hegar and Scannapieco, 1999;
Nisivoccia, 1996). This informal practice of
kinship networking provided a strong method of
support from a variety of family members,
friends and the community, and historically has
been the black family's oldest and most
traditional response to caring for children.
Informal responses to children in need were
conventionally the domain of family and
relatives who provided care outside the legal
welfare system (Stack, 1974; Hegar and
Scannapieco, 1995). It became a well-recognised,
established and accepted family response to
problem solving, thereby providing immense
benefits for children. There were clear benefits in
terms of identity and sustenance within their
own family circle and community who took a
keen interest in and responsibility for their

upbringing. In some instances informal kinship
care was also provided as a temporary measure
when parents were unable to care for their
children and this has remained a phenomena
within black and minority families. Gleeson
(1996) refers to this type of care as 'a type of
family preservation or home based service or a
type of foster care' (p. 3).

Nobles (1985) showed that Du Bois, one of
America's most celebrated black authors and
academic commentators on black family life style
observed as early as 1909 that charity was of such
among Africans that they shared the common
fund of land and food. The notion of kinship
networks provided for children through lineage,
and older brothers immediately became
responsible for children when a child was
orphaned. Similarly, relatives and friends took
over the care of children when it became
expedient for them to do so. These forms of
support not only provided care for children in
need, but also kept them within the family
network, offering protection and safety in the
most natural environment. It established family
links that made it possible to avoid separation
and loss between parents, children, siblings,
extended family and friends. Castle (1996) noted
that in African societies children were often given
over to grandparents for weaning, as the
upbringing of children had never been
conceptualised as the sole responsibility of
parents. Therefore, it became common practice
for the first-born child to be given to
grandparents who naturally and informally took
over caring responsibilities for their
grandchildren. Martin and Martin (1983)
demonstrates the imperatives facing African
families who had to find strategies of survival as
slavery took them to the United States, and in so
doing they developed elaborate kinship
networks based on interdependence and
partnership. According to Nobles (1985) Edward
Wilmont Blyden recognised the strengths within
African families and strongly advocated the
preservation of what he termed 'the unique
characteristics of African people'. Further, he
explicated the soul of the people as lying within
their customs and institutions, which were of
central importance to their 'development and
well-being' (p. 19). The notion of family rested
within a particular understanding of 'oneness of
being, the family was an expression of the centre
of the individual's existence'. In other words the
family constituted the axis on which all members
of its unit revolved. The family was seen as the

community, indeed all children became the concern of the community with the notion that 'it takes a whole village to raise a child', and this reinforced a sense of interconnectedness (Scannapieco and Jackson, 1996).

It is not unusual to hear many adults from the Carribbean talk about the role their grandparents and extended family had to play in their upbringing. Many families who immigrated to Britain left their children behind with relatives and friends until it was possible for them to join their parents. The role of grandmothers was so strong that they often lived with their daughters, or their grandchildren were reared within their households. Children developed a strong and significant bond with grandparents, particularly grandmothers and often acknowledged and referred to them as if they were their parents. It is important to note that women had a strong and influential role to play in developing kinship networks. Barrow (1996) noted that kinship networks were the 'basic building blocks which provided continuity and stability within the black community. In a number of the Carribbean islands where her study was conducted it was found that the sexual relationship between men and women provided a strong impetus for the development of kinship networks. Such relationships provided women with sustained support from men, but even more important was the production of children, which was crucial to the continuing strongholds developed within kinship patterns and relationships. Women had a strong role as carers and developed it by relying on each other for support. Parents expected children to discharge their responsibilities towards them after entering adulthood, particularly girls who, when they emigrated, were expected to maintain their responsibility and send money back home to support their parents and siblings who were left behind until eventually reunification was possible.

American Responses to Children in the Welfare System

American social work agencies have begun to recognise the family's role in caring for children and to adopt it within their legislation and practice guidelines. Part of the reason for using kinship foster care in a more organised fashion, was the recognition that children can benefit from remaining in their extended families even when their parents cannot provide appropriate caring environments for them. There was also the

recognition that African American children are at higher risk for out-of-home placements than Caucasian or any other minority ethnic children.

Like African Caribbean and mixed heritage children, African American children are more likely to come into care earlier and remain there for longer periods and are therefore over-represented in the child welfare system. (Brissett-Chapman and Issacs-Shockley, 1995). According to Curtis *et al.* (1995) the national average stay in care for children was reduced from 2.4 years in 1977 to 1.7 years in 1990 and in 1990 of all children who left temporary placement only 8 per cent were adopted (p. 47). Concurrent with this activity, the numbers of African American children in out-of-home placements were increasing to unprecedented levels. Scannapieco and Jackson (1996) observed that the growth of kinship care was influenced by an increase of African American children in substitute care and within the youth justice system. McFadden (1998) draws attention to the ways in which African American organisations 'criticised the foster care system for its failure to meet the cultural and developmental needs of African American children' (p. 8). Professional responses to black families devalued the strategies they had adopted for preservation evidence by removing and placing their children with stranger foster carers. Additionally, there was greater awareness of institutional racism, lack of a model based on cultural competence with concomitant impact on policy and practice. Thus the numbers of African American children in out-of-home placements increased rapidly. (National Commission on Family Foster Care, 1991). Brissett-Chapman and Issacs-Shockley (1995) noted that there was a strong correlation between 'race' and the black child's 'exposure to the child welfare system' (p. 2). They drew attention to the fact that whilst Caucasian children represented 75 per cent of the child population only 42 per cent of these children were to be found in out-of-home care situations (or what is known as foster care or residential care). At the same time African American children only made up 15 per cent of the population, but 43 per cent of out-of-home placements were utilised by these children (Woodley *et al.*, 1997). This analysis of the outcomes for African American children is not dissimilar to that made years earlier in the works of Billingsley and Giovannoni (1972). They had drawn attention to the plight of black children within the state welfare system, showing that the forces of racism had been a major obstacle to meeting their placement needs. They noted a lack of culturally competent models of practice and lack of positive reinforcement of cultural values. They demonstrated that the welfare system had consistently denied black children services, thus forcing the black community to develop its own services for children to bolster parents who could not satisfactorily meet their parental duties. The self-help measures to which Billingsley and Giovannoni (ibid.) referred was the willingness of families to offer their homes to children who for a multiplicity of complex factors could not remain with their parents. They argued that despite oppression black families had shown a 'spirit of benevolence deserving of appreciation' and support within the welfare system (p. 46).

Professional responses to black children in the American child welfare system

Professional solutions to providing care for children who cannot live with their parents have been rooted in the concept of kinship foster care in the United States of America for over a decade. Changes in attitude towards this method of family preservation were largely haphazard and did not come in direct response to research and scholarly work but rather out of the need to find alternative solutions for a growing number of African American children within the child welfare system. Thus, kinship foster care became an extensive placement response for 'children of colour' (a term used in the American literature) who were placed with relatives and fictive kin, and in so doing it revived and rekindled some of the oldest and most honoured methods known to be of value within black families. This rapidly growing phenomenon within the state welfare system was enhanced and largely developed within a black professional rationale, which helped to change the legal context of child care practice. The Association of Black Social Workers argued that little was being done to reunify black children with their families or to promote their cultural heritage. They posited the view that ethnocentric values in child-care did little to promote ethnically sensitive social work practice or culturally competent practice. (Brissett-Chapman and Issacs-Shockley, op. cit.)

Kinship care as an option received little or no research attention until the early 1990s when according to Thornton (1991) it began to appear in professional journals. Early research studies funded by the US Bureau focused on how kinship care could provide permanency for those children who were most vulnerable to being placed within the child welfare system (Gleeson, 1999). With the benefit of research there is now evidence to show a national increase and a widening gap in the use of formal kinship care, and those most likely to be offering it are people of colour, namely African American families. The major concern for policy makers is that the families most likely to offer kinship care are those who are already suffering hardship and disadvantage. They tend to be those who are economically unstable, live in poverty and who are most dependent on state benefits (Harden *et al.*, 1997).

Research evidence indicates that there are several reasons for the development of kinship foster care in America, among them are:

- Dramatic increase in the reporting of child abuse and neglect during the 1980s and 1990s (Wiese and Daro, 1995).
- The numbers of children who had been assessed as seriously harmed and maltreated (Sedlak and Broadhurst, 1996).
- Drug abusing parents who systematically left their children with grandparents (Minker and Roe, 1993).
- A correlation between race and the African American child's exposure and status in the child welfare system. (Brissett-Chapman and Issacs-Shockley, 1995: p. 3).

The factors which appeared to promote the growth of kinship care included dwindling resources, decreasing welfare budgets and increasing social work caseloads. Welfare reforms were put in place to reduce federal spending and children in foster care became the most likely area for reductions in spending. This was to have a major impact on out-of-home placements and the formal development of kinship care. The Personal Responsibility and Work Opportunity Reconciliation Act (1996) required the state to give priority to relatives when considering the placement needs of children (GAO, 2000)

The legal framework and policy development became the impetus for change and the focus for adopting kinship care as an alternative to non-relative foster care. Deliberate attempts were made to isolate factors contributing to the preponderance of black and minority ethnic children in out-of-home placements and to offer more positive solutions for the survival and preservation of the black family. In Illinois, where there was a high frequency of black children entering the state welfare system, there arose a drive to provide alternative avenues of care for children in need. The Relative Reform Plan took as its starting point the need for the wider family network to provide care.

All of these factors pointed to the need to promote the welfare of African American children and to provide services that would enhance their abilities to survive childhood and make a contribution to their society. Some states began to formalise family arrangements into kinship foster care. According to George *et al.* (1996) it was reported that 50–75 per cent of children were placed with grandparents. In New York for example, in the last seven years, the numbers of children placed in intergenerational homes have quintupled. In June 1995, 42 per cent of children in foster care were in kinship foster homes (Selected Child Welfare Trends, 1995) In so far as kinship care has been a positive response to African American children, they have benefited from it in many ways. McFadden and Downs (1995) argue that kinship foster care is capable of effective family preservation and that it offers a new model of child care practice from which professionals can learn. The unique nature of this model encourages professionals to work in partnership with the extended family network and at the same time protect children who are at risk of abuse. Further, where children are maintained within their kinship networks it acts as a protective mechanism against separation and loss and in effect protects them from a care system that can be full of inconsistencies and one which leads to poor outcomes for black children.

A research survey conducted by Beeman and Boisen (1999) made some interesting findings in relation to professionals' views on the value of kinship foster care. They found that over 261 welfare professionals had a positive view of kinship care, though they found differences in perceptions between black and white professionals. Most agreed that children were better off when placed within their kinship networks. Relatives were reported to be more committed to the children, and by the same token the children demonstrated a stronger sense of belonging. In particular immense benefits were reported for the children's identity. Social workers participating in the study acknowledged that kinship care was better able to preserve family ties, the children were less troubled and were not stigmatised by the welfare system.

The strongest disagreement amongst social workers related to the role of adoption within kinship care. Over 62.6 per cent of professionals believed that kinship foster carers were reluctant to adopt because they felt that it would be the source of conflict within the family and with the birth parents. Other studies have suggested that the complete severing of ties does not sit comfortably with relatives who find this to be in opposition to their cultural beliefs. (Gleeson, 1993; Testa *et al.*, 1996; and Berrick *et al.*, 1994). Since a number of studies have demonstrated that children placed with kin are more likely to remain in the care system longer, it is argued that they create a greater burden on state welfare funds. Some research studies have reported no significant differences in well-being between children in kinship foster care and those placed with non-related foster carers (Dubowitz *et al.*, 1993, 1994). On the other hand there is evidence to show that part of the reason why African American children stay in kinship care longer is largely due to the fact that the kinship carers receive fewer services and have less access to professionals than children who are placed with non-related foster carers. (Berrick *et al.*, 1994; and Thornton, 1991). Those who support kinship care report more commitment and ability by kinship carers to meet the child's emotional and identity needs. (Wulczyn and George, 1992; Gleeson, 1999).

As might well be expected there is considerable controversy surrounding the rights of a family to be paid on an equal footing with non-kin foster carers. Gleeson's (1996) description of the development of kinship care policy within Illinois is clearly important in showing how the state had attempted to place children with relatives without remuneration. The law courts held that the practice of excluding relative homes from becoming family foster homes was in direct contravention to the law. The reforms made it possible for the state to strengthen and recognise the validity and importance of the family's contribution to the child's daily care. Thus it was through legal processes that measures were taken to offer families the same financial support as non-relative carers if they met the same criteria and licensing standards for claiming federal funds. Although the numbers of children placed with relatives were initially small, from 1986 onwards there was a rapid increase in the use of kinship care, not only in Illinois but also in New York and California (George *et al.*, 1995). These states began to show more reliance on families and thereby decreased the numbers of children being placed with non-relative carers.

Intervention by the state to assist families has grown as a result of federal intervention placing the spotlight on a developing trend of kinship care. Boots and Geen (2000) argue that during the 1980s when the Child Welfare Act was passed it was unheard of to place children with relatives who officially acted as foster carers. Now some twenty years later approximately 200,000 children are to be found in state supported kinship care placements. This means that the growth of kinship care has outstripped all other types of care provision. There is variation from state to state, but the general trend points to an increasing willingness to access resources within the family. Indeed, this action has led to the changes in the law (Statutes, 1991), which amended the Family Services Act to 'select the family as the preferred caregiver' (Gleeson, 1996).

Kinship Care Developments in Britain

In total contrast kinship care has not had the same impact or relevance in child care policy in Britain. The position of black and minority ethnic families is somewhat different historically to African Americans. It must be noted that UK immigration legislation has played a significant role in the lives of people from the Caribbean and Asian sub-continent. This makes comparisons difficult because in many ways the experiences of African Americans and African Caribbeans are qualitatively different and spring from different historical milieus. Immigration is much more meaningfully applied to this discussion in terms of understanding the political imperatives, which actively promoted migration from the Carribbean and later from the Asian subcontinent. Jackson and Penrose (1993) assert that Britain places considerable emphasis on the reunification of families, and promoted it as 'the building blocks of nationhood' (p. 70). At the same time there was destruction of the black family through immigration policies and recruitment of workers linked to British Colonialism, which effectively separated families. Family and nation were central concerns of successive governments. However, the developing policy on family reunification was to occur within a conceptual framework of exclusion. One popular debate within political parties during the 1980s was that reunification should be achieved through immigrants returning to their countries of origin. Miles (1989) argued that such policies were designed to restrict dependants from entering

Britain and contained a political agenda, which was consistently applied to the kinfolk of people who had earlier immigrated to Britain from the New Commonwealth. Immigration laws, which were consistently and relentlessly aimed at restriction, had a major impact on developing black family formation and certain implications for tried and tested models of child-care. To some extent and through no fault of their own families began to lose sight of, and connection with, the very networks which had provided a strong sense of identity for children. The lack of support and lack of sensitive services to help and assist families actively promoted the alienation and deconstruction of kinship networks. Viewed from this perspective, immigration has had a major impact on family organisation. The growing numbers of children who have been born within dual heritage relationships have had implications for the transferring of family values, including kinship care. Notwithstanding, James (1992) argues that black families have been able to maintain some of their strong survival skills and kinship bonds even when family members have been separated and live in different parts of the world.

In so far as scholarly work and research is concerned, evidence demonstrates that policy developments in Britain have paid scant attention to the needs of black and minority ethnic children who are looked after. In recent years there has been a growing awareness of the need to develop research into fostering and adoption and this has resulted in a number of interesting research studies and reviews. However, there remains a void in terms of placing kinship care for black children within the research knowledge that is developing. The work of Greeff (1999) whist offering an international perspective does not offer a black perspective and seemingly, black children are subsumed under all children looked after by local authorities. Nevertheless, it is clear that recent studies are beginning to develop a knowledge base from which professionals can learn. Examples of new development are in the works of NFCA (2000), Waterhouse and Brocklesby (1999), Laws and Broad (2000) and Hunt and Macleod (1999).

The paucity of research on black children in all aspects of child care, points to gaps in knowledge and a lack of understanding on the part of most professionals about the integration of a black perspective within the delivery of services to black and minority ethnic children and their families. Lamentably, black and minority children are conspicuous by their absence from research and to date there are certainly no studies which focus on the need to reinforce cultural competence in working with black children and their families. The only example of early research, which really connoted the relevance, and positive value of kinship foster care came from the work of Rowe *et al.* (1984). This research gave indications that children who were placed in kinship foster care arrangements were achieving better outcomes in practically all aspects of their lives as a result of being fostered by relatives than those who were placed with stranger foster carers. There have been frequent references to the poor outcomes for children looked after in terms of their health, education, identity, self-esteem and preparation for leaving care. (DoH, 1991), Broad (1998) and First Key (2000). It is clear that the loss of contact with a family, to which many black children have been subjected, militates against the development of kinship bonds, neither does it promote or support kinship networks within the black community.

The Children Act 1989 recognised that children are best placed within their family and community setting. It gives credence to the notion of kinship care, in terms of the imperatives placed on local authorities to work in partnership with parents, and to place children within their own local communities and family settings. However, what has not developed as a result of this legislation is the formal response to families in terms of kinship foster care. Whist some local authorities place children with their relatives who are registered as foster carers, this is not a widespread practice or one which promotes the need to place black children in kinship care settings. Thus, the Children Act 1989 with all its good intentions has had very little impact on black and minority children. Ten years after it was implemented Richards and this author (2000) found that few local authorities could indicate that they were producing better outcomes for black and minority ethnic children. In their study of the policies of 52 local authorities they found 'very patchy provision was made for the involvement of black families in planning for their children' (p. 46). There are clearly some vital issues which are related to power differentials, which can have implications for families. The Children Act 1989 reinforces the need to work in partnership with families, but when professionals are faced with working with black and minority ethnic families, differences can be accentuated, and in practice makes partnership difficult to achieve. To the extent that professionals can and do make decisions about the placement needs of children, they can invoke vulnerabilities within parents who may feel unable to compete on equal ground with them. Different cultural values, language, belief systems and differences in child care practices may lead professionals to opt for stranger foster carers as opposed to looking within the family to find alternative solutions. It may also be easier to work with stranger foster carers than relatives simply because professionals may find it more complex and difficult to engage and work collaboratively with families in a professional working relationship. Family and community options may not be explored because professionals are afraid to take risks, lose control (in child protection work) or venture into new and unexplored territory.

A recent and ongoing study in the London Borough of Wandsworth has just begun to produce some interesting findings. Broad (1999) points to the need for local authorities to enforce the legislation when making plans for placing children. In the area where his study was conducted he found the children most likely to be in the local authority monitoring system by ethnicity were children of Guyanese backgrounds. He found a higher number of black than white children were placed with extended family members. Broad reported that it was not clear why this practice was developing and concluded that it could be 'a good or bad thing' (p. 80). The research points to the need for further investigation to make discoveries about the underlying reasons for placement in terms of quality of service and levels of support which are offered to black families who offer kinship placements. Broad raises two important issues in his research. The first is the relationship between financial support and the ethnic origin of children since those who are placed with kin cost less in terms of provision of services. The second issue, and one which warrants further investigation is the form and processes which decision making takes in relation to placement type. The perspective of ten carers proved interesting since the study was able to take into account their views and opinions. This study reinforces the need to take account of families who are working at the coalface and providing services for children in need. (Laws and Broad, 2000)

It is certain that policy makers and practitioners need to know much more about the premise on which placement decisions are taken and the factors which influence social workers to opt for or against kinship foster care. In this contributor's view any development for black children looked after, needs to be steeped within a black perspective and one which clearly acknowledges the need for change as well as valuing the meanings which black families place on kinship networks.

Policy and Practice Implications for Professionals

Black and minority ethnic families face particular challenges in terms of the structural disadvantages which they face in Britain. The MacPherson report (1999) recognised that institutional racism is a major barrier to receiving equitable and fair services and that it is:

> ...incumbent on every institution to examine their policies and the outcome of their policies and practice to guard against disadvantaging any section of the community.

Further he rightly advised that there must be an:

> ...unequivocal acceptance of the problems of institutional racism and its nature before it can be addressed.
>
> (p. 1)

Many professionals need to learn how to overcome their prejudices which effectively stop them from seeing the strengths which black families can offer. Some may feel that because one section of the family cannot provide care, that all parts of the system are dysfunctional and pathological, which is of course not the case. Recent policy debates which will clearly have an impact on the quality of services to be delivered to children who are looked after have paid little or no attention to developing quality services for black and minority ethnic children. *The New Assessment Framework* (DoH, 2000) is very general and whilst it includes identity, this too could be interpreted by professionals within a very narrow frame of reference.

It is significant that in most local authorities there are no specific policies or comprehensive strategies for addressing and targeting services to black and minority ethnic families (Richards and Ince, 2000). As black and minority children enter the care system there are few indicators which suggest that the extended family might be the first and preferred placement option and that kinship care might be a strong placement

contender. It is clear from research that the over-representation of black and mixed heritage children in the care system is unacceptable and that the methods and responses to black families are not working. Research is only just beginning to highlight the need to pay more attention to this area of social work policy and practice.

The author submits that even when geographical and cultural differences are taken into account, it is still possible to learn some lessons from the American system. Notwithstanding the controversies surrounding some aspects of kinship care; it has largely been a successful attempt to find appropriate placements for black children. The first and perhaps most valuable lesson from America is that the family has been used as the first option, and this has undoubtedly supported the child's rights to remain within the black family and community. This was made possible through government and federal policies that clearly supported kinship care arrangements through financial assistance to poor families. The legislative framework is an important factor in bringing about change in policy and practice. Changes must be implemented if policies are to have any salience and meaning. It must also be remembered that even in Britain's multi-racial and multi-cultural society black and minority families are more likely to live in deprived areas, have less access to employment and good housing and are likely to face discrimination. Thus, they require tangible forms of support to assist them in their parenting roles and to reduce the numbers of children who are systematically removed from their families of origin.

Secondly, the development of research has proven very significant in showing the benefits of family care. The evidence points to clear benefits for the child's stability, psychological development, and knowledge of self, family and community. Research assists in understanding the tensions which kinship care can produce for professionals and the risk that they may have to take in order to support a child within the extended family. The gathering of information and the development of polices go hand in hand in terms of creating a reservoir of knowledge from which professionals can draw, learn and reflect on within their practice. When children in kinship care homes have been included in research studies this has been of benefit to policy developers and practitioners and has given them new insights into how to safeguard the interests of black children.

The third benefit is the way in which kinship care has empowered black families and relatives to make their contribution to caring for their children. The research evidence has shown clear benefits when the strengths and reserves within the black family are utilised. To reinforce families rights and responsibility for the balance of care is to locate black and minority ethnic children within their cultural roots. A valuable lesson which seems particularly pertinent from the literature is the development of strategies which work for black and minority ethnic families. In essence this means that black and minority ethnic families must be encouraged to take a greater participatory role in the decision making processes when their children are facing the prospect of being looked after. The first duty of the local authority is to ensure that children are protected, but this should not preclude them from considering a range of options including the extended family and friends' option. Black families are the custodians of information, of culture and of history and they are the child's link with the past and connection to the future. As such, they are in the best position to pass on the richness of their culture to their children and their grandchildren.

Fourthly, in order to capitalise on the strengths of black families, professionals must first adopt a positive attitude towards methods of child rearing different from their own. Clearly they must work towards eradicating some of the barriers which are reported to work against choosing family and friends as a viable option (McFadden, 1999). They must learn how to value different family forms and reinforce the survival mechanisms which are clearly present within the family and which are absolutely crucial to their survival techniques. They must work from a model of cultural competence and one which takes a holistic approach to family life. Kinship care begins within an ethnically sensitive frame of reference. As Devore and Schlesinger (1991) rightly argued, professionals who work with black and minority ethnic families must become aware of their own biases and attitudes which can create barriers and obstacles to working with black families. They must do so in order to provide better, more long term and lasting solutions for black children who come to the attention of professionals.

Fifth, to begin to explore the benefits of kinship care would be to acknowledge that the present options, which are currently available to local authorities, do not always work for black children. As their voices and stories have emerged in some of the most recent research findings, it is hard to ignore the way black young people define their experiences of being looked after in the care system. (Ince, 1998) Kinship care placements will not only build on the power base of parents, but will also empower children and young people to see their family as the focus and source of change. It will reduce separation and at the same time, provide an environment in which they can retain their ethnic identity, and cultural inheritance.

Conclusion

Finally, the social work professional has a long way to go and a lot to learn about the coping strategies of black families. Kinship care offers a way forward in terms of providing positive experiences for black and minority children who are at risk of being looked after. A good assessment system is clearly critical to considering the formal and informal aspects of kinship care and how it could work with the British Welfare system. In order to begin developing and facilitating this initiative some steps must be taken towards change, first at a policy level through legislation, and then ensuring its implementation at a practice level.

References

Barn, R. (1993). *Black Children in the Public Care System.* London: Batsford.

Barn, R., Sinclair, R., and Ferdinand, D. (1997). *Acting on Principle: An Examination of Race and Ethnicity in Social Services Provision for Children and Families.* London: BAAF.

Barrow, C. (1996). *Family in the Caribbean: Themes and Perspectives.* Kingston: Ian Randle Publishers.

Barth, R., Courtney, M., Berrick, J., and Albert, V. (1994). *From Child Abuse to Permanency Planning: Child Welfare Services Pathways and Placement.* New York: Aldine and Gruyter.

Bebbington, A., and Miles, J. (1989). The Background of Children who Enter Local Authority Care. *British Journal of Social Work,* 19(5): pp. 349–368.

Beeman, S., and Boisen, L. (1996). Child Welfare Professionals' Attitudes Towards Kinship Foster Care. *CWLA of America,* LXXV(5).

Beeman, S., and Boisen, L. (1999). Child Welfare Professionals' Attitudes Towards Kinship Foster Care. *Child Welfare League of America,* LXXV(5): pp. 315–335.

Berrick, D., Needell, B., and Barth, R. (1994). A Comparison of Kinship Foster Homes and Foster Family Homes: Implications for Kinship Foster Care as Family

Preservation. *Children and Youth Services Review,* 16(1/2): pp. 33–63.

Biehal, N., Clayden, J., Stein, M., and Wade, J. (1995). *Moving on: Young People and Leaving Care Schemes.* London: HMSO.

Billingsley, A. (1992). *Climbing Jacob's Ladder: The Enduring Legacy of African American Families.* New York: Simon and Schuster.

Billingsley, A., and Giovannoni, J. (1972). *Children of the Storm: Black Children and American Child Welfare.* New York: Harcourt Brace Jovanovich.

Boots, S., and Geen, R. (2000). Family *Care or Foster Care? How State Policies Affect Kinship Caregivers.* http://newfederalism.urban.org.html/anf_34.html

Brissett-Chapman, S., and Issacs-Shockley, M. (1997). *Children in Social Peril: A Community Vision for Preserving Family Care of African American Children and Youths.* Washington: CWLA Press.

Broad, B. (1998). *Young People Leaving Care: Life After the Children Act 1989.* London: Jessica Kingsley.

Broad, B. (1999). Kinship Care: Enabling and Supporting Child Placements with Relatives and Friends. In *Assessment, Preparation and Support: Implications for Research.* London: BAAF.

Castle, S.E. (1996). The Current and Intergenerational Impact of Child Fostering on Children's Nutritional Status in Rural Mali. *Human Organisations,* 55(2): pp. 193–205.

Child Welfare League of America (1994). Kinship Care: A Natural Bridge. *CWLA,* LXXV(5).

Clarke, E. (1979). *My Mother who Fathered Me: A Study of the Family in Three Selected Communities in Jamaica.* London: George Allen and Unwin.

Curtis, P.A., Boyd, J.P., Liepold, M., and Petit, M. (1995). *Child Abuse and Neglect: A Look at the States.* Washington DC: CWLA Press.

Department of Health (1989). *The Children Act 1989.* London: HMSO.

Department of Health (1991). *Patterns and Outcomes in Child Placement: Messages from Current Research and their Implications.* London: HMSO.

Department of Health (1998). *The Government's Response to the Children's Safeguards Review.* London: HMSO.

Department of Health (1999). *Quality Protects: Transforming Children's Services.* London: HMSO.

Department of Health (1999). *Statistical Bulletin: Children Looked After in England: 1998/1999.* London: HMSO.

Department of Health (2000). *The New Assessment Framework: Assessing Children in Need.* London: HMSO.

Devore, W., and Schlesinger, E. (1991). *Ethnic-sensitive Social Work Practice.* New York: Macmillan.

Dubowitz, H., Zuravin, S., Starr, R., Feigelman, S., and Harrington, D. (1993). Behaviour Problems of Children in Kinship Care. *Journal of Development and Behavioural Paediatrics,* 14: pp. 386–393.

Dubowitz, H., Feigelman, S., Harrington, D., Starr, R., Zuravin, S., and Sawyer, R.E. (1994). Children in Kinship Care: How do They Fare? *Children and Youth Services Review,* 16: pp. 85–106.

Ely, P., and Denny, D. (1989). *Social Work in a Multi-Racial Society.* London: Gower.

First Key (2000). *Leaving Care Provision: A Summary of Thirty Audits.* London: First Key.

Gallagher, M. (1991). Foster Care as Welfare. *The City Journal,* pp. 16–19. New York: Manhattan Institute for Policy Research.

General Accounting Office (2000). *Foster Care Quality and Permanency Issues.* GAO/HEHS-99-32 http://fewebgate.access.gpo.gov/cgi-bin/useftp

George, R., Wulczyn, F., and Harden, A. (1996). New Comparative Insights into States and their Foster Children. *Public Welfare,* pp. 12–25.

George, R.M. (1990). The Reunification Process in Substitute Care. *Social Services Review,* 64: pp. 422–457.

George, R.M., Wulczyn, F.H., and Harden, A.W. (1995). *Foster Care Dynamics 1983–1993 California, Illinois, Michigan, New York and Texas: An Update from the Multi-state Foster Care Data Archives.* Chicago: The Chapin Hall Centre for Children at the University of Chicago.

Gleeson, J. (1993). *Kinship Care: The Bridge Between Diverse Families and the Child Welfare System.* Paper presented at the 39th Annual Program Meeting of the Council on Social Work Education.

Gleeson, J., and Criag, L.C. (1994). Kinship Care in Child Welfare: An Analysis of State Policies. *Children and Youth Services Review,* 16: pp. 7–31.

Gleeson, J.P., and Harrison, C.F. (1999). *Kinship Care: Improving Practice Through Research.* Washington DC: CWLA Press.

Gleeson, J.P. (1996). *Kinship Care as a Child Welfare Service: The Policy Debate in an Era of Welfare Reform.* University of Illinois, Chicago; Child Welfare League.

Graham, M.J. (1999). The African Centred World View: Developing a Paradigm for Social Work. *British Journal of Social Work,* 29(2): pp. 249–263.

Greeff, R. (1999). *Fostering Kinship: An International Perspective on Kinship Foster Care.* Aldershot: Ashgate.

Gussler, J. (1980). Adaptive Strategies and Social Networks of Women in St. Kitts. In Barrow, C. (Ed.) (1996). *Families in the Caribbean.* Kingston: Randle Publishers.

Harden, A., Clark, R., and Maguire, K. (1997). *Informal and Formal Kinship Care.* Washington DC: US Department of Health and Human Services.

Hegar, R., and Scannapieco, M. (Eds.) (1999). *Kinship Foster Care: Policy Practice and Research.* Oxford: Oxford University Press.

Hegar, R.L. and Scannapieco, M. (1995). From Family Duty to Family Policy: The Evolution of Kinship Care. *Child Welfare,* 74: pp. 200–216.

Hunt, J., and Macleod, A. (1999). *The Best-laid Plans: Outcomes of Judicial Decisions in Child Protection Proceedings.* London: HMSO.

Ince, L. (1998). *Making it Alone: A Research Study of the Care Experiences of Young Black People Leaving Care.* London: BAAF.

Inglehart, A. (1994). Kinship Foster Care: Placement, Service and Outcome Issues. *Children and Youth Services Review,* 16: pp. 107–122.

Jackson, P., and Penrose, J. (Eds.) (1993). *Construction of Race, Place and Nation.* London: UCL Press.

James, M. (1992). Finding and Working with Families of Caribbean Origin. In Coombe, V., and Little, A. *Race and Social Work.* London: Tavistock Publications.

Kelly, S.J. (1993). Caregiver Stress in Grandparents Raising Grandchildren. *Image Journal of Nursing Scholarship,* 25: pp. 383–401.

Laws, S., and Broad, B. (2000). *Looking After Children Within the Extended Family: Carers' Views.* Leicester: De Montfort University.

MacPherson, Sir. W. (1999). *The Stephen Lawrence Inquiry: Implications for Racial Equality.* London: Commission for Racial Equality.

Martin, E.P., and Martin, M. (1983). The Black Extended Family. In Dodson, J.E. (Ed.). *Strengths of Black Families: An Afro-centric Education Manual: Towards a Non-deficit Perspective in Services to Families and Children.* Nashville: University of Tennessee, School of Social Work.

McFadden, E., and Downs, S. (1995). Family Continuity: 'The New Paradigm in Permanence Planning'. *Community Alternatives,* 7(1): pp. 39–60.

McFadden, E.J. (1998). Kinship Care in the United States. *Adoption and Fostering,* 22(3): pp. 7–15.

Miles, R. (1989). Migration Discourse, British Sociology and the Race Relations Paradigm. *Migration,* 6: pp. 29–53.

Minker, M., and Roe, K.M. (1993). *Grandmothers As Caregivers Raising Children of the Crack Cocaine Epidemic.* Newbury Park, CA: Sage.

National Commission on Family Foster Care (1991). *The Significance of Kinship Care: In A Blueprint for Fostering Infants, Children and Youths in the 1990s.* Washington DC: Child Welfare League of America.

National Foster Care Association (2000). *Family and Friends Carers' Handbook* and *Family and Friends Carers: Social Workers' Training Guide.* London: NFCA.

Nisivoccia, D. (1996). Working with Kinship Families: Principles for Practice in Community Alternatives. *International Journal of Family Care,* 8(1): pp. 1–17.

Nobles, W.W. (1985). *Africanity and the Black Family: The Development of a Theoretical Model.* Oakland, CA: The Black Family Institute Publications.

Richards, A., and Ince, L. (2000). *Overcoming the Obstacles, Looked After Children: Quality Services for Black and Minority Ethnic Children and their Families.* London: Family Rights Group.

Rowe, J., Caine, H., Hundleby, M., and Keane, A. (1984). *Long-term Foster Care.* London: Batsford.

Scannapieco, M., and Jackson, S. (1996). Kinship Care: The African American Response to Family Preservation. *Social Work,* 4(2): pp. 190–197.

Sedlak, A.J., and Broadhurst, D.D. (1996). *Third National Incidence Study.* Washington DC: National Centre on Child Abuse and Neglect.

Selected Child Welfare Trends (1995). New York City Human Resources Administration, Child Welfare Administration. In Nisivoccia, D. (1996). Working with Kinship Foster Families: Principles for Practice. *Community Alternatives International Journal,* 8(1): pp. 1–17.

Stack, C. (1974). *All our Kin: Strategies for Survival in a Black Community.* New York: Harper and Row.

Takas, M. (1993). *Kinship Care and Family Preservation: A Guide for States in Legal and Policy Developments. Unpublished manuscript.* Washington DC: ABA Centre on Children and the Law.

Testa, M., Shook, K., Cohen, L., and Woods, M. (1996). Permanency Planning Options for Children in Formal Kinship Care. *Child Welfare,* 75(5): pp. 451–470

Thornton, J. (1991). Permanency Planning for Children in Kinship Foster Homes. *Child Welfare,* 70: pp. 593–601.

Utting, Sir W. (1997). *People Like us: The Report of the Review of the Safeguards for Children Living Away from Home.* London: HMSO.

Waterhouse, S., and Brocklesby, E. (1999). Placement Choices for Children: Giving More Priority to Kinship Placements? In Greeff, R. (Ed.) (1999). *Fostering Kinship.* Aldershot: Ashgate.

Wiese, D., and Daro, D. (1995). *Current Trends in Child Abuse Reporting and Fatalities: The Results of the 1994 Annual Fifty State Survey.* Chicago: National Committee for Prevention of Child Abuse.

Woodley, B.A., and Bailu-Etta, B. (1997). An Out-of-Home Care System in Crisis: Implications for African American Children in the Child Welfare System. *Child Welfare,* 76: pp. 65–83.

Wulczyn, F., and George, R. (1992). Foster Care in New York and Illinois: The Challenge of Rapid Change. *Social Services Review,* 66: pp. 278–294.

15 Comparing American and United Kingdom Kinship Care: A Practitioner's View

Jean Stogdon

Introduction

1998 was a very significant year for me both personally and professionally. I reached the age of 70, celebrated 50 years of marriage, and witnessed the birth of probably the last of our four grandchildren. In addition I was coming to the end of paid work. I had worked for twenty years as a social worker and manager in an inner London borough Social Services Department, and 10 years as a Guardian Ad Litem.

I felt it was time to reflect on my personal and professional life; the School for Social Entrepreneurs founded by Michael Young provided this opportunity. In both areas my main focus has been family life. Now as a grandmother I was experiencing the joys, pain, complexity and changing nature of that role, but most particularly, the importance of it in my family. I was awarded a travel fellowship from the Winston Churchill Memorial Trust to develop my own interest and to explore how kinship care had developed in the US.

Anecdotally and through the help line of a small charity with which I was working, I could see that grandparents, with changes to family life through divorce, substance abuse, AIDS and mental illness, were vulnerable to losing touch with their grandchildren on the one hand, and taking full-time responsibility for parenting their grandchildren on the other. As a social worker and Guardian Ad Litem I was increasingly concerned about what was happening to our most vulnerable children in the public care system, when their parents for one reason or another could not bring them up. I had seen the public, and indeed the social work profession itself, lose confidence in the ability of the local authority to be an effective and safe parent to a child placed in its care through the courts or in a voluntary arrangement by parents.

Until very recently the position of grandparents, either in our private lives or in the public care system, had hardly been discussed. As the summary of child protection research put it (DoH, 1995: p. 49):

Myopia hindered discussion about a child's family. The common preoccupation was with the nuclear aspect, which more often than not consisted of a single female parent or involved step-parents…on the other hand the significance of wider patterns of kinship and other sources of emotional support was often overlooked.

I believe it is true to say to this day that the role of the extended family is substantially undervalued in social policy.

Questions

My visit to the United States was not simply to be a search for facts but for echoes and associations, signs and images of a sense of continuity that I was experiencing personally, a continuity I thought was being denied to at least some children in care. In the United States the development of kinship care, defined, according to the Child Welfare League of America, as:

> …'the full time nurturing and protection of children who must be separated from their parents, by relatives, members of their tribe or clan, godparents, stepparents or other adults that have a kinship bond with the child' had been gaining momentum since the recognition of the importance of the extended kinship networks of the African/American community.
>
> (Stack, 1974)

If, as many of us believe, it is a child's inalienable right to be raised in their family, be that with their own parents or by the member of the extended family or a person perceived by that family to be part of that family by friendship or marriage, i.e. godparent or stepparent, why was our welfare system not achieving that right for the child where humanly possible? This raises still further questions:

- Were we exploring the extended family systematically and in a culturally competent way when a child needed nurture and protection?

- If the answer to the above is 'no' as others and I sometimes experience it to be, what were the barriers preventing social workers achieving that goal?

- Were we looking for deficiencies rather than strengths in the extended family?

- Did younger workers understand the position and complexities of being an older person/grandparent in today's society where older people are often stereotyped as being weak, a burden, in need of services themselves?

- Were there the skills and, most of all, the time available for the task, particularly in today's 'child protection culture' of short term intervention and the move away from family support which occurred in the nineties?

From thirty years of professional work with families, I knew that one of the biggest issues obstructing true partnership with families was the power imbalance. Parents and families perceive social workers and the hierarchy in social services departments as having immense and overwhelming power. Ironically the social worker, most likely the least experienced in the hierarchy, can feel herself powerless in the face of the great and complex problems being presented to her by the family particularly, I suggest, if they are of an intergenerational nature. Grandparents are in transition as part of the wider family, and are caught up in the maelstrom of today's debate: 'what is a family?' At the latter end of the Third Age (said to be 55 to 74 years) we will have brought up our families when life was 'more settled', not necessarily more interesting. Much as my parents 'knew their place' in the class system, I was one of the thousands of 'housewives' and mothers in a traditional role, with at least eighteen years as a full time mother. Indeed, along with my peer group, we felt that raising children was a full time task for one person. In addition, we saw ourselves as 'Household Managers', with transferable skills that were to be invaluable when I became a manager of 200 staff. In time, in our personal lives, many of us were further blessed and became grandparents.

Yet what are the needs of grandparents today, and where are the voices raised to tell us? Are other voices, politicians for example, raised in encouragement and validation? The answer has to be, 'no', not so far. Although government is beginning to take an interest, a question must be: what role should government take in assisting families to raise children? So far the work of grandparents is unpaid and invisible because it is done for love isn't it? That will be a controversial area in future debates. To quote an assistant social services director from a recent article in

Community Care magazine, 'There was a time when there would have been no question that grandparents would take in a needy child from their extended family, but I suppose that's a reflection of the change in society these days'. This quote was in the context of help and support that some grandparents may need if they take on the care of a grandchild. Perhaps only our immediate sons and daughters know that, without our support, their lives and that of their children would be the poorer.

So, when I set off for the United States the two main areas I wanted to explore were:

1. Grandparents, particularly grandmothers in general like myself. What is our role in today's society?

2. What is the role of grandparents and other relatives and friends involved with the child welfare agencies?

These two main areas are embodied in the notion that grandparents constitute a great and growing reserve of care for children both formally and informally. Given that we usually follow trends from the States, I wanted to return from there prepared to disseminate what I had learnt.

What did I learn?

In Washington DC I attended the 10th Annual 'Generations United' conference for three days. True to the expression of, 'I thought I had died and gone to heaven', this is how I felt taking part in that conference. The concept of the 'can-do' attitude, the 'engine' a driving force, the energy, innovation and sheer *bigness* of the ideas and action was breathtaking, and it all seemed so *sensible*. Generations United (GU) represents more than 100 national State and local organisations on behalf of more than 70 million Americans. GU advocates for the mutual well-being of children, youth and older adults and acts as a resource for educating policy makers and the public about the economic, social and personal imperatives of intergenerational co-operation.

Three categories of grandparent care emerged:

1. **The Custodial Grandparents.** These have legal custody of their grandchildren. They provide daily care and make decisions. Typically, severe problems existed in the child's nuclear family. The focus of this type of care-giving is on the grandchild and providing him or her with a sense of security. These were typical of the group I had worked with professionally.

2. **The Living with Grandparents.** These provide daily care for their grandchildren but do not have legal custody. The child's parent may or may not live in the home. These grandparents focus on providing an economically and emotionally stable environment for the child and are often helping the parent. As the grandparent does not possess legal custody he or she has no way of protecting the child from an unsuitable or dangerous parent.

3. **Day Care Grandparents.** They focus on helping the child's parent and/or fulfilling their own needs. These grandparents tend to be the least affected by their care-taking role because the children return home at the end of the day. They function closest to the societal definition of a 'grandparent'. These are the grandparents, however, who may become the focus of the UK government attention soon as they are often filling the gap caused by the lack of business, family friendly work policies and lack of affordable daycare provision for children.

I attended this hugely satisfying GU conference and visited agencies in Washington DC, Michigan and Illinois and also several academic institutions. From sitting in on grandparents support groups there were a number of key issues raised.

Issues raised by grandparents:

- Health of grandparents: what happens if this deteriorates?

- Housing: accommodating a larger family?

- Money: what little money people have saved for older age may prevent them from obtaining government assistance.

- Legal advice: very costly.

- Their grandchildren's health: those who had suffered abuse, neglect, effect of drugs.

- Children's issues: angry with their parents for not being there or with grandma because she is there and the parent is not. Other children's taunts: making fun of them.

- Grandparent's loss of freedom/lifestyle, lack of respite care.

- The complexities of adopting grandchildren where adoption laws are designed primarily for families unknown to one another. Many kin carers are against adopting their own grandchildren.

Kinship care

The United Kingdom foster care system is designed for assessment by, administration by and care-giving by non-relatives. If we are to move to kinship care as a first and preferred option the barriers to approval of relatives' homes must be thought through very carefully and a new assessment and support system devised, otherwise we may begin to blame the kinship care givers for not adapting to the present system. All this depends on creating a concensus for society's response to vulnerable children and families, to clarify the definition of permanence. Permanent homes should function without the intrusion and supervision of social services if at all possible. We need a process of consensus building that includes Social Services, other government departments, business and the larger tax paying community.

My next area of study was in the State of Illinois, one of the 25 States that had researched what was happening to grandparents and their involvement with the child welfare system. In Illinois it was found that over 70,000 children under 18 lived with a grandparent with no parent present. 150,000 children under 18 lived with their parent in a grandparent headed home, the majority of homes headed by a grandmother. The Illinois Department on Ageing began addressing these issues in the following ways:

- Requesting government money to initiate a help line.

- Production of a 'Grandparent Resource Guide'.

- Establishing and funding support groups across the State.

- Developing model projects on mediation and advocacy.

- Sponsoring a symposium on legal and support services.

- Presenting workshops for professionals and grandparents.

- Encouraging private partnerships.

They worked in partnership with the 'Illinois Task Force on Grandparents Raising Grandchildren' to undertake the following mission:

> *Identify issues, challenges, needs and concerns of grandparents who are raising grandchildren. Positively impact programmes and services at local, State and National levels. Provide information on programmes/resources,*

services to grandparents, professionals and service providers. Promote media attention to the issue of grandparents raising grandchildren and programmes available to assist them. Build a strong coalition between Social Services/universities/government/health/voluntary organisations and grandparents.

Informal kinship care was used to divert children from the child welfare system. At that time only a small number of children in care lived with relatives. They had no public money except social security. A groundbreaking case, Miller v. Youakim (1979) stated that relatives should be paid as much as foster carers. Of the 26,500 children in informal kinship care in 1995, 87% were African American. 'Kin carers' had to be licensed. Many did not want that intrusion but wanted the money. Shades of this situation exist in the UK. They then began to develop new initiatives offering home-based services to relatives caring for children at risk to strengthen, support and preserve many kin families by means of family group conferences and mediation, in other words by a preventative philosophy and family support.

If the main aim of work with children and families here as well as the United States is to reduce conditions of risk and to increase the 'safety, permanence and well-being' of our most vulnerable children, then we need a broader vision. Social services departments become key in presenting this challenge to others in society who are much further removed from those who are most vulnerable. Social workers know about the needs of children and families, about the factors that contribute to family breakdown and about factors that strengthen and support families. Through contacts with the University of Chicago, Jane Addams College of Social Work, and the Social Work School at Grand Rapids University, Michigan, I was able to gain full insight into how they are training their social workers to look to the extended family (kin) as their *first and preferred* option for a permanent home for children who cannot live with their parents.

The first and most important message I was told was that there had to be a sea change in thinking and attitude in the US in order to begin to explore, facilitate and support extended family placement with all its complexities. I was informed that until the early 1980s when the African American grandmothers in New York fought to keep their grandchildren out of the child welfare system, which happened to coincide with a severe shortage of foster homes, the two main options for permanence for children was reunification with their parents or adoption.

I was puzzled by the fact that even though there had been similar thinking in both the US and the UK in relation to placement of children, as Diagram A illustrates, from the beginning of the 1990s many American states had concluded that placing kinship care at the heart of their family preservation and continuity philosophy was the way forward. In the UK by contrast our thinking has not evolved so fully as Diagram B shows.

What appears to me to be the most striking difference between the USA and the UK is that whereas in the 1980s in the American system they 'discovered' the extended family, mainly because of the push from the African American grandmothers, in this country we had the extended family well in our sights in the late 1980s and the notion was included in our Children Act 1989, but grandparents are not specifically mentioned. Yet in practice it appears that we have never fully acted upon this opportunity.

Kinship care in black families

Have we not been listening to the voices in minority ethnic communities? Black children are over-represented in our care system as they are in the States. Here are some views on the subject from the States in relation to kinship care in black families:

- Workers 'of colour' (an American expression) are more likely to agree that adoption is unnecessary in kin placements.
- Workers of colour generally have more positive perceptions of kinship care.
- White workers were more likely to believe that kinship homes were difficult to supervise.
- A majority of all workers believe that children in kinship care have a stronger sense of belonging and are less troubled about their status. (76% of workers surveyed in Minnesota believed children were better off in kinship care than non-kin care).
- Kin's relationship to parents is an advantage in facilitating permanency.
- Training needs: for workers cultural competence and facilitation of permanence in kinship network.
- Kinship caregivers need different kind of orientation, training and support.
- 83% of workers surveyed in Minnesota believed that kin carers' motivation was to hold the family together. From my experience I am quite sure this is the case in the UK.

Diagram A: A framework of child and family care reforms in the US since the 1970s

Time	Reform	Focus on	Contribution to field
1970s	Permanency planning	Adoptive family	Children belong in a permanent family: no child is unadoptable
1980 Family Preservation Adoption Assistance and Child Welfare Act		Bio family	Children belong with their biological parents: reasonable efforts must be demonstrated to maintain family
1990s	Family continuity	Extended/ augmented family	Children belong in a family network which continues relationships over time

Adapted from Downs, Costin, and McFadden (1996)

Diagram B: A framework of child and family care reforms in the UK since the 1970s

Time	Reform	Focus on	Contribution to field
1970s	Children Act 1975 (launch incorporated into the Child Care Act 1980)	Adoptive family	Children belong in permanent family. No child is unadoptable. Permanency planning
1980s	• Amendments to Children Act 1980 • Introduction of Guardians Ad Litem	Return to birth families or adoption	Parental contact is key to reunification. Social work ambivalence to contact as obstacle to adoption debate, leading to professional inactivity
1990s	Children Act 1989	Keeping children with birth families wherever possible. Working in partnership with parents. Promote contact	Assumption that it will now be possible for all children to remain or be returned to birth parents— purpose: Rehabilitation
2000	Extended family? Adoption? Clear vision?		

One of the Government's observations in *Quality Protects* is the recognition that a fifth of all looked after children are from minority ethnic groups. I propose that the evidence from the US is noted and acted upon and that the kinship care philosophy, so well developed now in the States is absorbed into our systems. Indeed it is hard to believe that a notion that is as old as the hills, kin caring for their own children, has to be presented as 'something new'. If social workers in the UK can be exposed to the creative training I observed in the States and the 1999 BAAF lecture tour with Professor Jean McFadden in this country recently, they will have the opportunity to marry the aspirations they would have for their own children in the event of their death, or if they were unable to care for their own children, with the children they know and work with in the care system. In all the workshops I attended no worker voted for foster care as their placement choice, all opted for kin care.

Aspirations for the families we work with are no different. Perhaps it is incumbent on us all, including Government ministers, to imagine what it would feel like for a child close to us, to be cut off from its family network.

An Agenda for Action for Kinship Care in the United Kingdom

First of all a summary of the general case for kinship care.

Why the need for kinship care in the UK?

- It is culturally relevant. Cultural competence in social work practice is of key relevance in the United Kingdom generally, and especially because children from minority ethnic groups are over represented in both countries' care systems.

- We have an ever decreasing number of foster carers as in the United States.

- Kinship care generally reduces separation trauma for children. As a Guardian Ad Litem for ten years representing children this aspect should never be underestimated. In our personal lives any mother knows this if she has to be hospitalised or even when her child starts school or nursery.

- Kinship care builds on family strengths and promotes family responsibility.

- Kinship care is a form of family preservation and provides knowledge of the child's past. It builds identity within their own family network.

- Kinship care affords accessibility to parents and other family members some of whom may have made positive life choices, the 'healthier' part of the network.

Social work practice issues

The two key phrases synonymous with kinship care are family continuity and family preservation. Family continuity refers to:

- The importance of family connections.
- The integration of all the child's earlier experiences of family.
- Refocusing on continuity and relationships.
- Integrating principles of family preservation.
- Involving extended family and other families in protecting children.
- Working with families in a holistic way, crossing traditional agency service boundaries.
- The legal status following new extended family connections.

Family continuity is, then, a unifying framework for: supporting families, protecting children, planning permanence, and providing continuity of attachment through the importance of relationships across the lifespan. It acknowledges that children need to be embedded in family and community networks of continuing caring relationships.

The principles of family continuity practice are: maintaining a child's existing attachments regardless of placement plan, ensuring family continuity work occurs within culture and community, and working to develop community resources and ensure that the legal status and the permanence plan follow existing relationships. It works to strengthen the core family and its practice begins at the first contact with the system. This is crucially important in our present system in Social Service Departments. If the family continuity practice does not begin at the duty desk and within the practice of the first social worker the family has contact with, delay will occur and impetus will be lost. Family placement workers coming in at a later stage, even if they advocate notions of kinship care will be at a disadvantage in placing the child and much time will have been lost. There can already be a good deal of tension in the system between field (child protection) social workers and family placement workers. It is strongly argued here that the slowly emerging 'Kinship care workers' or 'Placement with relative workers', will have difficulty in the system unless the whole system values family continuity and family preservation.

The disadvantages of kinship care also need to be recognised. These include:

- Imposing stress on family support systems.
- Changing and re-defining family relationships.
- Acknowledging the contribution of family dysfunction to parenting problems.

So having listed the positives and some negatives connected with kinship care placements, what are the policy changes that are needed in order for kinship care, and kinship care with grandparents, to be more fully considered and acted on as a positive placement choice for children by social services and families?

Social work policy issues

- **Learn from the US experiences of kinship care** and go on to pull out the similarities and differences in our systems.

- **Tackle ageism.** Governments need to take a lead in valuing older people and acknowledge their role in the strength of the extended family. Regarding age discrimination, the current administration has fallen short of its pre-election commitment to legislate against this in the same way as Equal Opportunities, Race and Disability Rights. Institutional ageism is endemic in local authorities as well as elsewhere and affects social work practice. Ageism works against many grandparent carers where, as in other areas of family life, deficits are emphasised more than strengths. The political power of the 'grey lobby' needs to assert itself.

- **Social services need to value the extended family.** There will need to be a sea change, a change in attitude that makes kinship care the *first and preferred placement choice* of children, both as a diversion from the care system and a placement for looked after children. Directors of Social Services will need to write their mission statements to that effect if they have not already done so. We need to explore within ourselves as practitioners and managers: why we have tried *so* hard to place children elsewhere; in foster care, back to parents (often when we knew it would fail) or adoption: why have we not put all our skills, creativity, commitment and energy into keeping children in the family network, a network

that is still there when the child is 18. Even though the father, for example, may be out of the picture, his family may still be a resource.

- **Generate research evidence** about what works and does not work in kinship care and about social services decision making We must look in depth at the bias and prejudice of workers who raise the barriers against placements with relatives summed up in the cliché in the United States as 'the apple doesn't fall far from the tree'. Jean McFadden points out there was a fairly widespread belief amongst caseworkers that the problems of the parents were most probably the result of the parenting they had received and that if one memeber of the family had problems then that whole branch of the family was compromised. We know that social workers make mistakes in judgement and reach decisions that harm children. The 'luxury' social workers have is making subsequent decisions following a mistake. This opportunity must also be afforded to the extended family. Initial solutions often require revision. The Department of Health funds ongoing projects between academic and social work departments until May 2000. The aim is to make sure that all decisions about policy and practice in social services are informed by good quality research. This is to be welcomed by all social workers. Hopefully we shall learn more about how social workers make their/our decisions, but also how we erect barriers against good research evidence.

- **Re-emphasise family decision making.** If social workers manage a sea change in attitude there must be clear policies that will enhance that practice. Family Group Conferences have been more widely used in the US than the UK, particularly when kinship care is the first and the preferred option. Perhaps we need to be reminded that social work practice normally assumes that the extended family has the greatest investment in the child, and that the role of the professional is to facilitate the family decision making process.

- **Change to a 'family-strengths' approach.** Through training, strengths based understanding of family problems resolution is needed, rather than a family-deficit based model.

- **Mediation services.** There is an urgent need for mediation services and skills to assist in family relationships and intergenerational feuds.

- **Assessment.** Social workers need to use a different form of assessment for relatives, (see Pitcher's chapter on an assessment framework for grandparents).

- **Best value.** Much benefit could be gained from authorities initiating a support group, perhaps in a family centre, to hear the issues being raised by grandparents and other relatives in order to tailor services to their needs.

- **Legal costs.** Many grandparents cannot afford legal fees and should not have to pay them in normal circumstances. If they have some savings they will want to keep them if they 'win' care of the child. Not being legally represented means court proceedings are not based on a level playing field. Local authorities pay legal fees for prospective adopters even if they are well off, in the event of contested adoption proceedings.

Conclusion

Since my 1999 visit to the United States of America I have spent time disseminating the findings through presentations on BBC radio, with Professor Jean McFadden (1999 BAAF lecture tour), the Department of Health, and with Michael Young, in connection with starting a new voluntary organisation for grandparents working in partnership with parent and child organisations. We hope to be able to contribute to the debate on the needs of children in today's society, and assert the value of the extended family to them.

As you will have gathered, I am convinced that kinship care has a lot to offer children and if they

had a strong enough voice, perhaps they would be telling us this. I suspect that most children want to be with familiar caregivers at a time of family crisis, within a familiar racial or ethnic community with historical patterns of family care. The kinship care model can be used at or before entry to the foster care system; clearly there have to be placement considerations about safety and relationship issues, but if these can be assessed in foster and adoption placements they can be assessed in kin families. Following the North Wales enquiry and the 37 other enquiries still to report there may be far greater risks for children than we were ever prepared to think about in the public care system. Certainly relationships with 'strangers' are notoriously difficult and complex to develop. I hope that what I have found out on my visit to the US and the ongoing contacts I have made can be of help in my profession and my community. I certainly have gained enormously in a personal capacity and will always be grateful to those involved in the Winston Churchill Travelling Fellowships for selecting me and sincerely hope that I have fulfilled their confidence in me. It was a wonderful opportunity, particularly at my age; reflecting on and assessing what can be passed on both personally and professionally, is uppermost in my mind.

References

Department of Health (1995). *Child Protection Messages from Research.* London: HMSO.

Downs, S.W., Costin, L., and McFadden, E.J. (1996). *Child Welfare and Family Services: Policy and Practice,* 5th edn. Longman Publishing.

McFadden, E.J. (1998). Kinship Care in the United States. *Adoption and Fostering,* Vol. 22: Number 3.

Stack, C. (1974). *All our Kin: Strategies For Survival in a Black Community.* New York: Harper and Row.

16 Kinship Care: Learning from the Past and Looking to the Future

Bob Broad

Introduction

This book set out to record the position about kinship care in so far as research policy and practice developments are concerned. There were many important outstanding questions about kinship care raised at the 1999 kinship care conference in Leicester. These included the following:

- What is kinship care?
- Does it include foster care by relatives?
- How are assessments best carried out?
- How can kinship care be supported?
- What is or could be the role of family group conferences?
- Should carers be supported and by whom?
- What is the legal situation for kinship carers?
- What are the most appropriate legal provisions?
- What differences do cross or inter-generational caring have on families and other children/young people in the family?
- How do courts deal with kinship carers in child welfare/custody cases?
- What are the particular issues for black families? and children of dual heritage?
- What do kinship carers say about what they do?
- What do the children and young people in kinship care say about their care?

This book's contributors have addressed many of these important questions here, and the kinship care debates, such as they are, have moved on quite quickly, with ever more challenging and sophisticated questions ready to emerge. This book has set out the arguments for kinship care, presented the real concerns of kinship carers, by implication, the effect on children in kinship care placements, and laid out agendas for action for local authorities and central government.

In the first part of the book the legal situation concerning grandparents and kinship care was clearly and comprehensively laid out (by Jenkins) and the shortcomings of the Children Act 1989 highlighted, followed by a summary of the 1998 British Social Attitudes Survey findings about, and an analysis of, grandparents who care for children (by Clarke and Cairns). The issue of grandparents, who although primary carers, were not able to participate effectively in court proceedings, from the beginning of those proceedings, due to lack of financial support is a key area highlighted by Hunt. This theme of lack of sufficient support (including professional guidance as well as financial support) for kinship carers, many of whom are often not earning an income themselves, also emerges in Laws' and Tapsfield's chapters. Suggested ways for social services to be more understanding of and supportive of kinship care were described in some detail in earlier chapters, whether concerned with training materials (see Flynn's chapter), an assessment framework (Pitcher), appreciation of family dynamics (Greeff), greater use of family group conferences (Nixon), or use of a new family network conceptual model (O'Brien). The key organisational themes 'supporting change' and 'overcoming obstacles to change' are identified in Wheal's, Tapsfield's, Ince's, and Stogden's chapters. Farmer's chapter usefully reminds us that the majority of children in need are reunited with their families, and examines an under-researched area, namely the management of the transition back home. Waterhouse's chapter, based on her original research, points to better outcomes for children in kinship care compared with those in stranger foster care, and points to the need for more developments to support kinship care.

In this final chapter I want to pull together some of the main issues that are beginning to emerge. First I want to summarise the child welfare context, which informs the Department of Health's Quality Protects Programme, especially its placement choice priority. Then I will move onto highlighting key issues for the future as raised by research and practice to date. The former primarily relate to the range and quality of child care options for social services departments and families for children in need and children at risk of serious harm. It is not intended to provide a full research based review of child welfare issues here, first because this is beyond the remit of this book and because, in any case, it has already been ably undertaken elsewhere (see, for example, Hill and Aldgate, (Eds.) 1996; and Iwaniec and Hill, 2000).

At the outset it is important to take note that the existing literature, whether relating to the USA or the UK, does not always distinguish between formal kinship care by relatives who are also approved foster parents, and those who are not foster parents. The focus of this volume has been *formal kinship care*, and not informal kinship care (i.e. private arrangements made within the family and not made through court or welfare routes). However, the emphasis of the contributions here has been mostly on those formal kinship care placements not subject to a fostering agreement. This distinction is important because formal kinship care placements falling outside fostering regulations are the ones most likely to produce placement choice, policy, resource and training issues.

Child Welfare Issues

Following the Children Act 1989, after an initial down turn in the total number of children looked after each year, there has been a steady increase, since 1994, from 49,100 children as at 31 March 1994, to 55,300 children as at 31 March 1999, the most recent figure available (Department of Health, 1999, Table A, p. 39). There have also been a series of major scandals about residential care (National Foster Care Association (NFCA), 1997), wider changes in family structures towards more diverse family types (Health Development Agency, 2000), continued poor welfare outcomes for children leaving care (Biehal *et al.*, 1995; Broad, 1998), a shortage of suitable foster carers (NFCA, 1997), and an over-representation of black young people in public care (Barn, 1991). Against this background, of increasing numbers of children looked after, pressure on existing services, and poor outcomes for those children, it seems that other appropriate arrangements for children in need warrant consideration. A formal kinship care arrangement, whereby a child in need comes to the attention of social services, and is placed, or supported in living, with a member of that child's extended family, or friend, is one such arrangement. It is known that kinship care is

developing in several local authorities, in some cases building on family group conference initiatives, in others within a kinship care placement strategy, and in yet others, in a local policy vacuum. A kinship care placement is the most positive for many children and young people in need by providing continuity of care, family, school and friends networks, and sustaining cultural and individual identities. Yet it is clear from some of the evidence presented here (as Laws' chapter details) that whilst it has benefits, kinship care is not without its problems and challenges, for social services, the children, and the kinship carers, with the latter group's life 'on hold' for the duration of the arrangement.

Next there is also an associated and ongoing placement issue concerning the search for more responsive and effective strategies for those children in need in the middle teenage age-groupings i.e. twelve-sixteen years of age (NFCA, 1997). The national foster care recruitment campaign, led by the NFCA, specifically demonstrates a continuing shortfall of appropriate foster carers as well as being testament to the shortage of a range of placement options facing local authorities. Also as Hill (1999: p. 2) adroitly observes '…fostering today is located within a child care scene which has a less certain sense of direction…' adding that it is also one in which permanency planning has been both promoted and, for adolescents in particular, questioned. Depending at what point in the child's life an extended family placement is initiated, why and for what length of time, kinship care might be seen as falling into the category of being an example of 'a more complex alternative arrangement which takes into account continuity, resilience, multiple identities and network support, as well as permanent belonging' (McFadden and Downs, 1995; Gilligan, 1997 quoted in Hill). The prominence given by government to urging local authorities to 'see adoption as a positive, responsible choice…' (Professional Social Work, 2000: p. 2) and the White Paper on adoption (Department of Health, 2000) are also indicative of what sometimes appears as a desperate search for other placement options. Other broader, and major, societal issues directly related to kinship care developments are concerned with the changing structure of families, inter- and cross-generational issues, and, at the micro level, family dynamics.

We have seen from the contributions here that kinship care placements constitute both a potential and actual breakthrough in terms of prevention of system abuse, provision of ongoing, familiar and willing support, and, not least of all, sustaining individual and family identities. I say 'potential' as well as 'actual' because although the selected literature quoted in this collection is positive about kinship care placements, we still need to be receptive to hearing messages about less positive outcomes and challenges. Additionally, we still do not have a child's perspective on this type of placement or comparative outcome studies. Although our kinship care research study (with funding by the Joseph Rowntree Foundation) seeks to obtain this 'users' i.e. children's perspective, it will still be very difficult to evaluate, compare and judge the outcomes as seen by them. There are also other limits to user focused research, including those concerned with improved service designs, policies and guidance, which require adult inputs, and judgements, which can be informed by users' experiences.

Defining and evaluating kinship care

Although I have defined the term 'kinship care' in this book, a basic though not straightforward matter, nevertheless, one of the problems that dog the literature, and therefore wider policy development, is that of an agreed definition of kinship care. As we have already seen, the term kinship care is often used quite loosely simply to describe both informal family arrangements, (whether or not the child or carer is known to social services), or formally approved foster care with a relative.

Arguably the definition of kinship care that eventually becomes agreed and accepted will become critical in terms of future policy and legislative developments in the policy area of service entitlement. For example, in relation to the latter, and drawing on the 'young people leaving care' field, the Children (Leaving Care) Act 2000 specifies a minimum period of time (three months) which a child needs to be looked after by the local authority for that child to be defined as 'eligible' for a leaving care service. Others who have been in care for less than three months are still care leavers but their needs, as statutory entitlements, will be 'defined out' by this eligibility criterion. Perhaps so far as future kinship care policy development is concerned, a child will need to have lived with an extended family member or friend for a minimum period to be officially classified as entitled to whatever

kinship care supports are available. I hope not. Whilst acknowledging the cash limits that face local authorities, the placing of any further limited financial and social services restrictions on kinship carers and children's needs would be unresponsive and unhelpful.

For example a denial of social services support at the beginning of a kinship care arrangement, initiated by a grandparent, could prejudice a potentially successful extended family placement, saving any further anguish and placement breakdowns. It would also fly in the face of what we already know from research findings presented in this volume, namely, that many kinship care placements are unplanned or unpredictable and made at a time of crisis for the child and family, and the option of having immediate help and support, rather than service denial, is what kinship carers say they need (see Laws' chapter on this point). Examples of crises include unavailability of parent as a result of a bereavement, court case and custodial remand. Categories of longer term crises from our research include 'serious child protection issues arising from parental mental health issues' and, in a surprising majority of cases, 'child protection issues arising from substance misuse by the birth parent(s)'.

Many kinship care arrangements continue from an initial temporary informal agreement often between the child's grandparent and birth mother, to a more permanent arrangement. This can occur when, for example, perceived short term parental problems become exacerbated and when living away from the parents home is seen as more desirable than an alternative. The 'seamless slip' between temporary informal and more permanent formal kinship care arrangements is one that could be readily assessed by social services departments. Also in ongoing formal kinship care situations it is clear there needs to be more and higher level support available, as initial social services involvement can often fall away once the formal kinship care placement is confirmed.

Research and evaluation issues

One apparently straightforward way of evaluating children in kinship care placements would be to produce a range of outcome indicators, making comparisons with other children in 'comparable situations' (see Waterhouse's chapter as she decided to make comparisons with those children in stranger foster care). In my view the impact of wider support services should also be included in any kinship care research and evaluation. In terms of evaluation criteria one possibility is to draw on the five general dimensions used in the *Looking After Children* (LAC) assessment materials (Ward, 1995). These are; health, education, identity, family and social relationships, and social presentation, emotional and behavioural development.

Thus if, as is the case and evidence presented here by the book's contributors, kinship care is a more positive alternative to public care placements, at least in the cases presented, one would also expect this to be supported by further research evidence. Such evidence could demonstrate one or more of the following positive outcomes, (subject to further refinement):

- better physical health
- better mental health
- better emotional health
- higher levels of educational attainment
- better placement continuity
- better placement stability
- fewer visits to 'problem' welfare agencies
- more support from the extended family for the child
- more stability and continuity of individual and family identity including:
  - ethnicity
  - culture
  - language
  - religion
  - class
- less call on the time of welfare agencies (benefits, social services departments) and punishment and rehabilitation agencies (probation and criminal justice system)

It is also accepted that there will not necessarily be an agreement about these criteria. These are nominal suggestions, and a framework, in this generalised research and evaluation context.[1] It can also be the case that a kinship care placement produces many of these positive outcomes over a sustained period and for a number of reasons, but that there is then a decreasing likelihood of the child returning to live with their birth parent(s). Is this a 'good kinship care outcome?' 'For whom?' The litmus test of kinship care, as with any other arrangement, is that it must be in the child's best interest (however that is decided upon) to be in such a placement. If the child remains with the extended family carer then this points to a new type of more permanent family arrangement. It begs the questions 'Is this what is intended by a kinship care placement?' and 'What is the purpose of kinship care?'

Theoretically and contrary to the evidence presented in this volume, if children in kinship care placements were evaluated as having poorer outcomes than children in a comparable situation then one would expect to see the following outcomes, which are the very opposite of the previous list:

- worse physical health
- worse mental health
- worse emotional health
- lower levels of educational attainment
- worse placement continuity
- worse placement stability
- more visits to 'problem' welfare agencies
- less support from the extended family for the child
- less stability and continuity of individual and family identity (see above)
- a greater call on welfare agencies (benefits, social services departments) and punishment and rehabilitation agencies (probation and criminal justice system)

There is no research evidence, at least known to me, which supports this latter 'poorer outcomes' scenario. So far as the child is concerned it is most likely to be the provision of a safe, loving home that matters most. It is also recognised that this may not always be possible, but perhaps not all extended family or other options have been fully considered in all cases. Yet those readers who still remain sceptical about kinship care should read Ince's powerful chapter here about kinship care. In that chapter the needs and strengths of black extended families are discussed, as well as the ways in which in American states the legislation and guidance have changed to bring about, legitimise, and properly support, kinship care placements.

---

1. For example one of our kinship care research projects took four months to decide on the questions to be asked to carers and young people and the criteria to cover and these needed to be further changed later on!

Concluding Observations

Given estimates of between 10% and 20% of children coming to the attention of social services living in formal kinship care placements (i.e. including same family foster care placements, non foster care placements, and others) there remains a paucity of research and development work in this field in the UK compared with this recorded level of activity.

At the heart of kinship care still remain many unanswered questions about public and private roles, rights and responsibilities and these questions are not taken forward or addressed in the Children Act 1989 or its guidance. Up until now a key question 'What is the role of the state, if any, in arranging, supporting and endorsing kinship care arrangements?' might seem to have defined the boundaries for the many practical questions and concerns. Yet the pressing issue of financial support, or lack of it, so far as most kinship carers are concerned, will not go away, and if social services 'care, support and protection' responsibilities towards children could be separated out from provision of financial support to their carers, for example by the creation of a 'carers allowance' or 'carers credit' for kinship carers, payable through the benefit or tax systems, then this might help.

The expressed needs of carers in our published study for more ongoing social work support and financial assistance presents a challenging agenda to social services child care departments driven by child protection concerns (Laws and Broad, 2000). More generally if, as the research from America suggests, outcomes for children in kinship care placements, are at the very least comparable with other 'stranger' child care placement outcomes, then kinship care merits a closer and more immediate examination by child care and family researchers and implementation by key authorities. For example our research study presents evidence of an over-representation of black families in kinship care placements (Laws and Broad, 2000). Although this is not in itself evidence of racism, given the extent of racial discrimination in other public policy fields, we need to be vigilant that discriminatory mechanisms are not repeated in kinship care work. It may also be that kinship care is the preferred choice for black, and also white, kinship carers. Yet kinship care should not and must not become a second choice and second-rate option for black and indeed white families in need but the placement selected as the most appropriate for the child, after all the due considerations, choices, and options have been weighed up.

It is also becoming apparent from our current kinship care study and to a lesser extent from another research study entitled *Improving the Health of Socially Excluded Young People* (work in progress), that for many young people living with extended family members, such extended family living arrangements are not exceptional. We have found, for example, that many socially excluded young people move around within their extended families outside the care system, and have done so for many years. Significantly, in both these research studies these kinship care arrangements were not with the consent of the child concerned but as a direct result of new reconstructed families arising from one of the birth parents living with a new partner. The ad-hoc nature of many of these informal kinship care arrangements, often outside the strictures of a clear legislative framework, makes the policing and supporting of them by social services all the more complex than a placement with a foster carer.

Kinship care is not simply another placement choice with a single function. It is multi-functional, carrying important child protection, family support, and placement choice functions. Thus at the national policy level kinship care can be developed, as a placement choice, under the auspices of the Department of Health's Quality Protects Programme (placement choice objective). Quality Protects bids made by local authorities for kinship care development workers are emerging as one practical, though insufficient, response to the growing interest and use of kinship care placements. Yet the social services' role is primarily child protection, and not a preventive, family support agency, or a youth support agency. It is also the case that the Home Office policy interest in the family needs, unless it is a passing or superficial one, be more fully recognised. Additionally the Children's and Young People Unit's (CYPU) focus on preventive services aimed at children aged between five and thirteen at risk of social exclusion might regard kinship care as preventive family support (Rickford, 2000). It is also possible that a family or children's voluntary organisation could take a lead in co-ordinating and developing, in partnership with others, kinship care in the UK.

Yet whilst policies and practices are being developed and evaluated, what should not get lost along the way are the principle ideas underpinning these kinship care placements.

These are, for a child or children for whom living with the birth parent(s) is no longer a possibility, for local authorities and families to fully and openly explore together, subject to proper checks and considerations, the possibilities for placing or supporting a vulnerable child or children within their extended family (or friends), in order to maintain continuity of care, relationships, family responsibility, and sustain cultural and racial identities.

Formal kinship care placements can offer a continuity of, and coherence in, relationships and identity often so cruelly severed through other options. As we have seen there are a number of important legal, anti-discriminatory, policy, training, financial, strategic and evaluation issues which contributors have addressed in this volume. The challenge now is to the relevant authorities, especially those in social services and the Department of Health, and perhaps the CYPU, to more fully acknowledge the scope and contribution of kinship care. In order to make kinship care a more coherent option will require more supportive and open responses. These will value the participation of family members in decision-making and acknowledge the strengths of extended families. It is the lethal combination of ageism, racism, professional autonomy, and social services child protection priorities, topped with ongoing financial constraints, which are likely to prove the biggest obstacles to kinship care developing properly and at the pace that is needed. Yet it is hoped that the wide-ranging and valuable contributions here, from experienced professional and academic colleagues, together with the words and messages of kinship carers, will help to overcome those obstacles, and inform and drive forward kinship care debates, policies and practice in an empowering way. An alternative whereby children at risk receive half-baked and under-funded child welfare interventions, or a denial of service, is not acceptable.

References

Barn, R. (1991). *Black Children in the Public Care System.* London: Batsford.

Berridge, D. (1987). *Foster Care: A Research Review.* London: The Stationery Office.

Berridge, D., and Brodie, (1997). *Children's Homes Revisited.* London: Jessica Kingsley.

Berridge, D. (1985). *Children's Homes.* Oxford: Basil Blackwell.

Biehal, N., Clayden, J., Stein, M., and Wade, J. (1995). *Moving On.* London: HMSO.

British Association of Social Work (2000). Adoption Takes Centre Stage. *Professional Social Work*, November.

Broad, B. (1999). Kinship Care: Enabling and Supporting Child Placements with Relatives and Friends. In *Assessment, Preparation and Support.* London: BAAF.

Broad, B. (1998). Kinship Care: Children Placed with Extended Families. *Childright*, 155: pp. 16–17.

Denscombe, M. (1998). *The Good Research Guide.* Buckingham: Open University Press.

DoH (1999). *Children Looked After by Local Authorities Year Ending 31st March 1999*, Table LA3. DoH.

DoH (2000a). *Quality Protects Placement Choice.* Seminar, 12th January. London: DoH.

DoH (2000b). *Framework for the Assessment of Children in Need and their Families.* London: DoH.

DoH (2000c). *Tracking Progress in Children's Services: An Evaluation of Local Responses to the Quality Protects Programme Year 2 National Overview Report.* London: DoH.

Gilligan, R. (1997). Beyond Permanence: The Importance of Resilience in Child Practice and Planning. *Adoption and Fostering*, 20: p. 2.

Greef, R. (Ed.) (1998). *Kinship Care: An International Perspective.* Aldershot: Avebury.

Health Development Agency (2000). *Changing Families, Changing Communities.* London: HDA.

Hill, M., and Aldgate, J. (Eds.) (1996). *Child Welfare Services.* London: Jessica Kingsley.

Hill, G. (1999). Introduction. In *Signposts in Fostering: Polic, Practice and Research Issues.* London: BAAF.

Iwaniec, D., and Hill, M. (Eds.) (2000). *Child Welfare Policy and Practice.* London: Jessica Kingsley.

Laws, S., and Broad, B. (2000). *Looking After Children Within the Extended Family: Carers' Views.* Leicester: Centre for Social Action, De Montfort University.

McFaddon, E.J. (1998). Kinship Care in the USA. *Adoption and Fostering*, 22(3): pp. 7–15.

McFadden, E.J., and Downs, S.W. (1995). Family Continuity: The New Paradigm in Permanency Planning. *Community Alternatives*, 7(1).

NFCA (1993). *Friends and Relatives as Carers.* London: NFCA.

NFCA (1997). *Foster Care in Crisis.* London: NFCA.

Rickford, F. (2000). Who is Flying this plane? *Community Care*, 19th–25th October.

Walby, C., and Colton, M. (1999). More Children: More Problems? *Community Care*, 15th–21st July.

Ward, H. (Ed.) (1995). *Looking After Children: Research Into Practice.* London: HMSO.

Who Cares? Trust (1998). *Remember my Messages.* London: Who Cares? Trust.